BIOG
LA MOTTA
AND
Anderson
Raging Bull II

Raging Bull II

Raging Bull II

by Chris Anderson
and Sharon McGehee
⊂≣ with Jake La Motta ≣⊃

LYLE STUART INC.   **SECAUCUS, N. J.**

Published by Lyle Stuart Inc.
120 Enterprise Ave., Secaucus, N.J. 07094
In Canada: Musson Book Company
a division of General Publishing Co. Limited
Don Mills, Ontario

Manufactured in the United States of America

Library of Congress Cataloging-in-Publication Data

Anderson, Chris.
  Raging bull II.

    1. La Motta, Jake. 2. Boxers (Sports)--
United States--Biography. I. McGehee, Sharon.
II. La Motta, Jake. III. Title.
GV1132.L3A63 1986   796.8'3'0924 [B]   86-24873
ISBN 0-8184-0407-8

In memory of my loving mother
ELIZABETH
And to my six children—
JACKLYN, JACKIE,
JOEY, CHRISTI,
LISA *and* MIA
And my beautiful, loyal wife
THERESA

ACKNOWLEDGMENTS

The authors wish to extend their sincere gratitude to the following for their personal contribution to the completion of this book:

Diana Adams, Dorothy Adams Anderson, Reverends Richard and Sahra Bennet, Dr. Paul Berguson, Marty Berkowitz, Emma Cappucci, Mr. and Mrs. Edward Fellini, Tony Foster, Joe Francis, Al Gavin, Mrs. Vincent Holland, Bob Jackson, Felice Lamden (Lynch Museum Industries), Mr. and Mrs. Albert La Motta, Debbie La Motta, Mr. and Mrs. Joseph La Motta, Theresa La Motta, Vickie La Motta, Richard Lieberman, David McGehee, Mrs. Eileen McGehee, John Mortimer, Mrs. Joseph Quish, Mr. and Mrs. Bill Ramaglia, John Staley, Barbara Szold, Mrs. Marjorie Thailer, and Mr. and Mrs. Augie Tumminia and family.

Raging Bull II

PART I

The Fix

One

It was raining hard enough to hurt as I stood looking up from the bottom of those long steps to the old Senate Office Building. I never did like Washington. All those over-sized buildings and monuments made me feel like some dumb bug crawling around a pyramid or something. I guess I was about as alone as any one guy could get. The Middleweight Champion of the World about to admit to the greatest sin in boxing. What a shit feeling—like going to confession for the first time. I was in a cold sweat. My body felt like a million pins were pinching my flesh. I felt I did nothing wrong. Everybody wants to be champ. What a great feeling to be champ of the world! All I ever wanted to do was to be champ. It takes connections to get what you want out of life. It takes two wires to connect a light bulb. All my life I only had one.

The steps were filled with all kinds of umbrellas and pushy reporters, all waiting for me to arrive. "Hey, Champ!" I heard in the background. Then, "Give 'em hell, Champ!" Some punk reporter shoved a microphone in my face. "Are you going to talk, Jake, in spite of mob reprisals?" "Did you really take the dive, Jake?" "Will your brother Joey testify?" I kept staring straight ahead, shoving my hands deeper into my pants pockets, trying to push my way past the crowd and all those creepy reporters. I never did like reporters, and they didn't like me. They never print what the truth is. You tell them the truth and when you read about it the next day, it's been twisted and turned around. So what's the sense in talking to them? Sure, they all liked talking to my wife Vickie—shoving those microphones in her face like they were big hard ons.

7

Reporters—bullshit! In my day they were all paid off with fat envelopes from the boys upstairs. That's how they created a demand for their boxers. The sports writers would go back and write up a bum who couldn't fight his way out of a paper bag. Then in a few months, with all the bullshit in the columns, they'd come up with a hot new contender. It wasn't that way with me. Nobody was handing out envelopes on my behalf. But I can remember guys like Dan Parker of the *New York Mirror* and Jimmy Cannon of the *Journal-American*—newspapers that aren't around any more. They always gave me a fair shake in their columns, calling me the uncrowned middleweight champ when the other bums were calling me names like "Jake the Snake" and "Jake the Rake." After today I guess they'd all be calling me "Jake the Fake." Ah, Who the hell cares anymore. . . .

I wanted to run up the rest of those steps and duck into the nearest hole, but all those people were pushing and shoving. All those flash bulbs popping off, like it was the night I beat Cerdan and Referee Johnny Weber held up my hand and told the whole world that Jake La Motta was the new middleweight champ. Maybe I liked what they were doing then, but as I think back, I kinda felt like a freak. Like a freak in a zoo—or better, like a geek in a carnival. You know what a geek is? You throw a geek a raw chicken and he'll eat it, feathers and all, and everybody outside the cage will laugh and applaud. Was I a champ, or was I a geek? Only God knows what I was . . . I never really thought that much about God, not since I was a kid and Mom would send me out to buy those little candles with the pennies she'd hide from Pop. Then I'd duck into the candy store and place another nickel bet with the local bookie, just to keep Mom in candles. She'd place the candles in front of four or five of those religious statues she kept in the house. "O my God I am heartily sorry for having offended thee and I detest all my sins for thy just punishment. . ." Those candles burned night and day. I can still remember the smell of those stinking candles. She really was religious.

My father on the other hand was really a mean son of a bitch. If I wasn't home before those church bells rang, he'd drag me up the steps and tie me to the foot of the bed and beat me with that broomstick he'd nailed nine leather strips to till my back bled. The mean bastard. Mom would try to pull him off me, and when that didn't work, she'd fake a faint. But he kept right on hitting me, with Mom lying on the floor next to me. "Maladrino, pedacuzo, s'fachimo!" he'd call me. Then there were the times he'd come home plastered and start choking Mom in the kitchen with my little sisters, Ann and Marie, crying in the corner and baby Albee bawling his head off in the crib upstairs. By the time I was twelve I was strong enough to pull him off her, but I never hit him. My brother Joey did that later on when he got big enough.

Joey was raised by our grandparents on the Lower East Side and wasn't around that much to get all the beatings. Except one Christmas I remember, when Joey was still a kid and was visiting with Grandpa and Grandma. They'd brought over a load of fresh fruit and stuff. Joey took an extra orange from the table, and Pop belted him across the room. I guess he was saving the fruit for himself. They didn't bring Joey over too much after that. He always felt left out because Mom gave him to her parents to raise, but I figured she did him a favor. If Pop ever loved any of us, he never showed it. I always thought that he hated my mother because of me. A bum, a bum kid. No beginning, no future, no end. That's what he thought all his life. Jake, a bum, just a bum—like him. Did he still think that now? I don't know, all my life I don't know. . . .

All this rain, you could drown in it. I felt that every drop of rain was a tear, a tear my mother cried. Every time it thundered and rained, Mom would hide herself in a closet, away from all the bad things that were happening upstairs. I used to hold her in my arms and say, "Mom, don't be afraid. God is just movin' the furniture around." Then she would smile and say, "I love you too, Giacobino." Pop always called her a closet case. She wasn't. I always thought he was. I don't know if I ever loved him or not. . . .

The pit of my stomach took another nose dive. For a second, I was that scared punk kid running from the cops through the back alley again. I felt like a cornered rat about to be clobbered. I tried to sink deeper into my soaked suit, like some stupid turtle trying to hide in his own skin. All those steps, it seemed like a thousand of them. I wished I could reach the top. I wished nobody would ever have to be in my position today—the Champ of the World being led by the nose like a common stool pigeon. I wished I could slip and fall and be taken to the nearest hospital. No such luck. I had to face what I did wrong. Help me, Mom. You see, Mom had God on her side. . . .

All these thoughts came to me in a flash as I kept walking up to that big courtroom. It was June 14, 1960—Flag Day. I remembered it was Flag Day because it was always my job to hang out that old American flag Pop kept folded in the top drawer of his bureau. All those colored rags sticking out of those tenement windows like a bunch of dirty laundry. Italians in the Bronx back then were proud to be Americans—even if most of them weren't even citizens. Pop was born in Sicily, but he must have gotten his citizenship papers somewhere because I remember they drafted him into the Army.

First, they tried to draft me. I had just beat Sugar Ray Robinson for the first time and was finally making enough dough to take the family off home relief. Now they wanted me to go off and fight a war. I didn't pass the physical because of my bad left ear. I'd dropped out of school in the eighth grade because I couldn't hear the teacher. I was eight years old when Mom wrapped my head in a scarf and walked with me in the bitter cold all the way to Marasenia Hospital in the Bronx. "I want to be a fighter," I told the doctor. "Forget it," he said. "You'll never fight with that ear." The doc didn't know who he was talking to. My brother Joey acted insane and went berserk and hit a sergeant during his physical. They had to take somebody from the family, so they wound up with Pop. He was 45 and had bad feet, but they took him anyway. "Imagine me," he said. "I gotta go and fighta my owna people. What a stupida country!"

Pop was off somewhere in Sicily now, living it up on social security. He took off, leaving my mother and sisters holding the bag, as usual. Way to go, Pop. If he was with me today, he'd probably be ashamed. He'd pull that wide-brimmed hat down over his eyes and slouch a bit, like he was tryin' to hide something—a poor man's Mussolini. I might even have cared how he felt, maybe for the first time in my life. But he wasn't here, and I didn't care. . . .

I kept looking around for my brother Joey. The cocky bastard. Here I was about to be hung on the cross and he's nowhere in sight. Wasn't he the one that said, "Ya open your mouth and they'll kill ya"? Simple as that. I still hadn't figured out how I was going to answer the D.A.'s questions and keep on living. I'm not the type that scares easy, but I'm not that stupid either. Nobody rats on the mob and lives to brag about it. Sure, some of them were dead by now. But the code of silence goes beyond the grave—way beyond. Besides, I wasn't a rat.

I'd pretty much decided to take the whole rap myself. I didn't even have a mouthpiece with me. I never trusted lawyers or managers. I never trusted nobody except Joey. The last manager I had I threw down a flight of steps for trying to double-cross me. And that was 20 years ago. He tried to sign me up for another four years so he could use his mob connections. He wouldn't sign the paper releasing me from his phony contract, so I choked him till he did. Then he sues me for attempted murder. I stood up before the grand jury and told them, "If I was gonna kill the guy, I could've done it in a minute." They dismissed the case.

After that I always figured I could take care of myself better than any lousy thirty percenter. I figured all I needed was a stamp. That's why it took me so long to get a title match. I wasn't giving the mob their fifty percent cut. I figured I could do it on my own. I figured wrong. I guess if I'd played ball with the wiseguys sooner I'd have saved myself a lot of time and made a lot more money. But that wasn't my way. I really believed I could be an independent fighter, and for a long time there, I was. A lot of good it was doing me now.

I gave one last shove past all the noise and the crowd and slipped through the huge metal door that a security guard cracked open for me. It was cool and dark and quiet as a tomb inside. The guard closed the door shut behind me. It sounded like the clang of a prison cell. I spied Joey at the far end of the empty hall. He was leaning up against the wall with his arms folded, listening to his lawyer. As I started walking toward them, the lawyer creep suddenly shut up and walked away. I could tell by the funny look on Joey's face that he'd been told to clam up around me. The creep lawyer just sat on that windowsill that was as wide as a love seat, puffing on some cheap cigar and staring at us, not saying a word, while Joey and I kept pacing up and down the corridor like two tigers in a cage. We were waiting our turn to get slaughtered. I'd look at him and he'd look at me as we passed each other. Now and then we'd shrug our shoulders at each other, each time thinking harder than the first. Should I lie about these mobster creeps to protect them? I didn't owe anything to any of them.

What I got I paid plenty for. I didn't mind admitting to my part in the deal. I wanted to come clean. I wasn't exactly proud of it, but I did what I had to in order to get my rightful shot at the title, and if I had to, to get the championship, I'd do it again. The statute of limitations was up on the whole goddam mess by now anyway. The D.A. couldn't touch me. But if I named names . . . They'd already put Frankie Carbo away—Jim Norris's top wiseguy—and in the fight game they didn't come any bigger than Norris and Carbo. I had no beef with them. Didn't they sign me for the championship bout like they promised? So Norris and Carbo were in the front row for most of my fights—so what? I knew I'd be deader than a doornail. Squealing on myself was one thing. In my world the golden rule went something like: "Thou shalt not squeal on others. . ." All my life I'd lived by that code of survival, and I wasn't about to turn rat now. And what about Joey? They'd get him, too. Sure, I okayed all the deals, but Joey was in on every deal I'd made. What a goddam bind we were in.

Suddenly we both stopped pacing and looked hard at each other. "What are you going to do?" I finally asked him. He looked at me like I was crazy. "I'm gonna take the Fifth all the way. What do ya think, I'm stupid?"

"What do ya mean, take the Fifth?" Joey had talked to his lawyer—I hadn't.

"I respectfully refuse to answer on the grounds I maka for myself a recrimination," he grinned. "Simple," he shrugged, "The D.A. can't touch me."

It was then that I knew what I had to do. If they couldn't nail Joey, then all I had to do was put the blame on him. That way we'd both walk out with our heads still attached to our shoulders. I didn't like it much, but what else could I do? I knew that those bastards set up the crime, and assholes like me go along and commit it.

This poker-faced guard came over and took me by the arm and led me through these gigantic oak doors into the Caucus Room. I was shitting in my pants, and I knew that if I did shit, somebody in that big room would clean it up. It made me feel important, and maybe sorry. I really did nothing wrong, at least nothing they were trying to prove. All I wanted to do was to be champ. What was I supposed to do—fight the whole stinkin' system? My hands were sweaty, almost as sweaty as the rest of me. I could have drenched a towel in two seconds.

Why do all court buildings have high ceilings? Maybe it's because they want to feel high and mighty, like God looking down on a bunch of ants. I was praying to Christ, but still I was as cocky as ever. I didn't give a fuck, and then again, I did. All the times I'd fucked up kept crying in my mind. Does anybody really give a good fuck about La Motta? Who the hell cares. . . . I'm not afraid of any of those rats!

There were microphones and cameras all over the joint. I sat down at the witness table before a panel of hard-looking faces. They probably didn't even talk to their mothers unless they were cross-examining them. Joey and his lawyer sat down at a table a distance away to my right. Behind me was a row of noisy reporters. The rest of the room was filled with nosy spectators. I tried hard not to look over my shoulder. I didn't want to see any faces I might know. I immediately noticed one face that was familiar to me. It was Assistant D.A. Bonomi. A big hunk of a guy with hands the size of catchers' mitts. The kind of hands I'd always wished I had. I automatically folded my girl-sized hands in my lap and started twiddling my thumbs, like a schoolboy waiting to see the principal.

I'd already gone a few rounds with Bonomi in the D.A.'s office a few weeks before. He was tough, and he knew a lot about the fight game. One thing was for sure, he didn't pull any punches. Senator Kefauver—the big muck-a-muck who started this whole mess— wasn't in the room, but three other members of the senatorial committee were sitting up on the dias looking down on me. The holier-than-thou assholes, I didn't know them and I didn't want to know them, and I'm sure the feeling was mutual. Senators—who the hell knew from Senators? All I knew was back rooms and stinking catacombs with creeps and mobster wiseguys.

They started reading off the preliminaries, going through all the phony motions like they had all the time in the world and nothing better to do than examine everybody's asshole. I wasn't listening much. I was too busy trying not to squirm off my seat. I was wearing this old black suit that was too tight across my middle, a wrinkled shirt and a crummy yellow tie that felt like a rope around my neck—a regular Beau Brummel of the fight world. On and on they droned with that legal mumbo jumbo. . . . Then I heard my name mentioned and my ears pricked up.

"The main witness at the present hearing will be Jacob "Jake" La Motta, former middleweight champion. Other witnesses will include several boxing managers and underworld figures. In this preliminary phase of the hearings, testimony will center on three boxing matches:

"1) A middleweight match between "Jake" La Motta and Tony Janiro on June 6, 1947, in New York's Madison Square Garden.

"2) A light-heavyweight match between La Motta and Billy Fox on November 14, 1947, at Madison Square Garden.

"3) A middleweight championship match between La Motta and Marcel Cerdan on June 16, 1949, in Detroit.

"New York authorities conducted investigations concerning possible bribe offers to La Motta in the two 1947 matches. The 1949 match was the first championship bout promoted under the sole or partial auspices of the International Boxing Club of New York and marked the beginning of 'exclusive contract' control of major boxers by the IBC."

What the fuck were they trying to do to me? I knew they were into the Fox fight. I expected that. But they were putting my whole career on the line—even the championship bout with Cerdan. I beat Cerdan square, and paid through the nose for it. What the hell did they care? They were out for blood—why not mine? This was going to be tougher than I thought. I tried to loosen my tie without being obvious. You show them you're scared and they automatically go for the throat. I ought to know. I could smell fear in a guy across the ring. It was that smell that drove me in for the kill.

The first guy finally sat down and another stood up—Senator Hruska from Nebraska. What the hell do they know about boxing in Nebraska? All of a sudden, everybody's an expert. What they'd never know would fill the whole room to the ceiling with transcripts. What they did know wouldn't scratch the surface of the whole stinking system. But here they all were, making expert testimony on something they couldn't see, smell, taste or touch. . . .

Senator Hruska: "It is well known to all of us that the American tradition in sports and in athletic contests generally is deeply founded in a background of fair play and an assumption that there is wholesome competition existent between the contestants, whoever they happen to be, whether they are individuals or whether they are teams. It is assumed and it is hoped that on each occasion in sports or athletic contests that the contestants will do their best and that they will sincerely and honestly try to prevail in the contest. And when sinister influences enter into the picture, when other motives enter the scene, then this entire purpose and goal is defeated. . ."

Who did he think he was kidding with that pretty speech? Was he talking about boxing or a beauty contest? A fighter goes into the ring with one thing on his mind—to beat the shit out of the other guy before he beats the shit out of him. Kill or get killed. But the fighters don't run the game, and the wiseguys that do are never in the ring. . . .

Mr. Bonomi: "At this time, Mr. Chairman, may we call Jacob La Motta. . ."

Here we go . . . what round is it?

Senator Hart: Mr. La Motta, do you swear that the testimony you will give in this proceeding will be the truth, the whole truth, and nothing but the truth, so help you God?

Mr. La Motta: Yes, sir.

Senator Hart: Mr. La Motta, will you state your name and address for the record, and then I will ask Mr. Bonomi to examine you.

La Motta: Jake La Motta, 345 East 52nd Street, New York City.

Bonomi: How old are you, Mr. La Motta?

La Motta: Thirty-seven.

Bonomi: And what is your present occupation?

La Motta: Actor.

Bonomi: And were you the Middleweight Champion of the World at one time?

La Motta: Yes.

Bonomi: And were you a professional boxer from 1941 to about 1954?

La Motta: Yes, sir.

Bonomi: About how many bouts did you have during that period?

La Motta: About 125.

Bonomi: What were some of the more important bouts that you engaged in during those 13 years?

La Motta: Well, I fought Ray Robinson six times, Marcel Cerdan, Fritzie Zivic four times, and a number of others.

Bonomi: Were you the first boxer to defeat Ray Robinson during his professional career?

La Motta: Yes, sir.

Bonomi: Can you estimate, Mr. La Motta, what your gross earnings were during that 13-year period from 1941 to 1954?

La Motta: About a million dollars.

Bonomi: Did there come a time when you won the middleweight championship of the world?

La Motta: Yes, sir.

Bonomi: When was that?

La Motta: 1949.

Bonomi: And who did you fight at that time?

La Motta: Marcel Cerdan.

Bonomi: Where did that fight take place?

La Motta: Detroit, Michigan. Briggs Stadium.

Bonomi: How long did you hold the middleweight championship of the world?

La Motta: Two years.

Bonomi: And when you lost the middleweight championship, whom did you fight?

La Motta: Ray Robinson.

Bonomi: Where was that bout held?

La Motta: In Chicago.

Bonomi: And did that bout take place on February 14, 1951?

La Motta: Yes, sir.

Bonomi: Now, for some time in the period before you won the middleweight championship, were you known as the uncrowned middleweight champion?

La Motta: Yes, sir.

Bonomi: And during that period, did you have difficulty in getting bouts?

La Motta: Yes, sir.

Bonomi: Is there any explanation for the difficulty that you had in getting bouts?

La Motta: I was too good.

Bonomi: You recall that in 1947 you fought Billy Fox, a light-heavyweight boxer?

La Motta: Yes, sir.

Bonomi: And that was in the period when you had difficulty in getting bouts, is that right?

La Motta: Yes, sir.

Bonomi: In fact, this was an over-the-weight match; isn't that correct?

La Motta: Yes, sir.

Bonomi: Where did you fight Billy Fox?

La Motta: Madison Square Garden, New York City.

Bonomi: And did that match take place on November 14 of 1947?

La Motta: I believe so.

Bonomi: On the record books, Mr. La Motta, that bout is listed as a knockout of you by Billy Fox in four rounds. In fact, the fight was fixed so that you would lose; isn't that correct?

La Motta: Yes, sir.

Bonomi: Now, will you state what happened in the ring during the Fox match?

La Motta: I would like to state from the beginning, if it is all right with you.

Bonomi: You may make whatever statement you want.

La Motta: When I signed for the Fox fight, after a couple of weeks I received an offer of $100,000 to lose to Billy Fox, which I refused. I said I was only interested in the championship fight. It was said it could be arranged, a championship fight might be arranged. That is all I heard for about a couple of weeks, and while in training I hurt myself and I went to a doctor and the doctor examined me and took X-rays and found out I had a ruptured spleen. He said I couldn't possibly fight, but I thought I could, and I started training again, and I instructed my sparring partners to concentrate their punches on my face, which they did. But as the fight kept getting closer, I found out—I realized that I had no strength in my arms. So, therefore, when I was told again if I would lose to the Fox fight, I kept stalling them off because I still felt I could win. But as the fight kept getting closer, I realized that it was going to be kind of difficult. But toward the end, when I realized that I couldn't possibly win, I said I would lose to Billy Fox, if I was guaranteed a championship fight.

I thought I'd beat Bonomi to the punch, thinkin' I'd get out of there a lot sooner. If the judges was scoring this one, they'd have to give the first round to me on points. I might've stunned him a bit, but Bonomi held his ground. He was just gettin' warmed up. . . .

> Bonomi: Mr. La Motta, you have stated, I believe, before this sub-committee that several weeks prior to the Billy Fox bout, you received a $100,000 bribe offer in order to throw the fight; is that correct?
> La Motta: That is right.
> Bonomi: From whom did you receive this $100,000 bribe offer?
> La Motta: From my brother.
> Bonomi: Your brother, Joseph La Motta?
> La Motta: That is right.

I shot a quick look at Joey. He knew I'd thrown him a curve, but I knew like always he'd go along with it. His lawyer just glared at me.

> Bonomi: Will you state in detail how this bribe offer was transmitted to you?
> La Motta: He just said that if I would lose to Fox, I could get $100,000. He knew that I wasn't interested in it, but he had to give me the message, and I told him that I wasn't interested in the money, and that I was only interested in the championship fight.

It was Tuesday night—fight night at the Park Arena—four days before the Fox fight. Frankie Carbo had never shown up at my club before, but there he stood at the door with Fox's crooked manager, "Blinky Palermo," and his sidekick, "Honest" Bill Daly. We walked down the steps to the basement past the fighters' dressing rooms to the end of the catacomb and made the deal. They couldn't believe it when I told them I didn't want the money. A hundred grand is a lot of dough, even when you say it fast. What they didn't know is that I would have paid them for a fair shot at the title. I'd been fighting forever, and I wasn't getting any younger. I knew they wanted the odds on the sucker bets so they could clean up, so I told them, if they could guarantee me a championship match, I'd lose to Fox. What they also didn't know was that with my ruptured spleen I'd have probably lost the fight anyway. So I figured I wasn't really doing them any big favor. I felt like a cockroach, but it was my only shot for the title, and I took it. I got the

word I was waiting for the day before the fight. I had to trust they'd
come through with their end of the bargain. They knew if they
didn't they'd have to kill me before I killed them. . . .

Bonomi: Do you recall that you were interviewed on April 28 of
1960 by me and by Mr. McShane at your residence, and isn't it a
fact that at that time you stated that you received a $100,000 bribe
offer from "Blinky" Palermo and Bill Daly through your brother, Joseph La Motta?

La Motta: I am sorry, sir, that was never said. It might have been
said in a different way, the way you put words into my mouth, but it
was never said that way.

Bonomi: How was it said?

La Motta: It was probably said, if their names were mentioned in
connection with the fight, I said, "Yes, Daly's and Palermo's names
were mentioned in connection with the fight," but not in connection
with the bribe offer because I know nobody that offered the bribe.
The only information I got from it was from my brother.

Bonomi: What did your brother say, who did he say was offering
the bribe?

La Motta: He did not mention any names. I wasn't interested in
any names. I was only interested in one thing, and that was the
championship.

Bonomi: How do you explain, Mr. La Motta, the fact that on May
11, 1960, when a stenographic statement was taken in your lawyer's
office, that you stated, to the best of your recollection, that a
$100,000 bribe offer came through your brother from Bill Daly and
Frank "Blinky" Palermo?

La Motta: I don't recall saying something like that. You know,
you guys start to ask questions and then you stop for a pause and
then you say some more questions and then you put them all together and you get a different kind of story.

Bonomi: Do you deny making the statement?

La Motta: I know in the statement I said that he definitely didn't;
then later on you said I did. I don't know how it works out.

Bonomi's punches were getting sharper, and they were beginning to hurt. I was sweating. My eyes were beginning to blur. I
yanked my tie loose and looked across at Joey and his lawyer. Joey
just looked up and shrugged his shoulders, then looked back down
at the pencil he was twirling in his fingers. I wished like hell that

he could give me the victory whistle he always blew from our corner that signaled the last thirty seconds of the round. That's when I
knew to pour it on and finish the guy off. I knew Joey was in my
corner, but he couldn't throw the towel into this ring. He knew
Carbo and his henchmen as well as I did, and what would happen
to both of us if Bonomi's lucky punches got much closer. All we
could do was hold our breath and wait for the next blow. . . .

I noticed Senator Hruska leaving the room—the guy from
Nebraska with the pretty speeches. I guess he figured he knew the
outcome. A real fight fan would know that the fight's not over till
the last round. Like the time I came back from a vicious beating to
knock out Dathuille in the last 13 seconds of the 15th round and
defended my title. Bonomi was punching this one out like it was a
title match. Maybe he wanted to be governor or something. What
did I know? Anyway, he wasn't letting up. . . .

Bonomi: Do you recall being asked on May 11 of 1960 as to why you
had made a false statement to the district attorney when he
questioned you concerning the Fox fix? Do you recall being asked
that?

La Motta: Yes.

Bonomi: I am reading from your statement of May 11 of 1960,
page 6: Did Alfred Scotti—and I will identify him for the record; he
is the Chief Assistant District Attorney in New York County—
question you and at that time did you deny you threw the fight?
Why did you deny it at that time and now you are telling me the
story?

Answer: I denied it at that time because I would get into trouble,
but at this time my lawyer tells me to tell the truth because I can't
get into trouble.

Question: In other words, because of the statute of limitations?
Answer: Yes.

Question: Were you also afraid that you might be hurt if you told
about the fix in the Fox fight?

Answer: I was not told, I just would not say because I would get
into trouble.

Question: Did you feel that you might be hurt by somebody in
the game?

Answer: I imagine so.

Question: So there were two reasons why you did not tell the
truth to the district attorney. One is that it would involve you in a

crime at that time and two that somebody in the mob might hurt you.

Answer: Three is that I still had a chance for the championship fight.

Question: When things cooled off?

Answer: Yes.

Do you recall making that statement to me on May 11 of 1960?

La Motta: Yes, sir.

Bonomi: Now it was the truth at that time and is the truth today, isn't that correct?

La Motta: Yes.

Another Senator got up and left the room. Maybe he had to take a piss; maybe he was bored; or maybe he knew I was telling the truth and there was nothing else they could grab me on. Or maybe he even thought I was making the whole thing up. Here I was about to get my head blown off and they didn't care enough to sit through the last round. These shadow boxing committees get together every few years because "boxing smells to high heaven" and they think they're going to spray a little perfume around and make the stench go away. But the fact is nothing ever changes. The wiseguys'll go on fixing the fights, and the punch drunk fighters will go on taking the dives, and the fight fans will go on betting the odds, like always. . . .

Bonomi: Do you recall, Mr. La Motta, that you won the middleweight championship of the world from Marcel Cerdan in a bout on June 16, 1949, in Detroit?

La Motta: Yes.

Bonomi: And two years had elapsed since the Fox bout, is that right?

La Motta: Yes, sir.

Bonomi: That was the cool-off period, is that correct?

La Motta: I guess so.

Bonomi: Will you state to the subcommittee the events leading up to the bout with Marcel Cerdan in June of 1949?

La Motta: I was told that if I wanted to fight for the championship with Cerdan, it would cost me $20,000.

Bonomi: What was that amount, Mr. La Motta?

La Motta: $20,000.

Bonomi: Who told you that?

La Motta: My brother.

Bonomi: And did there come a time when you gave that $20,000 to your brother?

La Motta: Yes.

Bonomi: Was that by cash or by check?

La Motta: Cash.

Bonomi: Will you please speak up, Mr. La Motta?

La Motta: Cash.

Bonomi: Where did you have the cash?

La Motta: I had it in a vault.

Bonomi: At a bank?

La Motta: Yes.

Bonomi: Will you relate to the subcommittee the circumstances under which you gave this money to your brother?

La Motta: Well, he said if I wanted a chance to fight Cerdan, that it would cost me $20,000, so I gave it to him.

Bonomi: You gave your brother, Joseph La Motta, the $20,000 in cash?

La Motta: Yes, sir.

Bonomi: And did you tell him where to bring the $20,000 in cash?

La Motta: I don't remember.

Bonomi: Did you tell him to whom the $20,000 in cash was to be delivered?

La Motta: Well, he was the one that told me.

Bonomi: You are stating that you gave no instructions to your brother?

La Motta: He just—

Bonomi: As to where the money should be delivered and to whom, is that what you are saying?

La Motta: No. He told me that I could get a chance to fight Cerdan, if I was ready to kick in with $20,000.

Bonomi: Did he tell you where the money would have to go?

La Motta: Where it had to go? Well, maybe he did, but I don't remember.

Bonomi: Didn't you have any interest in where $20,000 in cash was going?

La Motta: I knew it was in good hands.

Bonomi: In the hands of your brother Joey?

La Motta: That is right.

Bonomi: And it would be delivered?

La Motta: That is right.

Bonomi: In order for you to get the title shot, is that right?

La Motta: That is right.

Bonomi: You not only had to pay $20,000 in cash to a party whom you have not identified, but before you got the bout, you had to sign an exclusive services contract with the International Boxing Club of New York, did you not?

La Motta: Yes, sir.

Bonomi: And that agreement was made directly with Olympia Stadium Corporation?

La Motta: Yes.

Bonomi: And by the terms of that contract, if you won the championship from Cerdan, you would be required to fight for the IBC exclusively for a three-year period, is that right?

La Motta: Yes.

Bonomi: And did you have to sign a return bout contract with Cerdan?

La Motta: Yes.

Bonomi: Providing for a rematch if you won?

La Motta: Yes.

Bonomi: So that there were three things you had to do in order to finally get your match for the championship: You had to make a $20,000 payment to people connected with Cerdan; you had to sign an exclusive contract with the IBC of New York, and you had to sign for a return bout with Cerdan in case you won, is that right?

La Motta: Yes.

Bonomi: Mr. La Motta, do you recall that your purse for the Cerdan bout was approximately $19,000?

La Motta: Yes.

Bonomi: So that you paid out $20,000 in order to get the title match, and you received back a purse of $19,000.

La Motta: Yes.

Bonomi: So you were fighting for the middleweight championship for nothing, is that correct?

La Motta: Yes.

Bonomi: Did you try to cover yourself in some way?

La Motta: Yes.

Bonomi: What did you do?

La Motta: I bet on myself.

Bonomi: Do you recall that the odds on the fight were 8 to 5 in favor of Cerdan?

La Motta: Yes.

Bonomi: How much did you bet on yourself?

La Motta: To the best of my recollection, I think I bet $10,000.

Bonomi: And you won that match, did you not, by a KO in ten rounds?

La Motta: Yes.

Bonomi: So that you recouped some of your loss by winning a $16,000 bet, is that right?

La Motta: Yes.

Bonomi: You have stated before the committee about certain bribe offers that were made to you during that period. Was your experience a very unusual one at that time?

La Motta: I don't think so. Graziano was in trouble over a fictitious bribe offer when he fought Cowboy Shanks, I think it was, and they made a big thing out of it. It wasn't really nothing, because people in the fight game, we get all kinds of silly offers like that. A guy will come over to you and he will say, "Jake, I'll give you $100,000 if you lose this fight." You know what I mean, things like that. Some would say fantastic sums, you know, but you can't believe everybody. Some of it is true; some of it is not true.

Bonomi: Do you recall that at one time you managed a fighter by the name of Julio Mederos?

La Motta: Yes.

Bonomi: And did you manage him in the United States in the period between 1954 until Mederos knocked out Roland LaStarza in Miami Beach on March 2 of 1955?

La Motta: I think so.

Bonomi: You recall that you left as Mederos's manager when Mederos KO'd Roland LaStarza, do you not?

La Motta: Yes, sir.

Bonomi: What were the circumstances under which you left as manager or resigned as manager of Julios Mederos?

La Motta: I didn't like the environment.

Bonomi: Will you explain what you meant by not liking the environment?

La Motta: I didn't like the people he was associating with.

Bonomi: Who were those people?

La Motta: I don't know, a couple of phony tough guys.

Bonomi: Who were the "phony tough guys" that were connected with Mederos?

La Motta: I don't know their names.

Bonomi: Well, you remember that when you gave up the management of Julios Mederos, a boxing manager by the name of Jimmy White took over, do you not?

La Motta: I don't know. I guess so.

Bonomi: Don't you recall that, Mr. La Motta?

La Motta: He was with another manager, partners with me, a guy by the name of Black.

Bonomi: And that person's real name is Louis Sacarama, is that correct?

La Motta: I don't know his real name, but I think you are right.

Bonomi: What happened that created this unpleasant atmosphere? In other words, how were you pushed out as manager of Julios Mederos?

La Motta: I wasn't pushed out; I walked out.

Bonomi: Why did you walk out?

La Motta: I just didn't like the people that were involved.

Bonomi: Some tough guys had moved in on Julios Mederos at that time, is that right?

La Motta: I guess so.

Bonomi: Don't you know?

La Motta: Well, they didn't exactly move in. They was just around. I just didn't like the environment. I never did like the environment, and if you look back on my record, you will see that I never liked the environment of these guys, and that is why it was tough for me to get anywhere in the boxing business. I had to take matters on my own. Of course, I made a mistake and I am very sorry I made a mistake, but at that time I thought I was right when I lost to Billy Fox.

Bonomi: And it makes it difficult for anybody who wants to be independent because these people infest the game, isn't that true?

La Motta: There is quite a lot of them in it.

Bonomi: And they exert an awful lot of influence, don't they, Mr. La Motta?

La Motta: I think they do.

Bonomi: On the basis of your experience, you know they do, don't you?

La Motta: They never bothered me, they knew better.

Senator Hart (presiding): Mr. Bonomi, do you have any further questions?

Bonomi: No, I do not. No further questions at this time.

Senator Hart: Mr. Chumbris, for Senator Dirksen?

Mr. Chumbris: I have just a few questions. Mr. La Motta, what are you doing now? What is your profession?

La Motta: Actor.

This guy looked like he didn't believe me. What's the matter, didn't he ever see me fight?

Chumbris: What type of actor?
La Motta: All types.
Chumbris: Television shows?
La Motta: Well, I just finished doing a picture in Miami and I am working in a picture here in New York—I mean New York City.
Chumbris: Are you doing television shows, spot shows?
La Motta: No, not now. I was doing it, and I also do stage work.
Chumbris: Do you have any connection whatsoever with the box- ing industry now?
La Motta: No, sir.

I started fishing in my pockets for something to wipe the sweat off my face. I couldn't believe it was over. Bonomi was stuffing pa- pers in his briefcase like he couldn't wait to get out of here. He might have had me on the ropes, but he knew I'd never go down. There was nothing in my pockets but a scrap of paper I didn't know was there before. It was a note scrawled in pencil. Some creep must have slipped it into my pocket on my way into this joint. LA MOTTA—KEEP YOUR MOUTH SHUT. Who did they think they were talking to, some scared punk? It pissed me off. . . .

Mr. Dixon: Mr. La Motta . . . Mr. La Motta?
La Motta: Yes, sir?
Dixon: Since you talked to Mr. Bonomi and Mr. McShane, and since it was made public that you were coming down here to testify, has anyone contacted you directly or indirectly and suggested that you had better not give us any names?

I crushed the note in my fist.

La Motta: No.
Dixon: You are not afraid, if you give us these names, if you knew them, you might be threatened with bodily harm?
La Motta: No, I ain't afraid. I ain't afraid for myself, sir.
Dixon: Are you afraid for your family?
La Motta: No, I'm not afraid for—I am just not afraid of none of them bums.

Dixon: Are you afraid for your brother Joey? You must like your brother, like we all like our brothers.

La Motta: Uh?

Dixon: You are very fond of your brother?

La Motta: Yes.

Dixon: Are you afraid for Joey, if you give us these names?

La Motta: Well, there is no names to give, sir.

Dixon: No names to give. No one has told you, if you come down here and give us names, that something might happen to you or members of your family?

La Motta: No, sir.

Dixon: This is a pretty rough crowd, isn't it, Mr. La Motta?

La Motta: What is?

Dixon: These people engaged in this boxing business.

I looked hard at Joey and tore the note into small pieces. . .

La Motta: I ain't afraid of none of them rats!

Two

When I got on that plane back to New York, my mind was dead tired. I felt like I'd been back in the ring with Ray Robinson pounding me up against the ropes for thirteen rounds till Referee Frank Sikora jumped between us and stopped the fight. I was bloody, defeated, but still on my feet. I didn't know it then, but my career as a fighter was over. Now my reputation as a champ was over, too. All my life I fought like I didn't deserve to live. I guess now the whole world would agree with me.

I slumped down in my seat and looked straight ahead, trying to hide in my collar. I didn't want to be recognized by any more nosy reporters. They was having a field day with this one. FORMER CHAMP TAKES DIVE INTO TOILET. It was the first time in the history of boxing that a fix had been officially exposed, and probably the last. I might've been finished as a fighter a long time ago, but I had to clear the record. Not for all the creeps, not for the mob, not for the senators, but for me. Yeah . . . "La Motta's Own Story: Honest Fighters Finish Last." I gave that story to *True* magazine for a lousy $2500 bucks. I needed the dough, but more than the money, I had to get it off my chest. How did I know the whole mess would wind up sprawled across the front page of *The New York Times*?

There was testimony that Fox was in a Long Island mental hospital—punchy as a loon. Bet he wouldn't know who La Motta is. The dumb shmuck, he was probably the only one that didn't know the fight was fixed. His manager, "Blinky" Palermo, set him up real good with that string of phony knockouts. The poor slob never fought a real fight in his life. They use guys like him up and spit them out on the street like a wad of chewed tobacco. No pension, no benefits, no nothing. That's the way it is in the fight racket. Fighters are as expendable as toilet paper. If I had listened to all those wiseguys, I'd probably be Fox's roommate today. As my own manager, I called my own shots. I might have made some mistakes, but they were my mistakes, and I paid for them my own way. Even the wiseguys had to respect that. I guess I'd find out soon enough how much respect they still had.

Joey testified, too, and took the Fifth all the way home. That was the end of it—or was it? At this point, I didn't give a good fuck what happened. I was tired and I wanted to get some sleep. One good thing about planes, they have a certain hum that acts like a tranquilizer. So tired . . . I didn't care if I ever woke up. . . .

"Giacobino, I gotta sixa kids for you today."

"How many do I have to beat, Pop?

"All six. I know you canna do it. I gotta my friends comina down. They gotta lotsa money. They throwa dollar bills ina the ring for you. Remember—hit 'ema first, and hit 'ema hard!"

The kid is ten years old. I'm only eight, and he's taller than me. I'm punching as hard as I can, but I can't hit him, I wish they'd stop hitting me with those coins. . . . All those nickels and dimes and pennies are stinging my body. Everybody's yelling and screaming. I've got to finish him off. . . . "Go on, Giacobino—knock him down—you canna do it!" . . . "I can't hit him, Pop. . . . Something's holding back my arms. . . . I can't hit him!"

I try to pick up the coins with my gloves, but I can't do it. All those coins and I can't pick them up. Everybody's jeering at me; they're laughing at me. . . . "Pop, where are your friends with the dollar bills?" "Sorry, Giacobino, they couldn't come. Wipa your nose; it'sa bleeding. . ." I try to wipe my face with my glove, but the glove's too hard. The blood tastes so salty. . .

"Pop, why are you hitting me? Don't hit me anymore, I swear I'll beat all the kids. . . . Don't pull my ear, Pop—not my sore ear—stop hitting me . . . stop hitting me. . . . Pop, I don't want to hit you—leave me alone . . . I got this pipe, Pop, and I'll hit you with it. . . . Don't make me hit you, Pop!". . . It's Harry Gordon—the bookie I mugged in the back alley . . . I've got this lead pipe I wrapped in dirty newspaper and I'm hitting him over the head with it. . . . "Harry, don't let me hit you anymore. Your head is bleeding. Harry, please let me stop, let me stop. . . . Stop crying . . . stop crying . . . stop. . . . You're dead, Harry—you can't cry anymore—you're dead!". . . .

"Wrong," the judge is saying, "wrong in your attitude, wrong in the company you keep, wrong in your whole approach to life. I hereby sentence you to an indeterminate term of one to three years in the state reform school at Coxsackie, New York. Take him away . . . take him away . . . take him away. . . ."

It's Father Joseph. "Hi, Dad!" . . . "How many times do I have to tell you, Jake—you don't call a priest Dad." . . . "Okay, Dad. I told you I'd beat every kid in the joint. I want to fight more than anything in the world. I can beat them all—I know I can beat them all!" . . . "Jake, is there something you want to tell me, something else I don't know? I've never probed at you, Jake, but I can see something is troubling you. Trust me. Let me help you. Have faith in me. . . . Jake, you've got to trust someone." . . . "You don't understand how it is, Father. I can't trust nobody. I never learned how . . . I can't trust nobody. . . ."

Why aren't there any windows in this truck? It's dark, and hot and sweaty. There must be fifty other guys chained together in here. I can't see out—where are we going? I can't breathe in here! They're going too fast—it's going to turn over! . . . Slow down! . . . We're going to turn over in the swamp. . . . I hear water rushing in . . . we're all going to drown . . . get these chains off me . . . get me out of here . . . somebody break these chains . . . I'm drowning . . . get me outta here . . . I want to live, do you hear me—I want to live! . . . .

Someone was shaking me hard. I woke up in a cold sweat. Viola Carbo was standing in the aisle over me. She was still bathed in the same cheap perfume. The last time I'd seen her was five years ago. I'd closed the club early. There wasn't much action that night. She stayed behind. I always found her attractive. A real Mitzi Gaynor type—tough but sexy. Being around Frankie Carbo, and married to him, she had to be tough. She knew I wanted her—a broad can always tell—but she'd kept her distance. I don't know why she stuck around that night. Maybe she thought a champ's cock was special.

Viola must have been sitting in on the Kefauver hearings to report back to Carbo and the boys. Frankie Carbo had been sent up by the same clowns who grilled me. They let him out of jail long enough to give him three more years at Rikers Island for undercover managing. With his record, the judge was doing him a favor. He'd been indicted for murder five times, and that was only the ones they knew about. As Norris's top henchman and "Blinky" Palermo's boss, Carbo controlled the fight game from top to bottom. They might have told me who I'd fight, but I still made my own deals. Fighters are kind of like whores—they sell their bodies for a price. My price was $15,000 or 35 percent of the gate—and I'd fight anybody.

I'll say one thing for Viola; she sure was a lot more loyal to Frankie than Vickie was to me when I was on the chain gang. I'd heard she and Vickie was still palling around together. The years were beginning to show on her face, but I still wouldn't kick her out of bed. She looked down at me like she wanted to kick me in the balls.

"Why did you do it, Jake? Frankie was always good to you." I shrugged my shoulders. "I had no choice. They subpoenaed me." Bonomi never even asked me about Carbo, but Viola would never believe it. Bonomi didn't have to. He had already nailed Carbo to the wall, but good, months ago, calling him stuff like "the prime minister of the boxing racket" and "boxing commissioner of the underworld." He wasn't exaggerating.

Yeah . . . Frankie Carbo was real good to me. He and Viola hanging on his arm with the mink coat and the flashy jewelry, always coming around with gifts for Vickie and the kids, trying to bribe me into one tank dive after another. It was Carbo who finally got me into the Fox fix. Maybe it was some kind of poetic justice that I was sitting on this plane free as a bird and he was back behind bars. I couldn't feel sorry for him. For a fucking wiseguy, he deserved it. Viola must have read my thoughts.

"You know, you owe Frankie a lot, Jake. We spent a lot of money on you. You ungrateful son of a bitch—I hope they blow your head off!"

I closed my eyes. The last thing I needed was this cunt busting my chops. When I opened them again, she was gone.

I hated her guts. I knew she and Vickie were out running around in California with that pack of rats and wiseguys while I was sweating it out on a bum rap on the Dade County chain gang. I was railroaded on a morals charge by some fourteen-year-old hooker and her madam who came into my club one night. The D.A. had a ball with that one. I guess you could say I was a victim of being Jake La Motta. Everybody's looking for a handout. I probably should have paid off those rotten cops. I'd have gotten off on appeal if I'd shelled out another $10,000 to that hotshot lawyer for payoffs. Fuck it. They'd sucked enough of my blood. I'd rather do the time. Besides, the chain gang was a picnic after the hell Vickie was putting me through. I remember getting served the divorce papers while I was still on the work gang. It was April Fool's day, 1958, and I was the fool.

They had us loading logs onto a truck that day. There were too many guys on the detail. There were always too many guys and too little work, but they had to keep us busy. There was this one screw—a real mother-fucker. He was alway on my case. He saw me standing off to the side, brooding over Vickie and looking like my insides had just been kicked out.

"What's the matter, Champ Pimp? Havin' trouble with the little missus? Get over there, Mr. Tough Guy, and make room for yourself. Now!"

I wanted to belt the redneck bastard then and there. I went over to the crew and knelt down to get in on the act. In the process, my arm got pinned under one of the ten-foot logs. I let out a low moan. The other cons start to lever it off, and this screw prick starts in on me again.

"What's the matter—Champ Pimp got himself another boo-boo?"

I automatically doubled up my fists. "Lay off the name, ya fuckin' cracker!" I growled. He aimed the shotgun at my head. For a tense moment there, I thought he would pull the trigger.

"You goddam Yankee!" he screamed. "Get in the truck. Get in the truck!"

They threw me in that hole—7 by 7 by 3, with a shit bucket, a water bucket, and a blanket on the floor. They'd have let me rot there if I hadn't gotten word to Sally and told her that if they didn't let me out, to hire a battery of ten lawyers and blow their graft-ridden hole sky high.

Sally Carlton . . . She was a good kid—a real sweetheart. Everything that Vickie wasn't. When Vickie took off to play playmate of the year, Sally would bring my kids to the jail to visit me. She really stuck by me when the rest of them acted like La Motta was some kind of new social disease. Yeah, Sally was a real good sport. Like the time I set it up for us to be together while I was in jail. Each time she'd visit me, I'd go crazy, being stuck behind bars with her looking so sexy on the other side. I couldn't stand it any more. I told her I was going to do something, so I faked a fall in the shower—a back injury. I'd learned how to fall down since the Fox fight. So they took me to the county hospital. I had it all worked out with the doctor. Maybe he felt sorry for me. Anyway, he left me alone with Sally and closed the door. How much of a risk could I be with one leg chained to the hospital bed? She looked like a living doll. I could hardly wait to grab her.

"Jake, don't come near me. You need a shave," she said. If she'd told me to shave my balls right then, I'd have done it. We looked around the room and found a straight-edge razor. Maybe they hoped I'd cut my throat with it. Sally started to shave me, then she noticed the chain on my leg attached to the foot of the bed. When you're in a hospital—even a prison hospital—you're not supposed to be chained.

"What do they think, Jake—you're going to escape?" Sally laughed.

"Yeah . . . Come over here," I grunted. I grabbed her and threw her on the bed next to me. I tore off her clothes and played with her smooth white body for a while. The blood was rushing to my head with excitement. I had to have her then and there. Maybe it was because I hadn't had it in so long; maybe it was knowing that we could be discovered any minute, but that was the best lay I'd had in years. Maybe it was that way for Sally, too. I don't know, but she'd have done it for me anyway. Sally was that way.

I remember the first time I saw her. I was out on appeal on that phony morals rap in Miami Beach. Vickie and I were separated, and I was shacking up with the Playmate of the Month—at least that's what she told me she was. Sally was sitting at a table with this wimp in the Edgewater Hotel. They were celebrating her 19th birthday. I walked over to the table wearing my lucky red shirt and smoking a big cigar with a couple of broads on my arms. "Who's that broad?" I said. "Hello, you beautiful, gorgeous, lovely creature." I gave her my standard line. I remember she didn't like me much at first. I think she even told me to leave. Stuck up broad. The guy she was with—this hotshot New York agent named Jerry Katz—was sliding under the table. "Do you know who that is?" he told her. "That's Jake La Motta—a tough guy." You think she'd have shown more respect.

I saw her again later that night at the Fontainebleau's Poodle Lounge. She was sitting with some people I knew at the other end of the bar. I kept sending her drinks until she gave in and let me come over and talk to her. I found out her name was Sally Carlton and she was a model working between Miami and New York. If I didn't know better, I'd have figured she was a high class hooker— one of those $100 a night jobs—and her fancy agent was her pimp. But I could tell by the way she talked she wasn't the hooker type. She was too nice and polite. I really poured it on that night. I must have put away two fifths of scotch. I started telling her all my troubles with Vickie and the law. She didn't seem to mind listening to all my blubbering. I don't know. What makes a young beautiful chick go for a middle-aged slob who's drunk half the time? Maybe it's like beauty and the beast. I always had beauty queens go for me. Vickie could still walk into a room and give every man there a rise. I could never figure it out—an ugly dumb fuck like me. . . .

I knew I was too goddam drunk to drive that night, but I slid behind the wheel of my baby blue Cadillac convertible anyway and tried to drive Sally home. I must have been driving like a maniac, because Sally got out of the car at the light and started to hail a cab. She was going to leave me there like the drunken bum I was, but instead she got in behind the wheel and drove me back to her place. I was a real mess that night. I started to get the shakes real bad—shivering and sweating and burning up like a case of yellow fever. I remember Sally lying on top of me all night long just to keep me warm. She was a real angel of mercy. We had breakfast together the next morning, and we've been together ever since. I don't know what I'd do without her. She's the one good thing in my life now. I need her like blood.

The no smoking sign went on in the plane, and I knew we were approaching La Guardia airport. I looked out the window. All I could see was a blank wall of thick grey clouds. The rain must have followed me from Washington. I hated the rain. It always made me think of poverty and cold wet feet as a kid. The stewardess was checking all the seat belts. Mine wasn't fastened. "Mr. La Motta, please fasten your seat belt," she cooed, and leaned over to fasten it for me. How did she know my name? My stomach took a sudden lurch as the plane dove down to the runway. I didn't know who else would be at the airport to meet me. I only knew Sally would. I thought of her long slender legs and pretty face and soft brown eyes, and suddenly I was anxious to hit the ground. The young stewardess came back and leaned over me again. "Mr. La Motta, please remain on the plane until all other passengers have disembarked."

"What do you mean?" I said. I was getting suspicious.

"Security reasons, sir," she answered, and walked away.

At that point Viola Carbo came down the aisle towards me, putting on the gloves she always wore, probably to hide her age spots. She looked me right between the eyes as she passed by. "I hope you have a long and prosperous future, Jake." Her voice was as cold as ice. What the shit did she mean by that? Screwy broad.

The young stewardess was watching me the whole time. She was a cute little blonde, trim figure and big innocent green eyes. I motioned for her to come over. "May I help you, sir?" She gave me that phony stewardess smile.

"How long must I sit here? Everybody left the plane." I was getting impatient.

"I know, sir. We have received word from security that there might be a slight problem upon your arrival."

"What kind of problem?"

"I wouldn't know, sir." She left me again.

I sat there like some dumb asshole, waiting it out. I reminded myself of this old gorilla in the Central Park zoo—a lifer. He'd sit in the corner of his cage, bored shitless, and spit at all the spectators. I wasn't spitting, but I was getting mad. If they got me mad enough, maybe I'd start spitting, too. Everybody left me—the cute stewardess, the pilots, everybody. I was sitting in total silence, all alone like a jerk. Again, all alone. . . . I wanted to get up and see what was happening, but being a fighter, I'd learned to take instructions. So I sat. . . .

A few minutes that seemed like hours went by, then these three big guys in plain clothes walked up to me. I could tell they were some kind of cops. "Are you Jake La Motta?" the first guy asked me.

"No, I'm Mickey Mouse. You guys know who I am. I'm the only slob left on the plane. What the hell is going on here?" I was pissed.

"We represent airport security, Mr. La Motta." He flashed his badge under my nose. "If you'll come with us now, we'll escort you through a restricted area. We have an airport limousine waiting."

"What about my girl? She's supposed to meet me." I didn't know what else was waiting for me, but I knew Sally wouldn't disappoint me.

"That's all been taken care of, sir. If you'll just come with us now. . . ."

I shrugged my shoulders and started to get up. My seat belt was still fastened. I unhooked it and followed the security guys off the plane. I didn't know what to expect, but I figured it was going to be a bumpy ride.

The rain was coming down in a steady drizzle as we made our way down the steep slippery steps to the ground. It was cold for June. I wasn't wearing a coat, so I pulled the collar of my jacket up and shoved my hands deep into my pockets. Two of the guards flanked me, the other followed close behind. It felt like I was being led down death row. As we neared the terminal, I could make out a crowd of people standing behind the chain link fence. Some were carrying signs. They was shouting something at me, and as I got closer, I knew it was nothing good.

"Hey, La Motta, you phony bum! Did they buy the title for you, too?" . . . "How does it feel to be a stool pigeon?" . . . "Why'd ya do it, Jake?" . . . "Hey, it's Jake the Fake!" Then they all started shouting in unison, "Jake the Fake, Jake the Fake, Jake the Fake!"

I just kept on walking, staring straight ahead. There's nothing more loyal than a fight fan, and nothing more angry than a fight fan that feels betrayed. I couldn't really blame them. Nothin's sacred anymore. If they could fix the fucking World Series, they could fix anything. . . .

Hurrying past all the mad faces, I noticed out of the corner of my eye this one little Italian guy standing off to the side of the crowd. He wasn't shouting or anything, just standing there alone looking at me. Our eyes met for a second as I passed into the terminal. I couldn't believe it—the guy had tears in his eyes. I never saw him before in my life, but I'll never forget the look he gave me—like he had just lost his best friend. . . .

The security cops led me quickly through the terminal and out to a parked airport limo. I ducked inside as fast as I could. I couldn't wait to get the hell out of there. Sally was waiting for me inside. I took one look at her and grabbed her and kissed her hard on the mouth.

"Jake, honey, you're soaking wet," she mumbled, trying to pull away from me. The bunch of newspapers she'd had on her lap slipped to the floor. I read *The New York Times* sports page headline: "Jake Blows the Whistle—Tells Senate Group He Faked Knockout Loss."

"Let's go home, Baby," I sighed and sank back into the seat. I was sick of the whole mess. "Let's just go home. . . ."

Neither of us felt much like talking on the way back. The driver seemed to know where he was going, so I sat back and lit up a cigar—the first I'd had all day. I took six puffs and had to put it out. I was gettin' agita—a feeling like your whole chest is tightening up and you can't breathe. I started to think about tomorrow. Who would knock on my door and who would call on the phone. I knew I had done nothing wrong but tell the truth. "The truth shall set you free," Sally kept saying. Was I free? I felt more trapped than ever. I looked over at Sally and wondered why she loved me . . . if she loved me. I loved her, I thought, but who knows what love really is? I can love a ham sandwich, too. . . . The silence was getting on my nerves. All I could hear was the windshield wipers going back and forth, back and forth. . . . It was like they were saying, "Jake the Fake, Jake the Fake," back and forth like a chorus. I wanted to turn my mind off, turn out the lights and forget everything. I needed a good stiff belt of scotch.

It was still drizzling as the limo pulled up to my apartment building at 345 East 52nd Street. Jimmy the doorman ran up to the car door to let us out. Jimmy had been helping me out of cars and cabs for close to two years now—ever since I left Florida. I liked Jimmy. He reminded me of Tom Pedi, a fighter from Brooklyn who turned actor—short, a bit on the heavy side with an Italian face and a busted nose. Jimmy's a little rough around the edges, but he has a great Italian heart—like me. "Welcome back, Champ," was all he said. "Thanks, buddy," I muttered back.

Sally and I were silent all the way up in the elevator. The tiny studio apartment with its dirty bare walls was as dismal as the rain outside. It seemed to smell sour and damp, like my clothes.

"Are you hungry, Jake? There's some cold spaghetti in the fridge. I can heat it up for you, if you like." Sally's voice sounded strange and far away. She'd never seen me this miserable and sober before.

"Naw, I ain't hungry."

The silence fell again like a thick wall between us. Sally threw herself across the narrow bed and stared at the ceiling. I stripped to my shorts and went for the bottle of scotch I always kept in the kitchen cabinet. I grabbed a tall glass, plopped down on the worn pull-out couch, and poured myself two fingers straight up. I looked over at Sally. She was curled up on the bed with her face to the wall. I hoped she was asleep. I was never too good with words, especially when it came to broads. I looked at the phone, hoping it wouldn't ring. I wasn't in the mood to talk. I didn't even feel like watching TV. I'd probably see my ugly mug looking back at me on the evening news. I grabbed the worn deck of cards I always kept around and started playing solitaire. It kept me from thinking too much.

By midnight I'd finished off the whole quart of scotch, but I still felt nothing. I got up and put on my clothes. My jacket was dry now. I thought I would hit some of the local joints, just to sound things out. I got to the door, but my hand wouldn't turn the knob. I went over to Sally and sat down on the bed next to her. As I leaned over her, I saw she was crying.

"What the hell are ya cryin' for? You know I can't stand broads that cry."

"Oh, Jake, I'm sorry," she murmured meekly. "I didn't know what they were going to do to you. I just thought if you told the truth that everything would be all right. I'm so sorry. . . ."

"Sally Bird, what am I goin' to do with you? You're such a baby, just a little baby. It's not your fault, darlin'. Sometimes the truth can hurt."

I put my arms around her and curled up beside her. Sally sobbed in my arms for a while, then we both fell asleep.

PART II

Hard Times

Three

Sally stared blankly out her New York apartment window at the vicious wind and rain raging through the streets below. The tight knot in her stomach that appeared the moment she awoke refused to go away and only seemed to grow stronger with the increasing storm outside. This was her wedding day. She should be happy—deliriously happy—she reasoned with herself crossly. Wasn't this what she wanted? Her little girl dream come true—to finally be Mrs. Jake La Motta, Mrs. Champ, the wife of the legendary Bronx Bull.

Her mind flashed back to that day in the Pennsylvania orphanage when she first saw Jake clowning with Rocky Graziano on television on the Martha Raye Show. She was only fourteen, but something about his rough, raw unadorned image impressed her as real even then. She had felt a certain intensity in his presence that she had never forgotten. Perhaps it was that same sense of strength and power, that feeling of being safe and secure and protected that she instinctively sought in all the men she had known. She had always been attracted to fighters—strong, proud powerful men on the outside who could be surprisingly gentle and affectionate on the inside.

Her grandfather had been such a man, at least she liked to remember him that way. He was stern and unrelenting, but he was there more often than anyone else she could remember. Her parents—poor itinerant laborers who followed hard work around the country like modern American gypsies—had abandoned her off and on in one orphanage after another. Small wonder she often felt like a little girl in Jake's strong supporting arms. At 37 he was 15 years her senior. Maybe she really wanted him to adopt her rather than marry her. . . . Marriage had always terrified her. Her parents' marriage had been one long painful disaster. She would be Jake's third wife, she noted apprehensively. He would be her first and, she fervently believed, last husband. Orphanages had a way of inspiring awe around the notion of the sacred family unit, a kind of worship from afar. If she was going to do it, it was going to be for good. That's what made it so damned scary.

A sudden strong gust of wind rattled the windows and howled ominously around the tall unyielding gray buildings. The knot in Sally's stomach tightened another notch. It wasn't as if she and Jake were total strangers, she continued to reason with herself. They'd been through a lot together in the past three years, ever since those first miserable months with him in jail. They had fallen in love slowly, painfully, passionately, the way a strong, wild vine wraps itself around the nearest tree.

She had been totally dependent on Jake that first year in New York. He seemed to know everyone, but they were all strangers to her. His mother and sisters were kind, but aloof. They'd seen too many of Jake's girl friends come and go. When Jake made his rounds of the town's nightspots, she'd remain all alone in that dingy studio, afraid to initiate any new relationships on her own. Jake could be so possessive at times; she preferred her self-imposed solitude to the harrowing cross-examination that followed any attempt on her part to widen her social contacts. It was only in these past few months that she had felt strong enough to pursue her own interests.

She was working full-time now as a showroom model on Seventh Avenue. She got along well with her boss, Lenny Silverman, a hard-core dress manufacturer who had hired her on the spot. "You've got the perfect measurements for my line. I've been looking for a fitting model like you since I got into this business. Just two things, and you've got yourself a steady job—be on time, and don't get yourself knocked up!" he'd told her firmly. Lenny could be tough, but he was a real sweetheart to his girls. Sally was meeting new people every day, and she was beginning to enjoy her new-found independence and freedom. When her old friend, Laura Miles, showed up from Miami, she seized the opportunity to share an apartment with her. They had found a lovely one bedroom just a few blocks away from Jake's studio. Jake had been more depressed than ever after the Fox business. He started drinking heavily again. Nothing she said or did seemed to make any difference to him. She was sick and tired of all the pain and hurt. If she couldn't help him, why shouldn't she help herself? "You're miserable; I'm miserable. Let's just try it apart for a while," she'd told him.

The separation had been good for both of them. When they saw each other, it was to go out and have a good time. Jake seemed to make more of an effort to please her. He was funny and entertaining to be with again. It was as if they were two different people falling in love all over again, with none of the old miseries of the past to haunt them. When Jake stormed into her apartment that night and blurted out, "Sally, I love you. Let's get married," she had no more strength to resist him. It seemed the natural, inevitable thing to do. Jerry Katz, her long-time friend and erstwhile agent, was sitting on the couch waiting to take her out to dinner. Darling Jerry . . . He had asked her to marry him a dozen times, and she had turned him down as gently as possible a dozen times more. Jake recognized him from the night they had first met on her birthday three years before, when she had told Jake to leave and Jerry had slid under the table in fear of Jake's notorious temper.

"What's that little creep doing here?" Jake glared at Jerry.

"I was just leaving, Jake. Don't mind me," Jerry stammered. "I've always been a big admirer of yours, Champ. Sally, I'll see you around, uh?"

Poor Jerry. He sidled out the door so fast he forgot his hat.

So here she was on the Big Day. They had settled on September 12th as much by chance as anything, though Jake did say something about John and Jackie Kennedy being married on that same day. Just our luck to pick the day hurricane Donna hits the city to get married, thought Sally grimly. She tried hard not to be superstitious about things like the weather. She wouldn't have minded a little rain, but a full-fledged hurricane? "You're part of my destiny," Jake had told her. Why did that sound so depressingly final, Sally wondered now.

"A Lily Daché it's not, but it'll have to do." Laura emerged from the bedroom carrying a tiny white veiled hat. "Come over here,

Desdimona, and try this on for size. Your faithful maid of honor wishes only to serve her fair mistress on this, her wedding day. Where's Othello and Iago? They must have been swept away by the storm, poor lads."

Laura's wit and biting tongue were a perfect complement to her tall, slender, well-tailored good looks. She moved with the cool self-assurance and easy grace that come with an upper-middle-class-family upbringing. Sally envied her roommate's background and charm, but her constant sarcasm often got on her nerves.

"Cut the crap, Laura, and give me my hat." Sally smiled in spite of her nervous stomach. She knew Laura didn't approve of her marrying Jake. To Laura, marriage was strictly a business proposition, and that made Jake a bad risk. She couldn't understand the kind of selfless love Sally was capable of giving.

"Darn it. It won't stay on straight," Sally complained as she tried the hat on before the mirror.

"Here, let me do it. It's my creation," said Laura firmly as she adjusted the hat to Sally's head. "I ought to know. I've modeled enough of these things. There, that's better."

"Jake and Rick should have been here by now. They only had to drive a couple of blocks from Jake's place. Oh God, I hope Jake isn't driving. He's a terrible driver. What if they're in some kind of trouble, Laura?" Sally's voice rose in alarm.

"Relax. They're probably parked in some bar somewhere while Rick expounds to Jake on the virtues of bachelorhood. Not that Rick is one to talk. Hasn't he got a wife and kiddies stashed conveniently away somewhere, out of sight and out of mind? The Cesar Romero of the Bronx. . ." laughed Laura sarcastically.

Sally went to the window and looked out at the flooded streets below. Laura could be harsh, but she wasn't that wrong about Rick Rosselli. The four of them had double-dated a few times—just long enough for Laura to catch on to Rick's con game and put him on her list of least desirables. Rick could be as charming as a snake oil salesman, but there was something about him Sally instinctively distrusted.

She was especially suspicious of Rick's influence over Jake. In Jake's eyes, Rick could do no wrong. It was silly for her to feel jealous of their relationship, but too often Jake would take Rick's advice over hers. If it ever came to a showdown between them, Sally couldn't be sure that Jake would choose her over Rick. An involuntary shudder ran through her as she thought of Laura's earlier allusion to "Othello." Rick's opinion of women was less than primitive. He stalked them for sport, then threw them aside like so many discarded trophies. Jake was suspicious enough of the women in his life. He didn't need any advice on the subject from the likes of Rick. She could never explain this to Jake, of course. "Aw, all you broads are just jealous," he'd say.

Jake had been lonely when he first came back to New York. He and his former wife Vickie had never bothered to cultivate any real friends. They'd growl at fans who came up to them. Sally was young, but she knew that you always meet the same people on the way down that you passed on the way up. Rick Rosselli showed up from Jake's past, fresh out of a five-year prison term for armed robbery. Rick and Jake had trained together as fighters when they were both kids in the Bronx. But Rick didn't have what it takes to be a fighter. He respected and envied the fact that Jake was a Champ.

Tall, glib and street-smart, Rick could talk his way into or out of most situations, a talent that deeply impressed close-mouthed Jake. Rick always seemed to have money. Sally knew he had some sort of dress manufacturing business, but she noticed that he knew an awful lot of the wiseguys that Jake despised. Even that didn't seem to bother Jake. Rick was his best man, and that was that. . . .

"Hey, don't jump! You've been staring out that window all day," Laura broke into Sally's thoughts. "Jake must be crazy insisting you go through with this today. This hurricane is no joke, you know."

Sally left the window and curled up in a stuffed armchair. She let out a long sigh.

"Sally, are you sure you know what you're doing? I mean, you do love this guy, and all that, right?" Laura continued in a more serious tone.

"Can you love a lost puppy?" Sally responded. "It's funny how the tables have turned. I always thought I needed Jake more than he needed me, but now . . . Jake's broke, Laura. His acting career hasn't exactly soared. The fight game was all he knew, and now that that's over for good . . . He's like Ferdinand the Bull set loose on the streets of New York with no place to run and no place to hide."

"That sounds more like pity than love," Laura said quietly. "Watch out, Kiddo. Poverty may be good for the soul, but it's hell on the complexion." Laura walked into the kitchen. "You can bet when I say 'I do,' it'll be to the highest bidder. Would you like some coffee? I'll heat it up."

"No, thanks," Sally answered absently.

Laura heard the strain in Sally's voice and bit her lip, regretting her insensitive remarks. She walked over to Sally and took her gently by the shoulders.

"Look, Kid. You're a good showroom model with a damn good reputation. You'll continue to do well until Jake finds himself again. And whatever you do, don't get knocked up the first year!"

"Are you kidding? That's the last thing I need," Sally replied firmly.

Three loud bangs on the apartment door interrupted their conversation. It was Jake's favorite way of announcing himself. The moment Sally opened the door and saw Jake swaying with his cocky grin and huge cigar, she knew.

"Oh no, Jake. You've been drinking," Sally cried.

"Not really, my sweet Sally Bird. We just had a few little quickies for the road," Jake grinned back sheepishly in a poor imitation of W.C. Fields. Sally tried not to smile. Jake slipped his arm around Sally's waist and continued soothingly. "Aw, c'mon, Baby. It's our wedding day. It's rainin' so hard ya can't see a foot ahead of ya, but I know we'll make it all right."

"Are you sure you can make it, Jake?" Laura asked.

"Don't be a dumb bitch," Jake grumbled, annoyed. "I can drink anybody anywhere under the table," he boasted proudly.

"Bullshit!" retorted Sally as they all left the apartment.

Rick was waiting unperturbed behind the wheel of his blue Cadillac in front of the building. Jake hopped in next to Rick and the girls scrambled into the back seat as best they could, trying in vain to avoid the driving rain. There were no other cars on the road. The sewers were overloaded and the rushing water spilled over the curbs and onto the sidewalks. Several of the smaller trees on the block had fallen. Broken glass and torn branches strewed the streets. Sally and Laura surveyed the scene in mounting dismay.

"Hi ya, girls. Lovely day for a ride, uh?" Rick greeted them. "I think we're all out of our fuckin' minds—especially you, Jake, you bull-headed fuck!"

"Please, Jake, let's call it off for today," Sally pleaded. "We have the rest of our lives to get married. Why does it have to be today?"

"What are ya, afraid of a little rain? Ya think you're gonna melt?" Jake demanded, ignoring Sally's plea. "Rick is a hell of a good driver. He knows what he's doin'. Let's get goin' before I give you all a beatin'!"

Rick started the car and eased slowly into the street. "I think we'd be better off takin' the streets all the way down, Champ. I'm sure the East Side Drive is too fucked up."

"I don't give a shit how ya' get there, just so's we get there," Jake grunted back. "I made reservations at the Copa tonight, Sweetheart. We'll have a ball." Jake turned back to Rick. "Just like old times, eh Rick? The old hangout. . ."

Rick smiled condescendingly. "No standing ovations this time, Champ. You're just another jerk who got married."

Sally glanced sharply at Jake and saw the hurt on his face. It wasn't the smartest thing for Rick to say at such a time in Jake's life. Why didn't he just shut up and agree with him, she thought.

When they finally arrived at City Hall, the water was so deep it was seeping into the car. Sally's and Laura's feet were soaked to the bone, but they didn't complain. Sally was determined to make this a happy day for Jake, even if it killed her.

They each pushed open their respective car doors and stepped out into the furious wind and rain. Jake rushed ahead with the only umbrella to the revolving door entrance, leaving Sally and Laura to fend for themselves. Rick sauntered casually behind. Jake barged headlong through the door with the open umbrella, trapping himself between the narrow glass partitions. The sight of Jake struggling helplessly with the hopelessly bent umbrella in his glass prison, his wet cigar smashed against the pane, was too absurd for words. Sally and Laura collapsed into uncontrollable giggles, heedless of their soaking clothes. Even Rick had to laugh.

"Oh, my poor hat," lamented Sally between fits of laughter. "It's ruined, Laura."

Laura looked ruefully at the pathetic white creation with its mangled veil and collapsed into another fit of helpless laughter. By the time Jake had crushed the uncooperative umbrella into several pieces and extricated himself from his undignified predicament, they all stood wet and uncomfortable and thoroughly exhausted inside the large empty hall. Jake had grown serious and silent. His experience with the door had unnerved him. He was suddenly sober and not a little nervous. Sally and Laura looked at each other and stifled yet another impulse to giggle.

"Well, boys and girls, we made it. Let's get this show on the road." Rick's deep voice boomed and echoed through the silent hall.

The long low hallway on the third floor, usually lined with assorted couples patiently waiting their turns to be legally joined together, was deserted. The wordless foursome made their way down the dimly lit, musty wood-paneled passage to the far end, where a door marked Judge's Chambers in faded gold letters announced their destination. Sally half-wondered, half-hoped no one would be inside.

"Maybe they've all gone home," she mused aloud.

"Naw, the judge has got to be here. It's his job—hurricane or no hurricane," Jake insisted.

The judge was surprised to see them.

"You folks must be awful anxious to come out in this weather. You're the first couple I've had all day," he observed, eyeing their rumpled condition.

The standard ceremony was brief and simple. Rick handed Jake the large opal-studded gold band he'd gotten on a deal from a guy in the jewelry business, and as Jake slipped it on Sally's trembling finger, he said gruffly, "This will last forever, Sally Bird, I promise." He kissed her hard on the mouth, and Sally's battered hat tipped slightly more to the right. Jake and Rick hugged each other in bosom-buddy fashion. Rick bent over to kiss the bride—"Not on the mouth," Jake cautioned seriously—then they all kissed Laura. The judged beamed benevolently. He was pleased to have married a celebrity in his chambers.

As they exited through the all too familiar revolving doors to the street, the rain had subsided and a refreshing calm hung in the air. Hurricane Donna was well on her way elsewhere. The sun penetrated through the melting clouds and warmed their still damp clothing. Jake seemed relaxed and content. He grinned boyishly at Sally.

"Thank God it's over," Sally sighed to no one in particular as she gazed up at the clearing sky.

The foursome were feeling no pain when they arrived at the Copa in time for the last show, having spent the remainder of the afternoon and a good part of the night bouncing from one old hangout to the next in pursuit of serious celebration. The maître d' congratulated them warmly, then led them to a front table close to the stage. The club was jammed, and not a few famous faces filled the tables. The comic Joe E. Lewis, a regular at the Copa, was appearing as the star attraction. He and Jake were nodding acquaintances from their drinking and gambling days together. Jake ordered a round of drinks as Rick scouted the room for celebrities. Ambitious for fame and power beyond his means, Rick longed to bask in the limelight that seemed to follow Jake like a searchlight. Fame had become just another fact of life to Jake. He'd been in the limelight so long he felt he was turning green. Rick elbowed Jake.

"Look who's over there, Jake. It's Sinatra."

"So what do you want me to do—sing a song? Jake said. He raised his glass and made a toast: "To the most beautiful bride in the world."

"I'll drink to that, Jake," Laura agreed.

"Ditto," Rick followed. "Why don't you girls come by my showroom one of these days and you can pick out a few dresses on me. Strictly on the house." Rick was all smiles.

"Said the spider to the flies," Laura muttered under her breath. She thought she knew what Rick was up to. She had heard of Rick's Saturday afternoon "sessions." His freebie customers were always young and attractive and spaced conveniently three hours apart.

"Do you mean that, Rick, on the house?" Sally asked, impressed.

"Oh, he means it all right, don't you, Rick?" Laura said knowingly.

"Sure, why not? Call it a wedding present," Rick urged, ignoring Laura's meaning.

"Yeah, Sally," Jake agreed. "You and Laura go up together. Women always need new clothes."

A heavy drum roll from the orchestra stopped the conversation. A deep off-stage voice announced, "And now, ladies and gentlemen, the Copa is proud to present Joe E. Lewis. . . ." The room applauded enthusiastically as Lewis sauntered on stage with the drink in hand that was his trademark. The orchestra swelled into "All the Way," the theme song made famous by Frank Sinatra's portrayal of Lewis in the film based on the comedian's life story, *The Joker Is Wild.* Sally and Jake exchanged meaningful glances and held hands tightly. It brought back memories of their first meeting at the Fontainebleau when Sinatra sang the song that had become their personal favorite.

"All the way for both of us, Sally Bird," Jake said softly. Lewis raised his glass, toasting the audience with his traditional opening line, "It's post time, ladies and gentlemen, and welcome to the world famous Copacabana." "You know," Lewis continued in his raspy voice, "I love playing this joint, and everytime I do, I see all my friends in the audience. The waiters are my spies, so during intermission they bring me a list of suckers—I mean guys who are out there. I pick and choose them carefully—I don't talk like this for nothin', you know. Then at the end of the evening, I invite them all to my dressing room. That's how I put my poker games together. I see one of my old poker pals is seated directly below me. A man I'm sure you all know, and if you don't know him—watch out. Ladies and Gentlemen, the Bronx Bull himself, Jake La Motta! Take a bow, Champ."

Jake was pleasantly surprised. He hadn't expected Lewis to recognize him. He rose slowly and clasped his hands above his head in the sign of a champion. In spite of the negative headlines just a few months earlier, the audience gave him a warm reception, so much so that Lewis felt obliged to call him up on stage. As Jake left the table to join Lewis, he gave Rick an "I told you so" look. He was still the Champ. Jake felt at home on stage. He seemed to come suddenly alive, as if he were just plugged into some invisible electric socket. He looked out at the audience and beamed a rare smile.

"So what's new in your life, Champ?" Lewis asked him, sharing the mike with Jake.

"Funny you should ask me that, Joe," Jake began in his gruff baritone. "And all you beautiful girls out there are gonna be sad, but I gotta tell ya that I just got married today to a beautiful, gorgeous, sexy young princess named Sally."

The audience applauded politely, and Jake continued.

"Now, as most of you know, this is my third marriage. My first wife divorced me 'cause she said I clashed with the drapes. My second wife, Vickie—you all know Vickie—"

An angry male voice called out drunkenly from the audience, "Yeah, what happened? She get tired of bein' your punchin' bag, you phony bum!"

The room fell silent as Jake glared in the direction of the unknown heckler, his fists clenched and his body tensed in preparation for attack. Lewis grabbed Jake by the arm and spoke into the mike.

"Woa, woa there, Champ. This isn't Madison Square Garden. We're at the Copa, remember. I guess there's one in every crowd. . ."

"Ya know, it's guys like you that are gonna force me to make a comeback," Jake rasped, pointing into the darkened room.

The audience laughed nervously. Jake regained his lost composure and carried on.

"As I was sayin' before I was so rudely interrupted . . . my second wife came home and I told her, 'Darlin', your stockings are wrinkled.' How the hell did I know she wasn't wearin' any? But God keeps givin' me chances. So now I'm married to this beautiful young creature. I don't know what's gonna happen, but I'm gonna keep tryin' 'til I get it right."

A slight giggle passed through the audience. Encouraged, Jake continued.

"Now to answer your question, Joe, I am now considered an actor—I don't know by who, but that's what they tell me. Seriously, I been doin' some summer stock, and puttin' my comedy act together. As a matter of fact, it's somethin' like yours, Joe. It goes somethin' like this . . . Ya know, Joe, I've cut my drinkin' in half now—I leave out all the chasers. My doctor said to me, 'Jake, if you don't stop drinking, you're going to lose your hearing.' I said, 'So what, Doc, the stuff I'm drinking is better than the stuff I'm hearing.'

Lewis laughed along as the audience tittered at Jake's rough imitation of the comic's familiar lines. Enjoying the spotlight and attention, Jake continued.

"My wife, Vickie, never knew I was an alcoholic till one night, I came home sober. But as I always say, you're never drunk if you can lay on the floor without holding on. . . . Ya know, I'll drink whiskey from a bottle, or from an old tomato can, 'cause I know whiskey'll never kill ya, but an old tomato can. . . ." Jake was pushing for a few more laughs with Lewis's material and was barely succeeding. Lewis stepped in for the rescue.

"Jake, if you want my act, you're welcome to it, 'cause it ain't worth a plugged nickel."

"That's what you think," Jake rejoined. "It got you into this joint. . ." I want to thank ya, Joe, for askin' me up here, and as for you, Ladies and Gentlemen, I'd like to leave you with a few words of wit and wisdom: Don't ever get discouraged. When things look black, send 'em to the laundry. You know you only live once, but if you work it right, once is enough. . . ."

Before Jake left the stage, Lewis insisted that Sally stand up and take a bow. Sally rose hesitantly and nodded shyly to the crowd. She wasn't used to being in the spotlight. For the first time she understood the meaning of being Mrs. Jake La Motta, the thrill of being a celebrity of sorts. It would be a much better feeling, it occurred to her, if Jake were in a better financial position. This would probably be the last time she visited the Copa, she thought wistfully, gazing at the well-known faces around her.

As Jake left the stage amidst scattered applause, he walked by Walter Winchell's table. Winchell took Jake by the arm as he passed.

"Congratulations, Jake. And by the way, Vickie sends her regards," he said with a crooked smile.

Jake looked at him with fire in his eyes. Everyone knew that Vickie had become one of "Winchell's girls," traveling around the country on promotional tours. Winchell had been a close friend of Vickie's and Jake's in Miami. Jake had no doubt that Vickie was dating Winchell before their divorce, and was still seeing him on a steady basis. In Jake's book, taking a friend's wife behind his back was as low as you could get. It was an unwritten Italian law. He leaned both hands on Winchell's table and looked him straight in the eye.

"Some day I'm gonna punch your fuckin' head off," Jake rasped menacingly.

Winchell leaned back in his seat and smiled nervously as Jake strutted cockily back to his table, both hands clasped characteristically behind his back. He never should've moved to Florida, Jake thought moodily. In Miami he'd lost everything that he loved most—his wife, his kids, his home—even the dogs. But especially his family. A man was nothing without his family. They call Florida God's waiting room. In his case, it was by invitation of the Devil.

Rick noticed instantly the dark change in Jake's mood. "What happened back there with Winchell? Did the bum give you a hard time?"

"Nothin' happened. Nothin' " Jake snapped. "I just hate the fuck. I don't like him puttin' his crummy hands on me."

"Aw, forget it. The world's full of creeps," Rick responded hotly. "I'd like to get my hands on that asshole that bothered you up there. The worm doesn't have the guts to say it to your face. He knows you'd kick the fuckin' shit out of him. Ya can't let 'em get away with that shit, or ya lose respect."

Sally and Laura exchanged worried looks. The mood of the evening had suddenly turned ugly. Sally knew only too well how violent Jake could get when he'd been drinking. She wished to God Rick would stop egging him on.

"Come on, Jake," she said appeasingly. "Don't start anything. Let's just have a good time. It's still our wedding day."

The waiter appeared with a cold bucket containing a magnum of champagne.

"Compliments of Mr. Podell, Mr. La Motta," he announced with a bow.

Jules Podell was the host and nominal owner of the Copa. Before anything could be said, Jake got suddenly to his feet.

"Yeah? We'll drink it home," Jake said, grabbing the bottle from the bucket. "Come on. Let's get out of here," Jake announced unceremoniously to the table.

"Hey, hold on, Jake. We didn't get the tab," Rick protested.

"There is no bill, sir. Compliments of the house," the waiter answered politely.

Jake turned on his heel and headed for the exit. Rick and the girls exchanged puzzled looks, then filed meekly out of the room after Jake. The peals of audience laughter followed them through the lobby and out into the night as Joe E. Lewis continued his performance on stage.

It was close to one in the morning when Rick pulled the car around to the front of the Copa where the girls waited quietly with Jake, his complimentary magnum tucked tightly under his arm. A cool, refreshing breeze had replaced the earlier calm, awakening them slightly from their alcohol-induced stupors. Rick reached over and flung open the front door for Laura as Jake and Sally climbed into the back seat.

They lapsed into silence for the short drive across town. Sally could feel the knot in her stomach returning. She gazed steadily out the window, averting her eyes from Jake. "What had she gotten herself into?" she thought in mounting panic. Suddenly she wished the whole day hadn't happened, that Jake and Rick were just dropping her and Laura home like any other night. She thought of the comfortable apartment just a few blocks away that she and Laura had decorated together, and longed to be back in her very own bed. The thought of returning to Jake's dirty little studio repulsed her. "I'm still the same person I was yesterday," she told herself. "Nothing has really changed, except maybe my name. Oh, why couldn't it all have been a dream, or just a dress rehearsal? I want to go home," she cried to herself. Sally stole a look at Jake's stony profile. In the flickering night lights, his face resembled a cold primitive icon of some strange ancient god staring blankly into space. A shudder ran through her.

Rick pulled up before the building on 52nd Street and put the car in park, leaving the motor running. "Well, kiddies, this is your stop, I believe. Sweet dreams, you two. And don't do anything I wouldn't do."

Jake lumbered out of the car with his bottle of champagne and held the door open for Sally.

"Come on, Sally Bird; we're home," he mumbled.

Sally remained in the car.

"Rick, you can just drop me off at my place now, OK?" Sally said in a small voice.

Rick looked at her like she was crazy. Even Laura was shocked.

"What're ya talkin' about, ya crazy broad? We're married now. Get out of the car, Sally," Jake said impatiently.

"I want to go home now, Jake," Sally insisted in a little girl voice.

"You are home, you little nut. I'm your husband; you're my wife; that's the way it is. Now stop bein' stupid and come upstairs with me—now," Jake demanded.

Jake grabbed Sally by the wrist and pulled her firmly out of the car.

"Oh, Jake, I don't feel right. I'm so scared," Sally whimpered as Jake pulled her to him.

"There's nothin' to be scared of, Sally Bird. Everything's gonna be fine. Now let's go to bed," Jake said with finality. The wedding was over, and the marriage had begun. . . .

Four

It was almost four in the morning when the long shiny black limousine lurched to a stop. Jake got out, swayed precariously trying to regain his balance, then stumbled his way blindly to the entrance of his apartment building as the car sped away. He had spent that evening, as he spent most every evening, getting drunk with his socially prominent drinking buddies at his favorite hangout, P.J. Clark's—a Third Avenue saloon where the down and out could rub elbows with the rich and famous for the price of a beer. A faded autographed picture of Jake striking a boxing pose hung on the cluttered wall amongst a potpourri of famous names and faces framed in curling brown edges. Jake knew the three bartenders and the waiters as well as he knew his own brothers. He'd even stepped in on a few unruly occasions as a part-time bouncer. P.J.'s was Jake's home away from home.

Jimmy the doorman rushed to Jake's aid in time to save him from crashing through the glass door entrance.

"Let me help you there, Champ," Jimmy offered as he half carried Jake into the lobby.

"Ya know, this is gettin' to be a real habit with you, pal," Jimmy continued through the lobby over Jake's silence.

"Hey, was that really who I thought that was in the back of that limo?"

Jimmy gave out a low whistle, impressed.

"Wow, Robert Kennedy and Onassis himself! You sure keep some company, Champ!"

"Yeah, so what—that and fifty cents won't get me on the subway," Jake slurred bitterly.

"Yeah, sure, Jake," Jimmy appeased as he led Jake into the elevator.

"Bet you were at the big shindig for Sugar Ray Robinson at the Garden tonight, uh Champ? Must've been some night!" Jimmy continued on their way up to the fifth floor.

"Naw, I wasn't invited. I only fought him six times. I was the first one to knock him on his ass, too. Aw, who the hell needs that lousy chicken dinner, anyway. . ." Jake rambled on as they staggered down the hallway to his apartment door.

"Aw, that's a dirty shame, Champ. How soon they forget, eh?" Jimmy empathized as they reached Jake's door.

"You, uh, got a key, Champ? I'll just help you with the door here, and you can go in and sleep it off, eh pal?"

Jake fished in his pockets and finally produced the key. Jimmy took it from him gently and unlocked the door.

"Well, here we are, Champ. Give my best to Mrs. La Motta, uh?"

Jake stumbled into the dark apartment and fell back against the door, closing it with a loud thud. He fumbled for the light switch and clicked on the glaring ceiling light. Sally awoke suddenly and sat up in bed.

"Jake, for Pete's sake, turn off that horrible light," Sally said crossly, switching on the dim lamp beside her.

"What time is it, anyway? You know I have to be at work early looking like a rose."

Jake switched off the offending light and slumped into the nearest chair.

"Don't be mad, Sally Bird. Your Jakie Bird don't feel so good," Jake whimpered drunkenly and belched loudly.

"If 'Jakie Bird' throws up on the floor again, he's gonna clean it up himself," Sally said angrily.

"We've been married three months now, Jake, and you've stayed drunk for nearly two of them. Tell me, what's your excuse this time?"

"I got no excuse. I just feel left out of everything that's goin' on," Jake answered morosely.

"I'm the only champ that didn't get invited to Ray Robinson's dinner. I fought Robinson so many times it's a wonder I don't have diabetes. Rocky got a dinner . . . everybody gets a dinner. . . . Whatsa matter with me—I got leprosy or somethin'?"

"I wouldn't invite you anywhere. Just look at yourself. You're turning into a champion slob. Who would want you at a dinner table?" Sally persisted.

"So what—I don't give a shit!"

Jake got up and staggered toward the kitchen cabinet in search of his bottle of scotch. The cabinet was empty.

"Where the hell's my scotch?" he cried loudly.

"I threw it down the drain," Sally replied firmly.

"Are you crazy? Booze costs money!" Jake yelled.

"Not as much as your sanity!" Sally exclaimed back.

Jake began tearing at the kitchen cabinets in a drunken frenzy, knocking dishes, cups and pottery to the floor in a cacophony of breaking glass. Sally jumped out of bed and ran across the room to the tiny kitchen.

"Stop it—stop it, Jake!" she cried as Jake continued his pillage.

"The more you break, Jake, the longer it's gonna take you to clean it up—I'm not your maid, you know. I know Vickie always had a maid, but I don't!" Sally shouted angrily.

Something snapped in Jake's mind. He stopped and turned to Sally with a strange wild look in his eyes. His whole body started to shake with an uncontrollable rage. Sally backed away in mounting fear as Jake walked slowly toward her.

"I told you . . . I told you, Vickie," Jake growled menacingly. "I know that maid of yours is lying for you . . . lies . . . lies . . . nothin' but lies. . . . Where were you, Vickie? Don't lie to me . . . I warned you, Vickie. . . ."

"Cut it out, Jake," Sally said nervously. "I'm not Vickie. I'm Sally, your wife. Stop calling me that . . . you're scaring me, Jake. . . ."

Sally's voice trembled as Jake came closer. She could see the irrational fury in his eyes.

"My God, he's gone completely mad!" she said to herself in horror.

"You're lying, Vickie. . . ." Jake repeated threateningly.

"I told you . . . I told you I'd kill you this time. . . ."

"Jake, I'm not Vick—"

Jake suddenly grabbed Sally by the throat and began to squeeze down hard with both hands. Sally gasped for breath and tried to scream, but she could make no sound. Jake's face leered inches from hers like a swollen red demon. She struggled desperately and tried to pry his hands from her throat, but she was helpless in his vice-like grip. Sally felt she was going to black out when Jake's grip suddenly relaxed. His eyes rolled upward and closed and his body went limp as he slumped to the floor in an unconscious stupor.

Sally backed slowly away from the silent dark mass lying on the floor and leaned back against the wall, gasping for breath. Her whole body trembled and it was minutes before she could move. She stared at Jake's immobile body as if he were an animal that had entered her apartment to destroy her. In the dimly lit room he no longer looked like Jake to her, but like a bloated beast from another world.

It was daylight before Sally was able to pull herself together. She dressed quickly and methodically, tied a scarf around her bruised neck, grabbed her purse and coat and headed for the door. She stopped with her hand on the doorknob and looked over her shoulder at Jake still lying in the middle of the floor, snoring loudly, then she slipped quietly out of the room.

Sally entered the corner coffee shop, walked directly to the pay phone in the back and made two phone calls. The first was to her boss.

"Lenny, it's me, Sally. I can't come in today . . . I've got a sore throat—a very bad sore throat. I'll call you tomorrow."

The second call was to Jerry Katz. She hadn't seen Jerry since that night in her apartment when Jake had stormed in and asked her to marry him, but she had to talk to someone, and she couldn't think of anyone else she could trust. She had lost track of Laura after she had married some famous musical conductor and moved to Europe. Jerry would be sympathetic, she knew, but he would also be discreet. She didn't know yet what she was going to do, but she felt she had to do something. She desperately needed advice and comfort.

Waiting for the express elevator to Jerry's office on the twentieth floor in the large marbled lobby of Jerry's New York agency at Madison Avenue and 57th Street, Sally felt suddenly foolish and embarrassed. She adjusted the scarf around her neck nervously as the elevator doors glided silently open and she stepped gingerly into the polished wood-paneled car.

"Mr. Katz will be with you momentarily, Mrs. La Motta," the efficient secretary told her in a pleasant professional tone. Sally perched stiffly on the beige leather couch that perfectly matched the textured beige walls of the reception area and waited, feeling like an ingenue auditioning for her first Broadway role.

"Mr. Katz will see you now," the secretary announced crisply. Sally made her way through the labyrinth of closed doors to Jerry's private streamlined office at the end of the corridor. Jerry's diminutive features broke into a welcoming smile at the sight of Sally. He seemed the epitome of the Madison Avenue agent, nattily clad in an expensive three-piece suit complete with matching tie and handkerchief and sporting a birthstone pinky ring.

"Hiya, kid," Jerry greeted her amiably. "Long time no see. What's up, angel? I know you wouldn't look me up unless you had a problem."

Jerry walked over to Sally and put his hands gently on her shoulders, leading her to a handsome leather chair. "Geez, you look terrible, kid. Come on, spit it out. Tell Uncle Jerry all about it."

Sally looked up pitifully at Jerry and burst into tears. "Oh Jerry," she sobbed, unable to control herself any longer, "It's so awful, I shouldn't be telling you this, I shouldn't even be here, but I had nowhere else to go," Sally continued, crying uncontrollably.

Jerry sat patiently on the edge of his desk and watched her with genuine concern. The desk phone rang and Jerry picked it up abruptly.

"Hold all my calls for now, Martha," he said and hung up. "That's all right, kid. Get it out. You know you're safe here. Is it as bad as all that?" he asked, handing Sally his handkerchief as her sobs gradually subsided.

Sally looked up at Jerry wordlessly and untied the scarf from around her neck, revealing the ugly bruises on her throat.

"My God, Sally, did that bastard Jake do that to you?" Jerry exclaimed in shock.

"He'd been drinking. He didn't know what he was doing, Jerry. He just—went crazy on me," Sally explained lamely. "He thought I was Vickie," she added softly.

"I don't care if he thought you were Joe Louis!" Jerry exclaimed hotly. "There's no excuse for that kind of behavior, Sally. The man's an animal—he belongs behind bars!"

"He's still my husband, Jerry," Sally replied firmly. "He needs help. I just wish I knew what to do."

Sally twisted the handerkerchief in her hands. She should have expected Jerry's reaction, but it wasn't what she wanted to hear.

"Look, Sally, you know how I—how I've always felt about you. . ." Jerry paused and lit a cigarette. He offered Sally the pack. "Oh, I forgot, you don't smoke," he smiled.

"You know this guy has a reputation for this sort of thing," Jerry continued. "I'll try to refrain from saying 'I told you so' . . . Look, it's your life, kid, but if you don't divorce this bastard, you should have your head examined."

"You're probably right, Jerry," Sally said with a deep sigh. "I thought he'd changed. . . . This time I really thought he'd changed," she repeated sadly.

"The evidence says he hasn't," Jerry said evenly. "Are you willing to spend the rest of your life trying to prove otherwise?". . .

Sally pondered Jerry's words as she walked slowly back to the East Side. "Divorce the bastard" kept ringing in her ears. Why did she always have to fall for the wrong guy, she thought. Why couldn't she go for someone like Jerry? He was kind, considerate, gentle—and boring. If only Jake would stop drinking. He was like a different person when he drank. Booze seemed to bring forth all the demons from his past in an orgy of fury. Maybe it was her fault. . . . Maybe she wasn't the right woman for Jake. . . . Maybe she should have been more understanding, more compassionate, more . . . Yeah, and maybe Jerry was right. Maybe she should have her head examined. . . .

Sally was so lost in her thoughts that she almost passed her apartment building before she realized that all her ruminating had unconsciously led her home. She ducked quickly through the lobby and into the elevator, avoiding the chatty doorman. She was in no mood to talk to anyone. Her heart pounded as she opened the apartment door. She was far from ready to confront Jake.

The apartment was empty. Jake must have gone out, she breathed a sigh of relief. Everything was just as she had left it—the bed was unmade; the chair she had knocked over during her struggle with Jake was still on its side; the broken dishes still lay strewn across the kitchen floor. The scene of the crime, she thought grimly.

Sally began to straighten up the apartment with quiet determination. She had disposed of all but the last of the broken dishes when the phone rang. That's probably Jake, she thought, her stomach lurching sharply. Sally picked up the receiver.

"Yes?" she said. "Yes, this is Sally La Motta. . . . Are you sure? . . . Yes, I see. . . . Yes, I will. . . . Thank you, Doctor." Sally put down the receiver slowly.

"No, it can't be," she said to herself. "Oh, God, please, not now. . . . No, I can't be pregnant—not now!" she told herself in mounting panic.

Sally jumped and turned abruptly to the door as she heard the key turning in the lock. She stared wide-eyed like a scared rabbit caught at night in a bright beam of light as Jake entered the room. Jake stood motionless near the door, unshaven, unkempt and miserable—the picture of self-defeat.

"I'm sorry . . . I'm sorry, Sally. I didn't know what I was doin'. I must've gone crazy," he mumbled.

"I know," Sally answered softly. "Jake, let's go for a walk, OK?" She waited for his reaction.

"Sure, whatever you say," Jake answered quickly, anxious to please her.

They walked up Fifth Avenue in silence in the direction of Central Park. The cold grey January sky reflected harshly in the expensive shop windows, incongruously displaying the latest Spring styles and bikini beach wear for the winter jet set. Sally shivered in her plain wool coat several paces behind Jake, as he walked briskly before her, coatless with his hands shoved deep into his pockets and his gaze fixed straight ahead.

"Hiya, Champ," "How's it goin', Jake," several passersby greeted him familiarly along the way. Jake returned a brief forced smile and said nothing. He felt more like a chump than a champ this day.

They cut across the small square opposite the Plaza Hotel, past the graceful little fountain, and entered Central Park. Jake stopped at one of the street vendors and bought a bag of warm chestnuts, offering some to Sally. She shook her head and they continued in silence down the half-deserted winding walkway to the low, marshy man-made pond. Sally sat wearily on an empty bench and watched a lonely pair of white swans gliding lazily across the smooth surface of the placid water. Jake finished off his chestnuts and sat down stiffly next to Sally.

"Jake—", "Sally, I—", they both began together awkwardly.

"I want to be very honest with you, Jake," Sally started somberly. "This morning I had every intention of divorcing you."

Jake jumped to his feet. "Are you crazy? You must be out of your mind! All right, so I got a little out of hand. . ."

"No, Jake. You almost killed me last night, and I don't think I want to wait around for the next time for you to finish the job. My life may be worth nothing to you, but it means a great deal to me," Sally said quietly.

Jake looked down at his feet. "I'm sorry, darlin', he muttered softly. "I don't know what else to say. You know I'm no good with words, but that's the truth—I'm sorry. Please forgive me. But this divorce business is crazy. You know we love each other. I'd go nuts without you, baby. I'll do anything you say—just cut out this divorce crap."

"You've got to stop drinking, Jake. You just cannot drink. Something comes over you—it's like some demon inside you takes over and you can't control it. All your frustrations break out of you."

Sally looked up at Jake, her eyes full of pain. Jake could say nothing. He knew she was speaking the truth.

"And there's something else, too," Sally continued, upset. "It's this 'thing' you have for Vickie. You're still not over her, are you?"

"No, you're wrong—dead wrong," Jake protested. "Sure, I think about the kids a lot, but that's all. That bitch is out of my life for good—I swear it!"

Sally pulled the scarf from around her neck. "Look—look what you did, Jake. Isn't that Vickie?"

"No, no—it's not her, it's me! I love you, Sally. I'm just all fucked up. I don't know what I'm doin' half the time. It's like I wake up in the mornin' and I don't know what to do next. I don't even know who I am anymore," Jake confessed.

"Maybe you're right, Jake," Sally said. "It's not just Vickie I'm competing with, or any other woman. It's the championship. It's always been the championship. No woman in the world can compete with that, Jake. When are you going to realize that it's over—

it's all over for good. You've got to stop living in the past and start thinking about the future—about our future, Jake. What are you going to do with yourself? You've got to do something. What are you going to do?" she asked plaintively.

Jake looked skyward in exasperation.

"I don't know . . . I don't know. . . ." Sally said, holding her head in her hands. "Write a book. Tell your life story—get it all off your chest."

"Write a book? Are you nuts? I'm lucky if I can spell my own name!" Jake said. "Bullshit! Why the fuck do you think I get jobs? They're not just hiring some bum actor—they're hiring Jake La Motta, Middleweight Champion of the World! They can't take that away from me. I'm goin' to continue with the acting. I know it's gonna work. You'll see—you'll see. Why can't you have a little faith in me? Now cut out all this crap, and let's go home."

Sally got up and walked toward the pond. She stood for a moment with her back to Jake, looking out at the peaceful scene. Then she turned abruptly and blurted out what she had been wanting to say from the beginning.

"Jake, I'm pregnant," she said and waited breathlessly for his reaction.

Jake's face lit up like a Christmas tree

"That's great, darlin'. Are you sure?"

Sally nodded.

"Aw, that's terrific! Now we can have our own family. I love kids, you know that."

Jake walked up to Sally and took her in his arms, kissing her tenderly.

"I'm very happy, sweetheart. Eh . . . what do ya think, maybe we ought to get a little dog, too."

It started to snow gently as they made their way together out of the park. Jake held Sally close and hailed a passing cab. As they headed home, the snow fell harder.

Five

"Give me three cards," Jake said to Rick, holding two aces and hoping for at least one more. "Ya never can tell what Rocky's holding. He has the best poker face in the world," Jake commented grudgingly as he assembled his cards. "Ya never know what he's thinkin' cause he can't think."

Jake, Rick and Rocky Graziano were slumped around the used coffee table in Jake's and Sally's heavily lived-in apartment, half-engrossed in their afternoon penny-ante poker game. Except for the all too obvious fact that each player was spreading his way well into middle-age, the familiar scene could easily have been taking place twenty years before in the Italian sector of the Bronx, where the habitual trio fought and stole their way to a tough manhood.

"Gimme four," Rocky said dully.

"Ya can't take four—only three, ya punch drunk moron," Jake jumped down Rocky's throat. "Where do ya think we are— Vegas or somethin'?"

"All right, then give me three," Rocky agreed grumblingly. The two ex-champs exchanged stubborn glares as Rick doled out the cards in question.

"And no more cheatin', Rick. You been winning too many hands, and I know you ain't that good," Jake said, arranging his cards carefully.

"What cheat? You keep your lousy hand wide open. If we were in the ring, I could've knocked your fuckin' block off," Rick said, his cards held close to his chest.

"Bullshit! You couldn't even be my sparring partner. You couldn't take the punches," Jake shot back.

"Uh . . . uh . . . uh . . . Remember, Jake, nobody wanted to be your sparring partner," Rocky chimed in.

"Yeah, not even you, stupid," Jake grunted back. "Eh, Rick, Ya know I asked Rocky while we was out the other day, 'What the hell is that thing up there, the sun or the moon?' So he said to me, 'Uh . . . uh . . . uh . . . I don't know, Jake. I don't live around here.' How punchy can ya get?"

"I don't know what I'm doin' here wastin' my time with you two bums when I could be makin' some dough in Vegas in a real man's game," Rick complained.

"I gotta make a phone call," he announced, slapping his hand face down on the table and getting up abruptly.

"I gotta take a piss," Rocky announced in turn, getting up from the table after Rick.

"Hey, you guys—I finally got a good hand here. Where the hell are ya all goin'?" Jake protested.

Rick went to the phone and dialed as Rocky disappeared into the bathroom. Jake shrugged and got up to go to the kitchen in search of another beer. Rick spoke into the phone in low, serious tones, his back carefully turned to the room. Jake looked across at Rick suspiciously, guzzling his beer. He and Rick had few secrets from each other, but these mysterious phone calls that usually resulted in Rick's suddenly taking off for a few days for parts unknown were something Rick wouldn't talk about. Jake thought he knew what Rick was up to. He'd been around the kind of wiseguys Rick hung out with long enough to know they weren't exactly sending him on a three-day cruise.

Rick hung up the phone and took his seat at the table. "Fuck it—I've gotta leave town for a few days," he muttered, picking up his hand.

"But where the hell do you go?" Jake asked, annoyed. "Whatta ya got, a fuckin' mistress or somethin'? Ya holdin' out on me?"

"What are ya, my old lady all of a sudden? Even she doesn't bust my chops the way you do," Rick said. "It's business. Do ya think I'd leave town on my kid's birthday if it wasn't important? Fuck it. I'll make it up to him when I get back—buy him somethin' special."

Rocky emerged from the bathroom, stumbling slightly.

"Who do youse guys think you're kiddin'—you're both a pair of fuckin' whoremasters from the day ya layed your first broad in the back of your old man's Chevy!" he said, cutting in on the conversation.

"At least we're not a big fag, like you," Jake shot back.

"Are we goin' to finish this lousy hand, or what?" Rick interrupted impatiently, drawing one card to his two pairs. "I bet a buck," he added.

"Your buck, and two better," Jake countered.

"Uh . . . uh . . . uh . . . I'm out, guys," Rocky stuttered. "No more of this shit for me," he sighed, shoving his half-empty beer can to the side. "I just saw the little guy in the bowl, so I quit," he commented half to himself.

"What little guy?" Jake questioned.

"The little guy in the bottom of the toilet bowl when you're takin' a piss," Rocky explained. "Don't you guys ever see a face lookin' back at ya when ya take a real hard piss and ya been drinkin' too much, and ya look down into the john and this guy seems to be grinnin' up at ya and says 'Ya had enough, pal—ain't youse guys ever seen that?" Rocky asked ingenuously.

Jake and Rick exchanged long-suffering glances.

"Ya never shoulda had that last fight, Rocky. You're punchy as a loon," Jake stated sadly.

The apartment door opened and Sally waddled laboriously into the room, looking every bit of nine and a half months pregnant. "Just bring it in here," she called to someone outside the door.

A young kid came into view carrying a small wooden crib that had obviously seen better days.

"That's fine. I can take it from here," Sally told the boy as he set the unwieldy object in the room.

"Wait a minute—I'll get you something for your trouble," she added breathlessly.

"Jake, quick, I need a dollar for the kid," Sally said, turning to Jake.

Spying the money on the table, she grabbed a dollar bill and handed it to the boy.

"Here you are. Thanks for the help,'" she said cheerfully, pleased with her accomplishment.

"Sure, lady. Thanks," the boy muttered and left.

"What the hell are ya doin'? That's our pot!" Jake called to Sally, annoyed. "And what's that piece of shit doin' here? I told ya I didn't want ya draggin' things in off the street—people'll think ya gone nuts or somethin'! Ya know how embarrassin' this is? Ya'd think we can't afford decent furniture or somethin'," Jake shouted.

"We can't, Jake. Look around you. Where do you think that chair, and that lamp, and that poker table came from?" Sally replied, pointing to the objects around the room. "And it's not a piece of shit. It's a lovely old crib for the baby," she continued, stroking the crib fondly. "I found it on First Avenue ready to be thrown out. Just wait until I clean it up. It'll look brand new. Or do you suggest we keep her in a dresser drawer for the first year?" she added sarcastically.

"Eh, don't say her—it's gotta be a him, or I'm sending it back," Jake grumbled.

"I don't care if it's an 'it,' " Sally said wearily. "I just want to have it before I explode," she sighed, making her way slowly to the kitchen.

Sally took a box of prunes from the kitchen cabinet and propped herself against the counter, munching thoughtfully on the dull dried fruit. "I feel like a balloon full of water ready to burst," she thought miserably. She recalled the words of Lenny her boss when she told him she was pregnant: "You've destroyed yourself—you'll never be a perfect eight again!" She glared across the room at Jake. "Look at him. It's all his fault, and he sits there playing cards like nothing ever happened," she thought, sticking out her tongue at Jake's unheeding back. Sally gently rubbed her round belly, caressing the child within her. "Come on, my precious baby, let's get this over with," she whispered.

Rocky elbowed Jake confidentially.

"Eh, Jake, whatta ya think you're doin', havin' kids all over the place like a fuckin' jack rabbit? Ain't ya never heard of contraceptives?" he whispered hoarsely.

"What would you know about it, ya dumb fuck. A family's a good thing. Gives a guy somethin' to think about besides his own lousy ass," Jake growled back.

"What're we doin' here—are we playin' poker or house?" Rick boomed suddenly. "I'll see ya and raise ya five bucks—and ya owe

the pot a buck—that's six bucks to you, asshole. Put up or shut up!"
Rick challenged Jake.

Sally gasped sharply and dropped the box of prunes to the floor.
"Oh my God . . . Oh my God . . . I think this is it. Jake, Jake,
my water just broke!" she cried in alarm from the kitchen.

"Well hold on a minute, will ya?" Jake called back matter-of-
factly. "I gotta finish this hand."

"Here's five bucks," he said to Rick, producing a five dollar bill
from his pocket and tossing it on the table. "I owe the pot a buck.
Now, whatta ya got, smart guy?"

Jake!" Sally called in rising panic. "You'd better get me to the
hospital, or I'm going to have it right here!"

"Hey, I'm gettin' outta here— You guys are crazy! I'll go get us a
cab." Rocky said, alarmed, grabbing his jacket and exiting hur-
riedly out the door.

"Here—two pair, ya greedy fuck!" Rick said, slapping his cards
on the table. "For Chrissakes, Jake, you'd better go take care of
your wife!"

"Jake!" Sally screamed again.

"Three bullets. I got ya, ya bastard!" Jake threw down his cards,
grabbed the pot, and walked quickly over to Sally. "I'm comin'
darlin'; let's go. See? I just made us cab fare," he said proudly,
helping Sally out the door as Rick followed behind.

Jake paced nervously back and forth in the polished bustling corridor of the maternity ward in Doctor's Hospital. Sally had gone
into advanced labor by the time they reached the emergency
room, and the doctors and nurses rushed her frantically upstairs
with Jake following helplessly behind.

They almost hadn't made it at all. When Jake and Rick arrived
outside with Sally gasping desperately, the cab driver Rocky had
waiting took one look at Sally, muttered, "Not in my cab, you
don't," and started to take off. Jake had jumped into the front seat
of the cab, grabbed the driver by his collar, and growled menacingly, "Do you know who I am, asshole?" The driver nodded
meekly, his eyes widening in recognition. "Then take me and my
wife to the nearest hospital—now—or I'll punch your fuckin' head
off!" Rick and Rocky helped Sally into the back seat, and watched
blankly from the sidewalk as the cab sped away.

Jake stopped pacing, sat down on a narrow bench against the

wall, and lit his last cigar. There really was nothing to worry about, he reassured himself. Sally was young and healthy as a horse. Having a baby was nothing for a tough broad like Sally, he thought. He couldn't remember the last time he sat waiting in a hospital. It seemed he'd always been out of town on a fight or something when Vickie had the three kids. He'd stayed at home when Ida, his first wife, had Jacqueline. He never saw Jacqueline much after Ida left, and then he knocked up Vickie and married her. He hadn't seen Jack and Joey Junior for a couple of years now, except to talk to them on the phone once in a while. Little Christie was too small when Vickie left him to even remember him much. . . . This time it was going to be different, he told himself. He was older now, and he had more time to spend at home, to really get to know his kids from the beginning, and be there as they grew up. He would have a real family again—and this time he wasn't going to fuck it up, he vowed to himself. . . .

"Mr. La Motta," the young nurse interrupted his thoughts, "you have a healthy baby girl, and your wife is doing fine. You'll be able to go in and see her shortly."

Jake's broad, battered, beleaguered face broke into a wide grin, his eyes lighting up with a rare sparkle, as he beheld his baby daughter through the thick glass of the hospital nursery for the first time.

"God, she's beautiful!" he exclaimed in awe. "She's not red or wrinkled, or nothin'—she's a livin' doll—a real little doll!"

Sally sat propped up in bed in the private room, exhausted and spent, but beaming with a happy glow. It had been an easy birth with no complications. And that's exactly how she'll grow up, Sally resolved positively—nice and easy with no complications—as she happily contemplated her new daughter.

Jake sidled into the room, feeling awkward and clumsy and out of place, suddenly timid in the face of the awesome feminine power to give life.

"She's beautiful, Sally Bird, really beautiful," Jake said in hushed tones as he kissed Sally gently on the cheek.

"I know," Sally agreed with self-satisfied pleasure. "She has your eyes, Jake."

"Yeah, but she's got her mother's smile," Jake responded sheepishly.

"I've been thinking, Jake," Sally said with a sly smile, "that we ought to name her Elisa, after your mother."

Jake broke into a big grin.

"You mean that, Baby? That would make Mom so happy, you know that. Elisa La Motta—sounds like an Italian song," Jake mused happily.

"Well, then, that's settled," Sally said with satisfaction. "I just wish we could settle the hospital bill as easily," she added, a note of worry edging her voice. "Jake, how on earth are we going to pay for all this? This room must cost a fortune!"

"Don't you bother your pretty little head about it, Sally Bird. I'll take care of it. Don't you worry," Jake assured her firmly.

Sally returned a wan smile and closed her eyes wearily.

"I'd better go now, let you get some rest. I'll come back for you and the baby tomorrow."

He kissed Sally on the forehead and left her peacefully asleep.

Jake stood with his back to the doors and tried not to stare at the dark, desperate, despondent faces slumped wearily on the hard seats around him.

He hated the subway—especially the filthy, rattletrap, graffiti-ridden express train that swayed and clamored and lurched its way angrily all the way to the Bronx. He hadn't set foot inside a subway since he was a kid, but he promised Sally he would take care of things, and he had to take a shot.

Jake hadn't seen his father much since he returned from Italy a couple of years ago with a new young wife and set up house in the old Bronx neighborhood. He had plied the unsuspecting poor Italian village girl with photos and newspaper clippings of his son, the World Middleweight Champion, neglecting to mention his first wife and the five kids he left in the lurch back in New York. Having sold the Bronx apartment building Jake had given him for a handsome profit, he was living comfortably if modestly in the style to which he had lately become accustomed. Jake couldn't remember his father ever giving him much other than his name, but he had to get money somehow, and his options were few and far between. Accepting handouts from Rick was becoming a bad habit—one he wasn't sure he could afford.

"Giacobino—whata nica surprise. Hey, Bellisa, looka whosa

here—assetta, assetta. How'sa bout some spaghet—just ina time, que diche?"

Guissepe La Motta was pleased to see his eldest son. It was only on rare occasions that his sons would visit him these days. He hadn't seen his daughters or their mother in several years, but he knew better than to expect them to forgive and forget. Italian women never forget, he knew from hard experience.

"Ma que fai—fa zupito—getta Giacobine a plate!" Guissepe ordered his wife loudly, slapping her bottom as she scurried silently into the kitchen.

"No thanks, Pop. I'm not hungry," Jake declined, knowing a plate would be brought anyway. Jake was never fully at ease around his father, and he was especially nervous whenever he had to ask him for something as he did now, but he rarely turned down a plate of homemade pasta.

"Howsa Mamma?" Guissepe asked pointedly as Bellisa returned with two steaming plates and placed them before the two men, her typical Italian peasant features registering a brief, timid smile before she disappeared back into the kitchen. "She's OK, Pop. Not bad," Jake answered noncommittally. Both father and son were naturally men of few words. They knew from long practice the less said the better.

Jake watched his father greedily consume his dinner as he cleaned his own plate in silence. He couldn't help thinking of all the times the man had sat in the kitchen devouring the only meat and fruit in the house, while his family dined on leftover rice. Somehow it didn't seem fair that this unknown girl should reap the benefits of his father's new financial stability gained from the blood and sweat of his son. Jake wondered how his mother had been able to manage all those years with five kids in that bare tenement. No woman could replace his mother, he thought bitterly. He remembered the day he had finally thrown his father out of the house, his mom crying, "Please, please make him leave before there is blood shed in this house!" He had convinced her to divorce him after that, though he knew she always regretted it. He wondered now if it had been so wise to free his father to remarry so easily. It had never occurred to him that he might one day be in the unlikely position of having to ask his father for money. . . .

"Eh, hava soma vino," his father offered as Bellisa returned with a carafe of homemade wine and two glasses, removing the plates and efficiently wiping the oil-clothed table before she retreated to her woman's domain.

"Everybody's gotta hava little dope," Guissepe remarked philosophically as he lit up his favorite Italian stogey.

Jake knew he couldn't put off the moment of truth much longer. It was an old family joke that you didn't try to talk to Pop after he'd had his evening jar of wine. Jake gulped down the strong red brew and cleared his throat importantly.

"Pop, I uh, got some good news. Sally and me, we just had a baby—a little girl. You're a grandpa again."

His father puffed on his little cigar in stony silence.

"Eh—whatta ya wanna from me? You wanna have babies alla over the country—whatta ya wanna me to do?" Jake lowered his eyes, hiding the hurt he felt like a sudden punch in the gut. His father's blows always caught him off guard.

"Nothin', Pop. I don't want ya to do nothin'," Jake answered in a low voice. "It's just that the hospital bill . . . I'm in kind of a hole right now. I need to borrow some money. It's about 400 bucks."

"A fa gullo a te e mamida e Jesus Christ, qui te fat! Whatta you, crazy—400 dollars!" Guissepe shouted.

"I know, Pop. But you sold the building. I gave that to you with no mortgage or nothin'—that's gotta be worth somethin', Pop," Jake pleaded.

"A sure, you giva me the building—una palaza di merde! I paint; I clean; I fix witha my owna hands. You, the biga shot, give me alla di agita, becausa you and your brothers, too proud to dirty your hands. Now, you wanna my sweat—a fa gullo!" Guissepe shouted.

"If that's the way you feel, Pop. Just forget it."

Jake rose sorrowfully from the table, ready to leave, broken-spirited and empty handed.

"Asperte, asperte," his father said softly.

Guissepe disappeared into the bedroom and returned a few moments later, check in hand.

"This isa the best I canna do," he said, handing Jake a check made out for ten dollars. "I gotta troubles ofa my own."

Jake looked at the paltry amount, suppressing an impulse to tear the check into tiny pieces and throw it in his father's face. No matter what else he might feel, Jake still bore a deep respect born of early fear for his father.

"Is this all I'm worth?" he asked, his eyes glued to the check. "Ya know, Pop, how soon they forget . . . the good times, the money—all that money I made, and I helped everybody. I supported the whole family. And most of all I helped you. What were you, Pop? What the hell were you but a cheap little peddler? You dragged the family from one slum to another, and pimped me off to fight every kid in the neighborhood. Did ya forget all those nickels and dimes I made you? And this is your answer—a lousy ten bucks. How heartless can ya be? Look at yourself—you're a broken down old man with nothin' but broken memories. . . . What do ya want from me—another championship? I'm an old man, too, now. I come to you begging for help, and you give me a kick in the ass like I was still eight years old. Why did you always hate me, Pop? All those beatings, and for what? Where was I so bad, Pop? Tell me, how was I so bad? I can remember ya beatin' me in my sleep when I was a little kid and I wet the bed 'cause I was always so cold and scared all the time. Was that a crime, Pop? Did it make me a criminal? Why do you hate me, Pop?"

Jake was almost in tears. His father bowed his head.

"I donna hate you, Giacobine," Guissepe muttered. "Maybe I justa donna understand. I justa wanted you to be a man. I didn't wanna you to be un maljulio—a cheapa gangster—so I beat you. . . . I didn't wanna you to be a murderer—un capitano di morte—so I beat you. . . . I didn't wanna you to be a failure like me—un cavone—so I beat you again, harder than before!" he yelled, pounding the table with his fist. "Maybe I wasa wrong—I donna know—but maybe the beatings, They mada you un champione. . . ."

"Naw, your beatin's didn't make me a champ, Pop. None of the beatin's made me a champ. I made me a champ!" Jake said, beating his chest defiantly.

Jake's anger was building inside him. For the first time in his life, he felt like punching his father—punching him just once for all the senseless beatings and meaningless hate and years of neglect. As the unbidden tears rolled down his face, Jake suddenly turned and punched the kitchen wall with all his might, putting a hole in it the size of his fist.

"Ma que fia—but whatta you do? Are you crazy?" Guissepe cried.

"Ya know, Pop, I love you, but I don't respect you."

Jake picked up the check with his bleeding hand and waved it before his father. "Is this all I'm worth, Pop?" he repeated. Without waiting for an answer, Jake stuffed the check in his pocket and left.

It was a perfect Manhattan October evening as Jake emerged from the 59th Street subway station and made his solitary way past a shadowy, deserted Central Park, East Side and homeward bound. The autumn splendor was lost on Jake as he stalked past the horsedrawn carriages waiting patiently for adventurous tourists before the Essex House and the Plaza, past the swinging new Playboy Club and the darkened 59th Street shops, beyond the lights and nightly hustle of the city carriage trade, all the way to the 59th Street Bridge and down quietly residential Second Avenue. Jake deliberately avoided his usual route down Third Avenue to the familiar corner of 55th Street, where the low friendly lights of P.J. Clark's beckoned him to pass away the hours in careless oblivion till dawn crept its cold white fingers under his swollen reddened eyelids.

No, tonight he didn't feel like drowning his problems in a bottle of booze. They only surfaced the next day like so many dead, bloated fish floating on the murky surface of his besotted mind. Tonight he wanted to be alone and think—think about who and what and where he was, and why he wasn't who and what and where he wanted to be. The confrontation with his father was a sobering reminder of past transgressions and present humiliations that bode an even more tragic future if he didn't do something to change his life. What had become of the tough, determined Bronx Bull who stopped at nothing and no one to get what he wanted, who gave up everything that made most lives worth living in order to win? He felt like the bull who had been stuck over and over again by the picadores, the blood oozing from his wounds in constant pain, waiting for some merciful matador to plunge the sword in just the right place to put him out of his misery forever, but until then, stubbornly refusing to go down. "I'm too strong to go down: you can beat the shit out of me, but I won't go down; I refuse to go down," he told himself. Where was the demon who had powered him past mortal pain and weakness to superhuman strength and endurance—to the championship. Why had his demon left him now?

Jake interrupted his thoughts as he slowed his pace past a closing liquor store. "In the old days," he mused, "Rick and me would've knocked off a joint like that for a lot more than a lousy 400 bucks. We'd've left the jerk behind the counter face down on the floor and took off, thinkin' nothin' of it. But those was different days. . . ." He continued past the liquor store and stopped at the corner newsstand. The ten dollar check was burning a hole in his pocket, so he cashed it in for a few cigars and a copy of the Daily News. The aging news dealer recognized him.

"Hey, Champ—good luck! I saw it in the *News*—a baby girl, uh?"

Jimmy the doorman greeted him warmly as he sauntered through the lobby.

"Hey, congratulations, Champ! Ya did it again, uh? Manacha, but whoever would figure you wanted more kids? You're all right, Champ—you're all right! My regards to the missus, eh!"

Jake stood alone in the middle of the darkened apartment and stared bleakly around at the shabby objects dimly reflected in the glare of the street lights below. He looked at the pathetic crib Sally had salvaged from the street and blinked back the tears that suddenly came to his eyes. The room began to melt in the flickering light, conjuring up depressing images from his childhood. "I might as well be back in the Bronx slums," he thought miserably. "Please God," he prayed aloud, "Help me. Get me outta here. Help me get my family outta here. . . ."

Six

"Hey, Mom, whatta ya doin' to my kid, there? You're gonna drop her on her head or somethin'!" Jake addressed his mother with affectionate concern.

Elizabeth La Motta held her tiny granddaughter upside down at arm's length; the miniature face turned pink as the blood rushed to the baby's head. It was an old Italian practice insuring proper circulation for the newborn, and Elizabeth was nothing if not a firm believer in family tradition and custom.

"Stop makin' such a big deal. I did this to all you kids, and God made you all strong," she stated firmly. "There now, Beleza mia, don't start cryin' in front of your Papa. He was no crybaby, you know."

The elder Mrs. La Motta delivered her suddenly vocal namesake into Sally's anxious arms. "Let's go to Mama. She has just what you need, plenty of good milk."

Sally cradled her daughter tenderly as the child began to nurse contentedly at her mother's freely offered breast. Jake contemplated the intimate scene with pleasure. It had been a long time since he had experienced so close a family setting.

"Don't you two go spoilin' her and feed her too much, now," Jake said in gruffly tender tones.

"Aren't you supposed to be at work, or something?" Sally prompted.

"Yeah, I'm goin'; I'm goin'. Leave you girls together to do your thing."

Jake kissed Sally and the baby goodbye, giving his mother a duti-
ful peck on the cheek as well.

"Now don't you go tellin' Sally nothin' bad about me, Mom."

"Now what could I tell her she doesn't already know? Go—go to
work. You're not going to feed your family hanging around here,"
she chided, shooing Jake out the door.

Elizabeth smiled warmly at her daughter-in-law. She approved
of Sally's simple good-heartedness and straightforward honesty, a
far cry from the treachery of the past that constantly stirred her
formidable son into fits of jealous frenzy. She only hoped that
Jake's fortune would improve quickly enough to support his new
family in a decent style. She knew only too well the toll that poverty and unemployment took on a marriage. And she knew her son
well enough to know that without the anchor of home and family,
he was as lost as an empty ship in a storm-tossed sea, destined to
self-destruct. She also knew how blindly selfish and demanding
Jake could be . . . . She hoped for the best, but something told her
not to expect too much.

"Why don't I make you some nice hot tea," she offered, her
short but generous frame bustling toward the tiny kitchen. "Tea is
very soothing, especially when you're nursing your first baby," she
insisted.

"Don't go to any trouble, Mom. I'm fine, really," Sally protested
politely as she gently tucked her sleeping baby into the foundling
crib.

Sally liked her mother-in-law's warmth and kindness—
everybody loved "Mom"—but she wasn't used to the Italian matri-
arch's unquestioned domination of those around her. Sally's
mother had been a shadowy presence, preoccupied with her own
considerable problems of survival, leaving Sally to rely on a tough
emotional independence of her own, developed at an early age.
She was careful, however, not to offend the older woman. Now
that she was a mother, she wanted her marriage to work out more
than ever, and Mom was the only real link she had to Jake and his
turbulent past.

"Why don't Jake get you a bigger kitchen? You can't move in
here. I don't know how three people can live here," Elizabeth
complained as she brought the promised tea. "When I think of all

the big houses and fancy cars he used to have. . . ." She sighed heavily.

"We plan to move into a bigger apartment in the building as soon as we get enough money together," Sally answered with a confidence she didn't feel. "Now that Jake is working steadily . . ." Sally's voice trailed off. With Jake, she never knew how long anything would last.

"Thank God he's finally come to his senses and taken a real job," the older woman said as she planted herself on the corner of the bed on which Sally was comfortably curled. "All that acting business is good for a hobby, but it doesn't put bread on the table. But what kind of job is this? He never tells me anything any more."

"It's something to do with the Park Commission. Some friend of his got him the job. He doesn't talk about it much," Sally answered vaguely.

"He's like his father. They never say too much, and you never know what they're thinking. I gave up trying to figure them out years ago," Elizabeth said. "Even as a little boy, I never knew what Jake was doing. Always the calls from the neighbors—'Mrs. La Motta, your son is fighting in the streets again,' they tell me. He must've been born a fighter. It must've been God to make him fight so good. He fed the whole family. God knows his father didn't do it," she added with a tinge of bitterness.

"What was Jake like as a little boy?" Sally asked, sipping her tea.

"You know something," Elizabeth answered thoughtfully, "I don't think Jake ever was a little boy. There was no time. His father was so hard and bad to him, and the times were bad. He grew up like an animal in that tenement on home relief. All those problems and troubles from the beginning. Poor Jake, he was so quiet and serious, always kept to himself, sitting alone with that black look on his face, thinking, always thinking so hard. Jake was a good boy, but life punished him so much, he felt guilty for just being alive. . . ."

The early November sky loomed overhead, heavy with blue-black clouds as Jake wandered aimlessly through the paths of Central Park, clad in drab green regulation overalls, a canvas bag slung carelessly over one shoulder, broomstick paper pick in hand. Occasionally he would stop to spear a stray piece of litter dropped by some passerby, depositing his find into his bag of discarded paper products, and then resume his listless journey through the civilized trees and shrubs and shaded sidewalks. Eventually he sat down on a deserted bench and stared disconsolately out over the empty Wollman Rink, where just two short summers ago he had played "Big Julie" on stage with Lloyd Bridges in a summer production of *Guys and Dolls.*

"The Champ of the World out here with a paper pick shoved up his ass. That's show biz," he muttered to himself. Maybe he would always be just an ex-freak and a part-time ham, a born loser and a no good bum—one very used ex-champ for sale at the local flea market.

Jake set slumped on the bench, a lone figure in a lonely setting, and pitched his paper pick randomly into the ground. He thought of the ice pick his father had bequeathed him as a kid—"Hit 'em first and hit 'em hard, hit 'em first and hit 'em hard. . . ." It rang in his ears like a schoolboy chant. That ice pick had taught him survival in a jungle world that had disappeared as completely as the dinosaurs, leaving him as alone as the last forgotten woolly mammoth.

Lost in his stupor, Jake dimly noticed the figure of an elderly man huddled in an old overcoat making painfully slow progress across the grassy field a distance away. Silhouetted against the bleak wintering sky, the small form of the stranger seemed to dramatize Jake's feelings of helplessness and despair. From the odd manner in which the older man carried himself, Jake could tell he was ill and probably in pain. As he watched the man's private struggle, he saw the lone figure suddenly clutch at his chest and collapse to the ground. Jake dropped his idle pick and bag and ran toward the fallen stranger. A conviction that he must act to help this unknown victim overwhelmed him, speeding him on to the man's side. He was out of breath when he reached the still figure, and for a moment panic hit him as he knelt beside the gasping man. What could he possibly do for this poor guy? Jake loosened the man's coat and necktie, recognizing the probable signs of a heart attack as the man's right hand grasped his left side in obvious pain, his eyes rolled desperately upward in a silent scream for help.

"Okay buddy, it's goin' to be okay. Take it easy now," Jake said soothingly as he carefully helped the sick man to a half-sitting position.

Somehow he knew he could save this guy. He wasn't sure why, but he was certain he could keep this man alive by the sheer power of his will. Jake grasped the man's right hand firmly in his own and looked skyward in sincere prayer.

"Please God," he said aloud, "Don't let this man die. Make him live. Don't let him die."

He looked intently into the stricken man's frightened eyes and repeated in slow, deliberate tones, "You're not going to die; you're going to live. You're not dying; you're going to live. . . ."

Several tense moments passed as the man fixed his desperate gaze into Jake's unblinking eyes. Gradually, the man's rigid form relaxed and his labored breathing subsided as the pain diminished and the blood began to pulse freely again through his body. Jake finally breathed a long sigh of relief as he noticed the bluing fingernails of the man's hands return to their normal pink. Incredibly, his prayer had worked.

Jake helped the man slowly to his feet. Wordlessly, the bewildered old man looked at him with a mixture of gratitude and disbelief, then he shrank into his coat and walked away. Jake stood and watched him until he disappeared behind the trees, then he turned and headed slowly back across the field, a certain smile fixed on his face. Maybe it had really happened, and maybe it hadn't, he thought calmly. But he knew he hadn't felt such an inner peace and satisfaction and sure faith in himself since the night he won the championship. That certain knowledge and cool-headed confidence that he would win had suddenly returned to him from out of nowhere. A phrase he had read somewhere came to him with sudden clarity—"Whatever the mind can conceive and believe, the mind can achieve. . . ." It would be his guiding motto from then on. Maybe he would finally begin to enjoy being Jake La Motta again. . . .

Jake retrieved his discarded tools and resumed his routine duties with the renewed conviction of a condemned man saved by a last minute reprieve. Suddenly freed from the trappings of self-pity, shame and guilt, he seemed to move again with the ease and dignity and skill of the champion athlete he had once been.

Seven

It was a fine sunny Spring afternoon and the street vendors were out in full force, hawking their wares to the bustling sidewalk traffic and the young secretaries and office boys enjoying their lunch al fresco in the crowded city parks. Jake strolled contentedly through the midtown Manhattan scene with three-year-old Lisa perched happily on his shoulders and their little dog Skippy trotting faithfully by his side. The familiar trio could be seen most any afternoon on their daily walks around the city as friends and strangers alike greeted them with a hearty "Hiya, Champ."

"Daddy," Lisa addressed her father seriously from her lofty perch, "why does everybody know your name, and nobody knows mine?"

"Well Darlin', I guess it's because Daddy has lived a little longer than you," Jake answered his daughter tenderly.

Lisa had become Jake's favorite person. He had devoted the last two years to her daily care and upbringing while Sally provided the main support of the family with her Seventh Avenue modeling job. There were few things Jake could refuse his pert, pretty daughter. He had even developed an attachment to Skippy, the ugly but endearing little mutt Lisa had chosen from the pound with whom Jake was at first embarrassed to be seen, and who since had become his constant companion. Jake noted with pride and satisfaction the reflection of the three of them as they passed a mirrored storefront. Taking care of Lisa had changed Jake's worst habits. He hardly took a drink any more, and he had slimmed down to a trim 168 pounds—almost back to his fighting weight. He was making real progress in his acting classes at the Bert Lane Theatre Work-shop in the old Variety Arts Building, too. At least that's what this young actor/director there, John Cassavetes, had told him.

Jake smiled with happy anticipation as he thought of the act he and Rick had cooked up for Sally's birthday. He couldn't wait to see the look on her face when she entered the theatre at the Barbizon Plaza and read on the marquee, "An Evening With Jake La Motta." Rick had put together a few Seventh Avenue guys and managed to raise enough to produce the one man show—a "one night only special." Jake was to perform nine scenes from nine dif-ferent plays, requiring him to memorize over 10,000 words. Of course, Rick would do a couple of scenes on stage with him too. Rick had always fancied himself an actor, so he just had to get in on the act, but what the hell, he was putting it all together. Rick was good at pulling off deals.

"But why me?" Jake kept asking himself. Rick was probably his closest pal, but Jake was constantly aware of a kind of unspoken rivalry between them. When Sally told him that Rick had made a play for her once when he was out of town, he shrugged it off. Rick had pulled his old trick, bringing some of his dress samples up to the apartment for Sally to try on while Jake was away. It was Rick's way of testing out Jake's women for him, like he was doing him a favor. "I never give a broad more than ten days without it—and that's on the outside," Rick would say. Ever since Vickie, Jake had figured if that's what they wanted, they were welcome to it. But Sally would never do anything—she knew better. Still, it had to make a guy wonder. . . .

It was impossible for Jake to ever fully trust anyone, especially anyone close enough to really hurt him. Like "Blanche DuBois" in *A Streetcar Named Desire*, he thought, "I've always depended on the kindness of strangers. . . ." Jake had seen Rick con a lot of peo-ple, but he was sure he'd never be one of them. Rick would never try to take him—he had too much on him. Besides, they shared a respect for each other born of their mutual survival in the tough Bronx streets.

Jake grinned to himself as he thought of the time Rick and he had "liberated" all the dogs from the neighborhood pound. The truck had picked up Rick's kid sister's pooch off the streets. Rick got so mad he pulled a gun on the jerk at the pound and made him

let all the dogs loose. All those yelping mutts running in every direction into the Bronx streets. . . . Six foot tall, hard-as-nails Rick
rescuing a bunch of mangy dogs. . . . Rick was real loyal to his
own. Jake knew he could count on him to be there whenever push
came to shove. It was one of the reasons Jake put up with all his
bullshit and wiseguy attitudes. . . .

"Daddy, I wanna ice cream," Lisa interrupted Jake's thoughts.

"Sure, Baby. Daddy'll have one with ya," he responded.

Jake purchased two frozen confections from the corner vendor,
handing one up to his eager daughter. The two continued their
walk, consuming their ice cream in mutual contentment.

"Daddy," Lisa interjected into their comfortable silence,
"When's Mommy coming home? I wanna see Mommy."

Sally had been spending more time than usual at her job lately.
Sure, it was the busy Spring season and all, but what the hell did
he know? Jake had never seen the inside of a showroom. He had
never bothered Sally at work; he trusted her. But then, as Rick always said, "Ya never know with broads; ya gotta watch 'em very
carefully. Ya just never know, Pal. . . ." What if she was modeling
bras and girdles or something and she had told him ladies' dresses?
Then Rick had said something about that hotshot Jew boss of hers,
Lenny Silverman, who hired her back after she quit to have the
baby. He was banging models three at a time and probably pimp-
ing them off to buyers on the side according to Rick. But then a
thief will always think like a thief—he ought to know. . . . But not
Sally. Maybe all the other broads, but never Sally. . . . Too much
thinking can be dangerous, he thought.

"Sweetheart, how would you like to go meet Mommy at work
and surprise her?" Jake announced, more to himself than to Lisa.

Jake made a fast turn toward the West Side, his pace suddenly
brisk and determined. Rick's ominous warning echoed in his foot-
steps. "Ya never know, Pal. . . ." Ya never know. . . ." It was
difficult making headway with Lisa and the dog through the tangled garment center traffic, dodging the recklessly pushed racks of
clothes and the heedless nine-to-fivers rushing blindly to the sub-
ways and trains and busses and cars that daily carried them home.
Jake stopped and took Lisa down from his shoulders, holding her
tightly by the hand as they entered the dark arcade of shops that
ran through the building at 1407 Broadway to Seventh Avenue.

Skippy heeled close behind. Sally's showroom was somewhere on the eighteenth floor.

Jake froze in his tracks, his whole body tensing angrily as he spied Sally sitting with her boss in a booth for two in the arcade coffee shop.

"Daddy, you're hurting my hand," Lisa complained as she tried to free herself from Jake's strong grip. "Look, Daddy, there's Mommy over there!" she cried excitedly, recognizing Sally through the glass front of the shop.

Lisa broke from her father's grasp and ran ahead to the booth, jumping onto Sally's lap. Jake stalked stiffly into the shop after her, Skippy cautiously dogging his tracks, and stood belligerently over Sally and the prematurely balding Seventh Avenue manufacturer.

"What's goin' on here? Are you fuckin' my wife?" Jake challenged the unsuspecting man.

"And you," Jake continued, pointing at Sally. "Are you fuckin' this guy? Answer me!"

"Jake, Darling," Sally anxiously tried to calm Jake down, "This is Lenny, my boss. Please stop—you're making a scene," she stammered.

"I don't give a shit. I wanna know what's goin' on with you and this asshole. Ya better tell me the truth!" Jake persisted in menacing tones.

Sally looked helplessly back and forth at Jake and Lenny, too stunned to say a word.

"Look, fella, we're just havin' a cup of coffee and goin' over the Fall line. What in hell is wrong with you?" Lenny protested, stomping his cigarette butt irritably into the ash tray.

Jake leaned both hands on the table and glared at the man.

"Come outside with me right now, fuckhead, and I'll show ya. I'll wipe up Seventh Avenue with ya!" he growled threateningly.

"I suggest you walk out of here right now, Pal. You come any closer and I'll blow a hole right through you. I've heard about you, and I'm not taking any chances," Lenny replied in a low, serious voice.

Jake noticed the man's right hand move slowly inside his pinstriped suit jacket as he spoke.

"What're ya, crazy? You're gonna pull a gun out with my kid here?" Jake responded.

"Your big shot boss here carries a rod—thinks he's a real fuckin' wiseguy!" Jake said to Sally. "Come on. Let's get the hell outta here before I really kick the shit out of this asshole!"

Jake grabbed Sally by the arm and pulled her to her feet with frightened Lisa clasped tightly in her arms.

"And don't expect her back, ya fuckin' pimp!" he added as he dragged Sally and Lisa out of the coffee shop, Skippy trotting faithfully behind.

Jake strutted ahead in stony silence as Sally struggled awkwardly trying to keep up with him in her uncomfortably high heels with Lisa still in her arms.

"Now you've really done it, Jake," she called after him. "How are we going to pay the rent now that you got me fired? That was real smart—the big champ just won another round. Your stupid jealousy is going to ruin us!"

"Shut up!" Jake said without looking back as he ploughed steadily across town.

"Mommy, why is Daddy so mad?" Lisa questioned her mother innocently.

"Never mind, Darling. It's not your fault. Everything's going to be fine," Sally reassured her daughter. "Daddy's going to go to work and support us now, aren't you, Daddy?" she added.

Jake gave Sally a dirty look over his shoulder as he led his family home in stubborn silence.

Eight

Jake had walked all the way to 106th Street, crossing the invisible border from Upper East Side prosperity into the no man's land of Spanish Harlem, before he reversed his purposeless course and headed back down Fifth Avenue past the long dark edge of Central Park towards the beckoning lights of the more privileged side of Manhattan society. It was Christmas Eve, and the lavishly decorated stores were just closing their doors to last-minute shoppers as Jake emerged from the shadows above 59th Street and continued his solitary sojourn past the commercial splendor of Bergdorf's and Tiffany's. Jake turned up his flimsy jacket collar against the cold and jammed his hands into his thin pants pockets as he continued morosely through the holiday glitter toward Rockefeller Center. He had about fifteen cents in his pocket. As he passed a lone imploring Salvation Army missionary clanging dolefully on the corner, he tossed his last coins into the familiar red bucket with a futile shrug. "Merry Christmas," he murmured gloomily.

Jake stood by the rail overlooking the Rockefeller Plaza skating rink and watched the skaters as they moved beneath the giant, multi-colored fir that loomed annually over the scene. As people rushed by him, Jake thought dejectedly of Sally sitting with four-year-old Lisa and baby Mia in their larger but still barren one-bedroom apartment. He couldn't even afford to buy them a Christmas tree this year. He'd walked the streets since sundown rather than face their silent disappointment across the cheerless room.

Money had been tight ever since Sally lost her job and got pregnant again, and they had had to get by on the sporadic gigs where

Jake performed his marginally successful comedy act. His "Evening With Jake La Motta" had fetched a few grudgingly favorable reviews, but he hadn't exactly become the most sought after actor on Broadway. His two-bit agent must've booked him into every small joint in the five boroughs, but the couple of hundred here and there was better than nothing. OK, so his act wasn't perfect, but what was? At least he kept trying.

Jake looked up at the towering Christmas tree and wished that he had a million presents to place under it for Sally and the kids. He thought of those boyhood Christmases in the Bronx when the guys got together in the dirty snow and cold and lit a big fire and threw the few potatoes they promoted or stole from somewhere into the coals till they turned black and crunchy on the outside and white and warm and delicious on the inside. Mickeys, they called them. Mickeys were the only good thing he could remember about being poor.

Jake turned his back on the holiday scene and headed reluctantly back across Fifth Avenue. There was an anxious crowd milling around the steps of Saint Patrick's, vying for a view inside the packed cathedral where the faithful patiently awaited midnight Mass. Jake hesitated for a moment, half-wishing to duck inside the warm sanctuary, then he continued slowly past the noise and lights and crowd through the nearly deserted midtown streets. As he neared Third Avenue, his feet by force of habit led him to the friendly doors of P.J. Clark's. He peered through the windows at the mostly empty tables inside. Noticing Al's familiar Irish face behind the bar, Jake decided to step inside and wish his favorite bartender a Merry Christmas.

"Merry Christmas, Champ," Al greeted him on sight.

"The same to you, Pal," Jake rejoined. "The place is pretty empty," he added, looking around.

"That's to be expected on Christmas Eve, Jake. How about a drink on the house?" Al offered.

"Sure, why not," Jake quickly accepted.

"What'll it be, Champ, the usual?" Al started to grab the bottle of bar scotch.

"Naw, it's Christmas. Give me a shot of brandy," Jake ordered.

He downed the shot in one gulp and held out his glass. "Hit me again, Al," he said.

Brandy was like poison to Jake, and he knew it. Some reckless urge within prodded him relentlessly toward disaster.

"The last time I had any brandy, I lost the championship," Jake confided.

"Yeah, I remember that fight," Al said. "I lost a bundle on you that night, Champ. I was sure you could take Robinson. You were beatin' him, too, till the tenth round, and then you just ran out of gas. I never saw anyone take such a beatin' as you that night." Al shook his head sadly.

"Yeah, but I never went down. Robinson never got me down. If the referee hadn't stopped the fight, Robinson would've collapsed from hittin' me," Jake protested weakly.

He downed another shot and stared morosely into his glass.

"What the hell's the sense in talkin' about it," he said to himself. He had failed then just as sure as he was failing his family now. He should have taken Robinson that night—February 14, 1951—the Saint Valentine's Day Massacre. He told the reporters, "I'm not stopping this fight for any reason. I'm prepared to die," and he meant it. He bet $10,000 on himself. Three days before the championship match in Chicago, he was in top shape. He had made the 160-pound limit that made it so hard for him to stay in the middleweight class, and if he had listened to old Doc and flown directly out there from New York the day of the fight, he might have retired a champ. But he took the train out with Vickie instead. Three days of boozing and partying with her was all it took to put him eight pounds over the limit. He spent the night before the fight sweating it out in the steam room. He lost the eight pounds all right, but it left him weak as a kitten. He took a few shots of brandy before the fight to give him some strength, and it was working until the tenth round, when he suddenly ran out of steam. He didn't have enough energy to raise his arms. Maybe if they had had some brandy in his corner, he could have made it through those last five rounds. Robinson was punching him at will, but his punches were weak. He was wearing Robinson out. If the referee hadn't stopped the fight in the thirteenth round, he might have outlasted him. Robinson would have had to kill him to get him down. But it was all ancient history now. . . .

"Last call, Champ. We're closin' the place up early. Gotta get

home to the wife and kids, ya know," Al broke into Jake's reminis-
cences, pouring him a final brandy.

"Yeah, sure . . . me too," Jake slurred, downing his last generous shot.

Jake stood swaying slightly on the corner as he looked blankly up
into the night sky at the steadily falling snow. The cold flakes felt
good as they melted on his battered upturned face. The brandy had
spread a warm, welcome numbness through his body and softened
the hard, rough edges of reality. As he made his woozy way down
the three blocks along Third Avenue toward his apartment, he
passed a little old Italian guy packing up the last of his unsold
Christmas trees on the now deserted corner. Jake stood and
watched the guy for a few minutes, eyeing the unwanted trees like
a lonely kid with his face pressed to the glass outside a candy store.

"Hey buddy, whatta ya gonna do with that little one over
there—that can't be worth nothin' much now, uh?" Jake addressed
the man thickly, pointing to a small scrawny fir off to the side. The
weathered old man gave Jake a long, hard look, a glimmer of recognition reflected in his sad wrinkled eyes. Wordlessly, he walked
over to the tree, picked it up and handed it to Jake. "Merry Christmas, Champ," he said softly.

Holding his prize tightly, a cocky grin spreading from ear to ear.
Jake could hardly wait to show Sally the tree. It wasn't much of a
tree, but it was theirs, he reasoned in his growing stupor. By the
time he reached his apartment door, the brandy had seeped well
into his soggy mind, fracturing his blurred perception into double
images. He fumbled clumsily with the lock and finally spilled
through the door, staggering awkwardly into the room, tiny tree in
hand. Sally was curled on the couch in her bathrobe watching television. Lisa and Mia were sleeping soundly with Skippy in the next
room. She looked up at Jake in silent accusation, her eyes red and
swollen from crying.

"Aw, Baby, whatta ya cryin' for, ya dumb broad. Look what I
brought ya."

Jake held out the naked little tree in pathetic offering, swaying
back and forth precariously.

"That's just wonderful, Jake. And what do you propose we put
on it, or under it for that matter," Sally replied testily. "How are

you going to make it stand up? You don't even have a stupid stand for it."

"Gee, I never thought of that." He dropped the tree unceremoniously on its side and staggered into the kitchen. He rummaged noisily in the cabinets, finally returning with a large pasta pot of water. He spilled it sloppily onto the floor as he attempted vainly to balance the tree in the uncooperative pot. The pitiful tree swayed from side to side as Jake struggled to keep it upright, swaying no less himself. Sally watched his feeble efforts in growing consternation. No longer able to control her mounting anger and frustration, she rose suddenly to her feet.

"Just get rid of it, you stupid fool! Get it out of here, and take yourself out with it!" she shouted, infuriated.

"Naw, I want the kids to see it in the mornin'," Jake replied dully, unperturbed by her anger.

Maddened by Jake's lack of awareness and concern, the constant disappointment of the last five years overwhelming her with unexpected fury, Sally grabbed the tree and threw it at Jake with all her might. The trunk struck him in the belly with a dull thud.

"Since when do you care about any of us, you drunken slob!" she sobbed, beside herself.

Jake staggered backward from the blow, shock and surprise registered on his blunt features.

"Hey, whatta ya think you're doin', ya crazy bitch!" he cried in sudden anger.

"I've had it with you! You're nothin' but a punch drunk has-been who can't even get a job. You're a mean, selfish bastard and I hate you!" Sally screamed hysterically.

"Hey, that's enough! Any more and I'll punch ya in the fuckin' mouth, ya crazy broad!" Jake growled back, his defenses mounting.

"Go ahead, ya phony loser, go ahead and hit me! All ya can hit are women, ya big coward! Go ahead and punch me—punch me!"

Sally moved in close to Jake, her contorted face shouting into his, challenging him with reckless defiance. Her threatening voice and posture triggered a deep, dangerous impulse in Jake. He reached out with both hands, grabbing Sally by her shoulders, and shook her violently back and forth in an attempt to snap her out of her uncontrollable hysteria. Dizzy and dazed, Sally stumbled backwards out of Jake's strong grip and fell, her head striking against the edge of the coffee table with a sickening crack as she collapsed unconscious to the floor.

Jake stared in disbelief at Sally's limp form. Her head was bleeding profusely, staining the collar of her white robe a deep crimson. He knelt over her, his panic rising as she remained still and silent, unresponsive to his frantic efforts to revive her.

"O my God, what have I done? She's dead!"

Jake moved in a dream-like trance. He removed Sally's robe and carried it into the kitchen, intending to wrap it in ice as a compress for her bleeding head. In his shocked confusion, he stuffed the robe into the freezer instead, He returned zombie-like to the darkened room flickering eerily in the light of the forgotten television, from which a full chorus of Handel's "Messiah" blared incongruously. Jake gazed in horror at Sally's ghost-like form clad in the thin white nightgown, lying so still on the floor, her pale image already haunting him. Gripped by an overwhelming sense of despair, he backed numbly out of the room, pulling the door tightly closed as if to shut out the nightmare within.

Jake ran blindly down the street into the frosty night towards the East River, his heart pounding with the fury of an escaped convict. "I've got to find Rick," he thought frantically. "Rick'll know what to do." The long-buried guilt over Harry Gordon welled suddenly within him, choking him with renewed fear. He had run to Rick then, spilling out the horrible confession of his gory crime in terror of a retribution that never came. Rick had cooled him down, and he had been right about nothing happening to him. But Jake had lived since the age of sixteen with the damning inner conviction that he had murdered a man in cold blood. It was that terrible secret that had given him the devil-may-care aggression in the ring that had so overwhelmed his opponents. He didn't care who he hit or how hard he got hit. He craved physical punishment like a starving man craved food. When he finally found out that Harry had survived and was alive and well and living in Miami, that he wasn't a murderer after all, Jake wasn't the same fighter as before. He started losing something with each fight. What he never lost was the self-hatred and shame and guilt he had learned to live with ever since that fateful night long ago in the back alley where he left poor bleeding Harry to die. Was he doing the same to Sally now?

The red glow of the traffic lights as he staggered through the

darkened streets made Jake think of police cars and sirens and relentless searchlights, the red and green of Christmas buried along
with all the pleasant memories of his past with one swift, careless
blow. He could see the morning headlines before him—"La
Motta's Wife Found Dead In Apartment." He found himself in the
shadowy darkness of Sutton Place Park. The small, quiet patch of
trees and wooden benches overlooking the East River was his favorite spot to take Lisa and Skippy on their frequent walks. He
headed toward the river's edge and looked out over the low railing
at the few tug boats chugging by, their long, low foghorns echoing
across the water. He stared dejectedly into the dark, cold river and
thought how easy it would be to slip over the rail and sink beneath
the swift, murky surface, drowning his sorrow and guilt forever.
The snow began to fall again, landing gently on the rail and ground
around him as the tears froze on his face.

PART III

The Lonely Years

Nine

⊂⧸ I was now living around the corner in a crap house called the Pickwick Arms. It should have been called the Pick-me-up Arms; this hotel housed more prostitutes than it had rooms. But what the hell, it was cheap enough. My room was the size of a closet—I had to step outside to change my mind—and the mattress felt like the one I had in jail. The bathroom was half a mile down the hall, but the phone and message taking was free, except for outside calls. I made them in the lobby phone booth. That was cheaper, too.

This had been home for the past eight months. I couldn't afford the rent any more on the last place. Who needed three rooms, anyway? I was pretty much alone. Rocky'd meet me once in a while and buy me a few drinks. Rick was still around, trying to get into show business through the back door—producing porno flicks.

Sex was a big thing now. Like nobody knew about it before and it was just invented. It was becoming so open you could buy it over any counter. People would be screwing on the street corners soon, like stray dogs. Rick caught on to the times and started making porno flicks on the side. The theatres around Times Square was buying them up like hot cakes. He had the nerve once to ask me to be in one of them. He figured the La Motta name would help sell the distributors. "I'm low," I told him, "but I ain't that fuckin' low." I like screwing as much as anybody, but I like it in private.

I was banging broads two at a time up in my room. All kinds of broads—white, black, Puerto Rican, Chinese—like the United Nations. Why the hell not—a broad is a broad is a broad. I didn't respect a goddam one of them. I picked most of them up in the clubs where I had my gigs. I lived from one gig to the next. It was like going to a party—lots of people, lots of booze and lots of broads trying to grab my cock. It paid the rent and kept me in cigars and scotch. I only had myself to worry about now. I was used to that. I had been a loner most of my life.

It seemed like the days were an hour short and the nights a year long. It was hot as hell and my room felt like a sweat box. I had opened the one window as far as I could, but it was one of those sticky still nights in late September that still feels like August. The room didn't come with a color TV, and I liked it that way. I'd seen enough crap on television to last me a lifetime. I'd taken up reading instead—and not those cheap dimestore novels that women like to jerk off with, either. I was getting into stuff like Ardery's *African Genesis* and Gibran's *The Prophet*—philosophical stuff like that. I even tackled some Aristotle and Plato. It got me to thinking about life and human nature and maybe why I kept fucking up all the time. I was still two characters, and I had to get rid of one of them. Before, I took out my frustrations on my opponents, and after that was over, I started thinking my wives were my opponents and I took it out on them. Sometimes I felt like a mad dog, like one of those dogs they trained in the war. People would donate their dog—a German Shepherd or a Doberman or something—and the Army would train them to attack and kill on command. Then after the war was over, they had to give these killer dogs back to their owners. Now, when the owner says "attack" when kidding, the dog starts and the owner pulls him back on the chain. The dog is all confused. He says to himself, "Before, when they said attack and I did, they'd praise me and give me something good to eat. What the fuck happened? I'm all fucked up." But it's very true, when you're taught one way, it's very hard to change. You keep on attacking because it's the only way you know how to survive.

I grabbed my old deck of cards and started playing solitaire—my old pastime—pazienza, or patience, they call it in Italian. I always had a lot of time on my hands during the lulls between fights. I would read the paper, go for long walks, go shopping, and still I had a lot of time on my hands. So I'd play solitaire. There's something about the action—picking up the cards and putting them down, picking them up and putting them down, that always helps me think. It's kind of like the rhythm you set up on a punching bag.

You get into the repetition and forget everything else and pretty soon you're feeling all right again. I reached over and switched on the little shit radio I kept in the room for company. Sinatra was singing "Strangers in the Night." It was me and Sally's last theme song. When I finally screwed up enough courage to go back to the apartment that fucked-up Christmas morning, she had already taken off with the kids and the dog and five bucks in her pocket to her grandmother's in Pennsylvania. It took me a while to find her. I figured she was trying to teach me a lesson and would come back soon enough. I figured wrong. When a broad like Sally makes up her mind, it's over for good. I learned that the hard way. Every time she and the kids moved, I'd find them, and every time there'd be an ugly scene. I knew this fucking wiseguy she started seeing was supporting her and the kids. I had told her often enough she ought to find somebody who could really take care of her instead of sticking with a bum like me. I guess she finally took me up on it.

The last time I saw her, I ran into her on Third Avenue. She told me to stay away from her and ran back into her car. I jumped into the front seat after her and grabbed her by the hand. She was still wearing the wedding ring I gave her. We started arguing again, and she took off the hat I was wearing and threw it into the street. When I got out to get it, she took off, leaving me standing there holding my hat like a jerk. Crazy broad. What's the sense in wanting somebody who doesn't want you? She got a Mexican divorce on our anniversary. I found out later that the asshole she was with told her that I had talked to the boys downtown in Brooklyn and had a hit put out on both of them. She must have known I didn't give a shit about the guy, but she must have been crazy to believe the rest of it—the mother of my children, I'm going to put a hit on her, too?

It beats me how two people can be so close and loving, with kids and all, and then all of a sudden they're like two fucking strangers . . . "Strangers in the Night." It was the same way with Vickie. Only broads can do that—just walk away without looking back. It was the kids I missed most, and being the head of a family. I guess I was a three time loser on that score now.

I figured I could use another drink to get me out of the crazy mood I was in. I went for the tiny closet where I kept my spare bottles of scotch. The door was stuck, as usual. I gave it a hard yank, and the door flew open, spilling out this box of papers from the top shelf. I had packed up this old box with all the other shit, not really knowing what was in it. I grabbed the last bottle of scotch off the shelf and poured myself a tall one, then I started going through the papers on the floor. They were all the letters I had written Sally from jail in Florida, and some she had written me. Sally must have kept them all this time.

Funny, I could still see that big sad-eyed look she gave me that last night just before Christmas when I went away to jail. I was standing at the door holding the shirts she'd just ironed for me. She looked so all alone, I think if she'd let me kiss her goodbye, I'd 've broken down. Then I left Sally and drove to the house to say goodbye to Vickie and the kids. Vickie followed me out to the car and kissed me through the window. That's all she had to do. I grabbed her and pulled her to me and kissed her hard on the mouth. Then she kissed me back. I got out of the car and picked her up in my arms and carried her back into the bedroom. I threw her on the bed and screwed her brains out. That was the last time I touched Vickie. I'll never know if it was love, or just lust. . . .

I poured myself a refill and sat down on the floor, reading the letters. Most of them were dumb shit, and the spelling was pretty bad, but some of them were good—stuff straight from the heart. . . .

My Heart, My Love,

I think the reason, Jake, that we will be happy together is we have a good communication between us. Communication doesn't always mean talking to one another, the greatest type of communication is selfless, warm, understanding love. I think that is what we are blessed with. I know you pretty well in such a short time I have known you, I feel things the way you feel them, mostly. When something goes wrong in your life, then my life isn't happy either. When you are contented and cheerful I am also. Even being separated hasn't changed our course of communication. I love you my precious beauty . . . My darling, winter is over. It was a long long winter; when you look back my lover it had a lot of storms, and bitterness. But winter is behind us now, we only have the Spring. The Spring is like a newborn baby, it comes softly, and with beautiful fragrances. The awakening of all nature is here and with it, it brings fresh happiness to people in all walks of life, that have weathered the long long winter. We have almost reached our Spring. Soon we will both be free, and we will love and play together again, only spring with her many enchantments gives to us these precious promises . . .

You are missed, missed and loved,
Your Sally Bird

My beautiful blue bird,

I miss you more & more as the days get closer & closer to me coming home. I want you to know without your love and compassion I would have been a very unhappy man. I won't forget darling. As I look back I should not be bitter. Either its faith or the act of god my being here because its done me a lot of good. Its given me plenty of time to collect my thoughts & its done something for my health that I could never have done on the outside & its made me fall in love with a wonderful girl, who is all women. She was lost & so was I & us two lost souls found each other . . .

All the way,
Me

The more I read the more I wanted to cry inside. The scotch was beginning to get to me. I couldn't remember if I was drinking the first bottle from today or the last bottle from the night before. All of a sudden I felt kind of weird. The room started to twist and turn all around me. I went into a cold sweat. The bed all at once was on the ceiling, and the walls were breathing in and out like a crazy Disney cartoon. I felt suffocated, like I was under water and I couldn't breathe. The closet door started banging open and shut, making a loud noise that kept getting louder, and it looked like a tornado was blowing through it. I started seeing all kinds of crazy things flying out of the black hole of that closet—Cadillacs in all colors, and hundreds of dogs in all sizes, all looking like Skippy running at me, then Vickie's face, and the kids' and Rick's, all laughing hard. Then I heard all these bells ringing in my ears and every fighter I'd ever knocked down bouncing off the ropes back at me, and millions of strange faces shouting my name—Jake, Jake, Jake. . . I tried to jam the closet door shut on all the demons and faces and noise, but it flew open again and blew me across the room like a feather in the wind. I felt like I was falling down this long black tunnel, and I just kept falling and spinning on my back faster and faster and faster. . . .

I'm sitting in this hot courtroom, and all these flies are buzzing all around, making a lot of noise. This lawyer that looks like my old manager is sitting next to me reading *Playboy* magazine. The judge is sitting high above me, picking his nose. There's a jury panel of six big rednecks wearing cops' uniforms staring hard at me. The D.A. is standing next to the judge, grinning at me. He leans over and whispers something in the judge's ear, then they both look at me and start laughing. I turn my head slowly and look back over my shoulder. There are a bunch of strange-looking faces in the seats behind me. In the back row I see Vickie. She's wearing dark sunglasses and a scarf around her head. She looks straight ahead, like she doesn't know me.

I turn back around and the D.A. calls out, "Your Honor, I now call Doris Ann Bridgmon to the stand . . ." This strange young chick in pigtails and bobby sox skips up the aisle. She's chewing bubble gum and smacking her lips. Her face is all painted up with lipstick and rouge. She winks at me as she passes by and sits in the witness box. Then she starts talking in this hi-pitched squeaky voice . . .

"I arrived in Florida from Alabama about October 7, 1956. I lived with my father under the name of Mr. and Mrs. Bridgmon. I am acquainted with a party by the name of Jake La Motta. I see him in the courtroom and I identify him."

She points at me and giggles, then she continues . . .

"I first met the defendant, Jake La Motta, at his bar on October 27th. I went over to the beach that night with Jim and we went to Flo's apartment. Then we walked to Jake La Motta's bar. We got there about ten o'clock. I met Jake La Motta at that time. Flo introduced us. He introduced me to the man he was with. He told the man this was my first time. The man said he could break me in. We danced a couple of numbers and left. We went back to the apartment house where Flo lives. We went to Apartment 8. I got in with the key Flo had given me. We remained in this apartment about twenty minutes. We had an unnatural act. He went down on me. I received $20—two tens—for this act. After I got the money we dressed. He carried me back to the bar and let me out at the red light. I went back in by myself . . ."

I stand up and try to say something, but nothing comes out. The whole room is staring at me. I want to shout, "No, I never saw her before! I can't remember none of that!" My mouth moves, but I can't make a sound. I try and try, but I don't have a voice. The lawyer gets up and walks away from me. I turn around and look at Vickie. She smiles at me, then she gets up and walks out of the room, too.

"Has the jury reached a verdict?" the judge is saying. The six rednecks stand up and shout in unison, "We the jury find the defendant, Jake La Motta, guilty . . . guilty . . . guilty . . ."

I'm standing alone in front of the judge. "Jake La Motta," he says, looking down at me, "It has been found that you did willfully, knowingly and unlawfully keep, set up, maintain and operate for the purpose of lewdness and assignation a place, structure and building located at 2300 Collins Avenue, City of Miami Beach, and that you did willfully, knowingly aid and abet a certain female, to-wit: Doris Ann Bridgman, to offer to commit, or to engage in prostitution, lewdness or assignation. I hereby sentence you to serve six months at hard labor in Dade County Jail and pay a fine of $500.00, and in default of payment of the fine, to be confined for an additional 100 days. Take the prisoner away . . ."

The judge bangs his gavel again and again and again, and suddenly he looks like my father and the gavel becomes this long whip and he's beating me with it over and over. . . .

All of a sudden I'm in this strange parking lot. All the cars are big Cadillacs. I'm surrounded by all these empty Cadillacs. Then I see my old baby blue Cadillac convertible pull into the lot. The D.A. from the courtroom is driving it. Vickie is sitting next to him. They start kissing each other. I see the expression on Vickie's face—she's enjoying it. I start toward them, angry as hell. They stop and look at me, then they both start laughing hard. They keep on looking at me and laughing. Then they get out of the car and walk away together. I want to follow them, but my legs won't move. I can't move an inch, and I can't say anything. . . .

I've got the D.A. on the ground in the parking lot and I'm choking the bastard. I've got both hands around his throat and I'm choking the life out of him. All of a sudden it's not the D.A. His face turns into Vickie's, and I keep on choking her. I'm so mad and her eyes are popping out and I'm squeezing down on her throat with all my might till she can't breathe. . . .

"Hey Jake, Jake, wake up, Pal. You're dreamin', Man. Come out of it, Champ . . ."

I opened my eyes. Rick was leaning over me, shaking me hard by the shoulders.

"Rick, what're you doin' here? I must've been dreamin'," I said woozily.

I tried to sit up on the hard floor, but I slumped back down. My head felt like it was the size of a basketball, and it felt like my mouth was full of cotton. It tasted like old vomit. I tried to swallow, but I started coughing instead. My clothes stank of stale sweat and dried piss.

"Dreaming? You've been fightin' the championship all over again. I've been tryin' to wake you up for the past half hour. Here, drink some of this crap."

Rick handed me a paper cup of cold black coffee. I gulped it down and started coughing all over again. Rick slapped me on the back till I stopped. Then he helped me to my feet and onto the bed. I was as weak as an old woman.

"Jesus, man, whatta ya tryin' to do—drown yourself in this shit?" Rick said, looking around the room at all the empty bottles of scotch on the floor. "Ya look like a piece of shit. Even your own mother wouldn't claim ya!"

"I don't know . . . I'm all fucked up," I said, sinking onto the bed.

By the amount of light streaming through the window, I knew it was afternoon. I must have been out for a good twelve hours.

"You're lettin' all these fuckin' broads ruin your life. I told ya never to trust a cunt. They'll fuck ya every time. Why can't ya just use 'em and leave 'em—do ya have to marry 'em every goddam time?" Rick said hotly.

I closed my burning eyes and wished I was somewhere else—anywhere else but here.

"So's how come you've had the same wife for the past 15 years?" I asked tiredly.

" 'Cause I never let my right hand know what my left hand is doin'. Family and business are two different worlds. Ya never mix one with the other. That's where you keep fuckin' up, Pal."

Rick walked to the door and put his hand on the knob. I knew he hated being here and seeing me like this. Rick liked everything neat and tidy and shiny—like in the movies.

"When ya didn't show up at El Morocco today like you was suppose to, I got worried. I had a couple of hot pigeons on the line who wanted to meet you. Ya fucked that up real good. I called the jerk at the desk and he said ya haven't been out of your room for days. Whatta ya got— shit for brains? Ya ain't shaved or washed for a week. Ya look like a fuckin' degenerate. Clean yourself up, for Chrissakes! I gotta go. I'll call ya later," Rick said, disgusted, and left.

I closed my eyes again, but the room started spinning and I had to open them to keep from feeling dizzy. Rick was right; even I couldn't stand the stench of my own body. Up till now I just didn't care—I didn't care about nothing or no one, because no one I knew gave a shit about me. I dragged myself down the hall and forced my stinking carcass into the shower. Funny, how a stupid shower can make you feel like a newborn baby, like your old self was washed away down the drain along with all the dirt and shit. Shaving in front of the mirror, I kept looking at my beat up old mug looking back at me. "Ya sure ain't no beauty, Pal," I said to myself, "and ya ain't gettin' any younger, neither. It's high time ya got off your ass and got your shit together." I did some shadow boxing at the mirror. My timing was a little off, but I still had it. "Once a champ, always a champ," I reassured myself.

Back in my room, I rummaged around till I found a clean pair of shorts. I put on my last clean undershirt, lay back on the bed and lit a cigarette. There was no one around I had to impress with my big cigar. I thought of all the things that had happened to me that don't happen to everybody. I made fortunes and lost them. I won the championship of the world when everyone thought I was through, then when I was losing the championship, I KO'd my man with 13 seconds left in the 15th round. I was the first man to lick Ray Robinson, and then I lost my championship to him. I had a return bout with him which meant $100,000, and I had to turn it down because I never thought I could make 160 pounds again, and then I went to jail and lost all that weight. I've had beautiful young broads marry me and give me kids. Maybe it's destiny, but when you think big, big things happen to you; think small, and small things happen. I had to start thinking big again. . . .

My eyes lit on this yellow pad of paper lying on the floor with all the letters I had been reading the night before when I passed out. I remembered Sally telling me that day in the park to write my book. I thought she was crazy then, but maybe she wasn't so nuts after all. If I could write all those letters, why couldn't I just put it all together and tell my life story? Who knew it better than me? Who knows, maybe it would even sell. If nothing else, at least I'd have the satisfaction of getting it all off my chest once and for all.

I found a stubby pencil on the floor next to the pad. I sat down at the wobbly little desk stuck in one corner and thought a while, then I started writing. . . .

". . . Now, sometimes at night, when I think back, I feel like I'm looking at an old black-and-white movie of myself. Why it should be black-and-white I don't know, but it is. Not a good movie, either, jerky with gaps in it, a string of poorly lit sequences, some with no beginning and some with no end. And almost all of it happens at night, as if I lived my whole life at night. . . ."

Ten

❑ I was dropped off at the Brasserie by the guys who owned this small club in Brooklyn. I had done my gig and left with 350 bucks, all in my pocket—cash. It was a nice warm Spring night and about three-thirty in the morning. Sometimes I liked breakfast to soak up some of the booze in me. The Brasserie was a 24-hour cafeteria with champagne prices in the East 50's where show bizzers and hookers and wiseguys hung out after hours. I sat down at the counter and ordered a couple of eggs over easy, fries and coffee. The joint was half-packed with jet set kids, tired hookers and big-nosed Mafiosa guys. Alice brought me my breakfast and gave me a friendly wink. I liked to kid around with her because it was no contest. Alice was about sixty years old, with a still pretty face and a great sense of humor. "How about comin' home with me, Alice. We'll get laid and maybe have a little Jake in nine months."

She laughed and went about her business. She was cute and streetwise. Alice knew every hooker in New York by first name and telephone number. That's how she made a living. Every out-of-town sucker wants to get laid, and Alice had the numbers.

As I was eating my breakfast, I felt a hand on my shoulder.

"Hey, Champ, it's me, Tony, remember? I met you through Rick at a party one time."

I looked at this guy and couldn't remember a thing, but I didn't let on.

"Oh yeah, how ya doin'?" I said with a mouthful of eggs.

"Come on over to the table and meet some of the boys," he said, patting me on the back.

"For what?" I asked him.

"No for what," he said, "They just want to say hello."

"OK, but let me finish my eggs."

I didn't know who this fucking guy was. I finished my breakfast and said so long to Alice, then I walked over to their table. There were six of them with the jewelry and the three-piece suits. They all greeted me with a nod, and I sat down. Then this slick-looking character in a black gabardine suit stood up and made himself known.

"My name is Jerry, Jake. Glad to meet you," he said, shaking my hand across the table.

"Yeah, thanks," I said, "I guess you know who I am."

"What would you like to drink, Jake?" Jerry asked me.

"Nothin', thanks. I just had breakfast."

"The boys and me was sittin' around talkin' when you walked in, and you sprung an idea in our heads."

"I sprung the idea?" I repeated curiously.

"Yeah, you see," Jerry continued, pointing to the rest of the group around the table, "all of us here, we're startin' a new club in New York. It's goin' to be kinda private, like if we don't know ya, ya don't get in. To give ya an idea, Tony here works outa Vegas mostly, Johnny out of Chicago, Lou out of L.A., Sal out of Reno, and I operate in New York. Phil here, he just looks after my ass. In any event, this is the idea . . ."

"Wait a minute," I said, stopping his spiel. "Why are you tellin' me all this?"

"Well, we feel we can trust you. After all, we know the same people. We know you know Rick Rosselli, for instance, and we know you was fightin' for Frankie Carbo and Associates when you took that little dive for the championship."

"I know a lot of people," I said, wanting to belt the fuck, "but I don't publish it in the *Daily News* on Sunday."

"That's what I mean." Jerry laughed a little. "You got a sense of humor and you got a way of keepin' your mouth shut."

"So what," I said, hard like. "Look, I'm tired and I just wanna go home and get some sleep."

I stood up, ready to take off.

"Wait five minutes," Jerry insisted.

So I sat down again to be polite. I hated his conversation already, and I had already figured out they were a bunch of button guys from all over the country. They'd as soon blow your head off as look at you.

"So look, Jake," Jerry continued smoothly. "It took us a long time to put a group like this together. Let's be honest with each other. We know you're not doin' too well at what you're doin'. . . ."

"You callin' me a lousy comic?" I shot back.

"No, no Jake, that's not what I'm tryin' to say," Jerry tried to con me. "I just mean money-wise, you're not doin' too good."

"I'm gettin' along," I lied.

"Sure, sure you are. But you could do a lot better. Hear me out, will ya? We've collected a list of high rollers all over this fuckin' country, and we know 'em like on a first name basis. The list can choke a dinosaur. We're in the process now of buyin' a small town house in the 70's on the East Side—wall-to-wall carpeting, free drinks and food, nice lookin' young chicks runnin' around servin' the pigeons, and some of the sharpest dealers around. . . . Come on, you get the drift . . ."

"In other words," I said before he said it, "you want me to front, or host the joint for ya, right?"

"That's it exactly," Jerry said.

"But why me?" I asked suspiciously.

"Let's face it," Tony chimed in this time. "Ya don't expect us to hire a schwartza. You're one of the only white champs left."

"Jake," Jerry started again, "we're willin' to pay ya one thousand bucks a week, free and clear. Come on, Pal, you don't make that kind of dough in a month. What do ya say?"

The insults was beginning to mount up, and I was getting more and more pissed.

"Let me tell you guys somethin'," I growled, "I told fuckers like you off before I was champ, while I was champ, and I can still tell ya now. Leave me alone and fuck off!"

I wanted to throw the cup of coffee he was drinking all over the motherfucker, but I was thinking these guys were carrying and they could blow my head off right in this joint. I tried to calm myself a little. I never should have sat down at their table. Jerry's face turned red as a beet, and the other guys stood up stiff, ready to attack.

"It was a good try, guys," I said, looking them hard in the eyes, "but find yourself another boy."

I got up from the table and walked out.

The next night Rick picked me up to go to this cocktail party. He said there were going to be a lot of big celebrities there and he didn't want to miss it. Show biz was fucking up his brain. That's all he thought of day and night. I said I'd go with him, but I hate cocktail parties. They're all the same—a bunch of stuck-up assholes boozing it up and all the cocks looking for a tail. Same old thing— misery reaching out to misery. The guy who was giving the party was a hot shot lawyer Rick had used to bail him out of some legal hassles with his films. He knew a lot of show biz people, and maybe publishers, too. Rick was hoping we would meet somebody there who might be interested in my book. He also had selfish reasons.

When I showed him the 200 pages I'd sat up four days and nights in my room writing, he started helping me with it, making himself a major character and a good percentage while he was at it. What the fuck did I care? I needed the money and I didn't give a shit how it got done. Rick knew how to put down words better than I did, so I thought it was a good idea to work with him. He was always giving me this shit about Cain and Abel or Becket. The movie *Becket* was just out, and Rick figured we could cash in on the idea by making the story about two friends instead of two brothers. I figured it was his way of justifying putting himself in the book. "We'll go with the Becket theme all the way," he'd say.

"Sure, Pal, whatever you say," I'd tell him.

When we got there, it was a big three-bedroom penthouse with terraces all around. People were all over the joint. Rick told me to maintain myself and not drink too much. Sometimes he talked to me like I was a sixteen-year-old kid. I walked over to where they was serving the booze and got myself a drink. Rick started to mingle, talking to most of the people. Mostly, I talk to people only if they talk to me first, so I stood in the corner by the terrace doors and watched. I had a good view of the scene this way. After a while, Rick walked over to me with this guy in a business suit that turned out to be the lawyer who was giving the party. He was serious and quiet-spoken, but he seemed like a nice enough guy. He said he liked the book idea and could probably get us a publisher if we let him agent the book. We made a date to meet him at his office and sign some papers. I was starting to feel better. Maybe now we were doing the right thing for once.

I got myself another drink and was feeling pretty good. I noticed this older dame sitting in the corner by herself. She must have been a real knockout when she was younger. She had long black hair over her shoulders, big green eyes and pure white skin. I was always a sucker for white skin on a broad. She was wearing a black velvet suit and a long string of pearls. I could tell she was real class all the way. She looked very familiar to me. I knew she had made lots of movies, but I just couldn't remember her name. I called Rick over. "Who's that broad in the corner?" I asked him.

"You asshole," he said, "don't you recognize her?"

When he told me her name I was shocked. This was *the* exotic siren of Hollywood in the late 30's and 40's. She'd made loads of pictures with big-name stars. She noticed me staring at her, so I walked over and introduced myself.

"Hello you beautiful, lovely, gorgeous creature. Ya know, you have beautiful legs—they run all the way up to your ass. I'm Jake La Motta."

I knew she'd probably heard that line a thousand times over, but broads are funny that way. They never get tired of being told they're beautiful. It works everytime.

"How nice," she said coldly.

"Whatta ya mean, 'how nice'?" I asked her back.

"What is so exciting about being Jake La Motta?" she said in this snooty foreign accent.

"What's wrong with you, lady," I said, insulted. "I'm Jake La Motta—the Middleweight Champ of the World."

"You mean the old middleweight champ, don't you?" she shot back.

"You're no spring chicken yourself, but I must admit, you're lookin' pretty good. I wouldn't kick you out of bed."

She raised one of her perfectly arched eyebrows at that one, so I figured I'd better stick to talking shop.

"I'm writin' my book now," I said to change the subject.

"You're writing a book?" she asked, like she didn't believe me.

"Well, my partner Rick is helpin' me out with it, but it's my life story. You wrote a book, too, I remember. What a zinger that was! Did you really do all those things you said you did?"

"I'm afraid I don't know what you are referring to, exactly," she said coyly.

"Sure, you know—the orgies, all the broads you screwed, all that stuff. Are you really a les or are you straight?" I asked her, calling her bluff.

"Is this an inquisition?" she said, batting her long dark lashes at me.

I wasn't sure what she meant by that, so I played it safe.

"No, I'm just tryin' to get some pointers from you for my book. Is all the truth necessary?"

"It depends on how you look at it," she said, evading me again. This broad liked to play games.

"How else can I look at it, but what really happened, otherwise, I'd be lyin'. Am I right or wrong?" I pinned her. "Come on with me for a minute."

I pulled her up from her chair before she could say no and led her into one of the bedrooms before she knew where she was going. I guess I had to prove something to myself with this stuck-up broad. I don't know why she came with me. Maybe she was curious, or maybe she never had a real man walk up to her and treat her like she was a real woman. I only knew that this was turning out to be a pretty good party. If she wanted to tease, then I was going to tease her the best way I knew how.

I threw some of the coats off the bed and sat her down. I walked over and locked the door, then I sat down next to her. A sudden whiff of her expensive perfume hit me, making me feel a little drunk.

"Where do you come from? You talk kind of funny, far away like," I said, taking her small white hand and holding it in both of mine. Something told me to take it easy with this strange broad.

"I was born in Vienna. I spent most of my adult life in Hollywood. Then I came to New York," she answered low and mysterious like, leaving her cold delicate hand in my hot rough mitts.

"Don't you miss Hollywood and all that movie star crap?" I asked her, trying to be nice. She looked cool as a cucumber, but I was getting so hot I was starting to sweat.

"I think what I miss most is my swimming pool. I just adore swimming pools. Do you have a swimming pool?"

Her voice suddenly sounded like a little girl's, and she looked up at me helpless like with those big green eyes. I could see that I could fuck her right then if I wanted to. I could also see that she was lonely as hell and probably a little kooky, too. All of a sudden, I didn't feel like screwing her anymore. She sounded so sad, I felt sorry for her. I missed my swimming pool, too. I said it before, and I'll say it again—misery reaching out to misery.

"I think I'd better go back out. My friend might be lookin' for me," I muttered, feeling like an awkward kid. I walked out and left her sitting alone on the edge of the bed. I never saw her again.

Back in the living room with all the noise and laughter and people, I felt I needed another drink. I headed for the bar and ran into Rick.

"Where the fuck have you been? I've been lookin' all over for ya. And Jake, lay off the sauce, will ya?" Rick said, playing baby sitter again. "I just heard about the Brasserie offer from Jerry."

"Jerry—is that fuckin' wiseguy here?" I said hotly. That was the last guy I wanted to see.

"Yeah, and keep your voice down," Rick warned, steering me away from the bar. "Madonna, are you a fuck-up! Why didn't you take the job? You could be on easy street for a change."

"Look Rick, if I told ya once, I told ya a million times, I don't like these creeps and I never will. I've been in enough trouble all my life. Don't you think it's time I smartened up? And what about the book? First you tell me don't worry, we'll have the book and maybe the movie, and now you want me to get mixed up with a bunch of fuckin' racketeers—are you crazy or what?" I was gettin' pissed.

"I was only being concerned with your present financial condition, Pal," Rick tried to smooth it over.

"Hey look," I said hotly, "You take care of your condition, and I'll look after my own ass!"

Rick was taking this Becket shit too seriously.

We were interrupted by this short young guy in blue jeans and a black leather jacket with a lot of hair who walked up to us. He was small, but built solid, kind of like me, and his big wide nose looked like it had taken a few punches. I liked the looks of the kid.

"Excuse me, you're Jake La Motta, aren't you? I'm Michael Cimino. I've been wanting to meet you. My father was a big fan of yours," he said in a calm, soft voice and held out his hand. It was small like mine, and when I shook it, I felt a firm, sure grip back. This kid was no pansy ass hippie.

"So you met me. What can I do for you, kid?" I said.

"I'm directing a few national TV commercials—United Airlines, Muriel Cigars . . . I do my own casting. I think you'd be perfect for what I have in mind. That is, if you're available," he said politely.

"He's available—he's available all right," Rick chimed in.

I gave him a dirty look. I wished Rick would stop answering for me.

"I might be available," I said to the kid. "Depends on what it is. I don't work for nothin', you know."

"Drop by my office next week when you get a chance," he said, handing me his card. "I think we can work something out," the kid smiled, then he walked away.

Something about him impressed me. He looked like a winner. I figured he'd make it big some day. . . .

Rick took the card from my hand and read it.

"Jake, this is a damn good agency—MPO. I've heard of these guys." He looked at me with a smirk on his face. "And you say you hate cocktail parties. This could mean mega bucks, and it's going to help the book, too."

"Gimme back my card. He wants me, not you, bozo," I said, grabbing the card from Rick and shoving it in my pocket. I looked around the crowded room. I never saw so many people in one apartment. By this time, the terraces were loaded with people too.

"Well, what do ya know," I said to myself. It was Jerry, the fuckhead from the other morning at the Brasserie, sporting Beer-Barrel Tony Galento on his arm like a prize size Teddy bear. They spotted me from across the room and were heading over.

"Hey Champ," Jerry said, holding out his hand. I didn't shake it, so he pulled it back quickly. "You know Tony Galento here . . ."

"Sure I know him. Who could miss him?" I said.

Tony had a glass of beer in one hand and a sandwich in the other. He looked like he weighed 500 pounds. It was hard to believe he ever fought Joe Louis. Louis kicked the shit out of him.

"Is this your new pigeon, Jerry?" I asked him, smiling slightly.

"Naw, naw—just an old friend," he lied.

He wasn't about to tell me. These guys never talk in public.

Everything is always a big secret. They never use last names, either. They have a habit of changing them all the time.

"Well, if ya hire Tony here, ya won't have to pay him a grand a week—just buy him a keg of beer a day," I joked.

Jerry forced a laugh, then he got to the point.

"Well, did you get a chance to reconsider our offer from the other morning, Champ?"

Jerry looked at Rick, who'd been keeping his mouth shut for a change, and gave him a wink. Rick just shrugged his shoulders back. I figured Jerry was counting on Rick to talk me into taking their lousy job. Rick should have known better.

"To tell ya' the truth, Jerry, it never entered my mind," I said coolly.

"I take it that's your final answer?" Jerry said. He wasn't smiling.

"Nothin' was ever so final," I said. I wasn't smiling either.

"Hey Champ," Galento said, putting down his beer and sandwich, "let's go a round or two."

Galento started to shadow punch me. I was in no mood to fool around. He tried to hold back his punch, but it caught me right in the gut instead. It pissed me off good. "Hey Beer-Barrel, you want to play tough? I'll pluck the eyes right out of your fuckin' head!" I growled, looking him right in the eye.

The conversation around us suddenly stopped and everyone looked our way. Galento was shocked.

"Hey Champ, I was only kiddin'," he said weakly.

Rick grabbed me by the arm. "Come on, Jake, let's get out of here before you fuck up everything we did tonight," he said, dragging me toward the door.

"But that fat fuck hit me in the gut," I said, still pissed.

"He didn't mean it—he's fuckin' drunk. Let's just get the hell out of here."

Rick shoved me out the door and we got into the elevator, leaving the party and the wiseguys behind.

Eleven

My life was starting to pick up again. I moved into a small furnished studio in a nice high rise on East 56th Street and finally got out of that crappy hotel. That whole time seemed like one long nightmare. The broads were fewer and farther between now, and my drinking was much better. A few glasses of red wine was enough for me. I was beginning to live my life from month to month instead of from day to day. It gave me a sense of security. My running pace had slowed down to a fast walk, and I liked it. That director kid, Cimino, came through for me with the commercials. The best one was for Muriel Cigars with Edie Adams. It ran the longest. It was great opening my mailbox and finding that residual check in the morning. I liked paying my rent by the month instead of by the week. It gave me a feeling of being more permanent, a feeling of belonging again.

That lawyer/agent came through, too, and we signed a book deal with Prentice-Hall. There were a lot of "if's" and "maybe's" before it happened. We had to hire this professional writer because they wanted a published author to polish up the book. It was coming out in the bookstores in a couple of weeks—*Raging Bull*. I wanted to call it *The Ice Pick and the Gloves*, but the publishers was paying for it, so I let them call the shots. Rick and I split a nice fat advance, considering Jake La Motta wasn't exactly a household word. We had a 60-40 deal, with the 60 on my end, but Rick kept squawking that he was doing all the work, so to make him happy I agreed to split 50-50 right down the line. I figured if we didn't make any money, it didn't matter, and if we made a lot of money, it still didn't matter.

What I couldn't figure out was how Rick always ended up making more than me. I figured he and that hot shot lawyer had some kind of deal on the side, but I couldn't prove it. What the hell, I knew I couldn't do any of this on my own. I didn't love Rick, but I needed him. He kept telling me, "Jake, nobody ever capitalized on your name. If we work it right, you could be worth millions!" I'd tell him, "OK, Rick, stop actin'—slow down—stop actin' all the time." But it was true—he was the only one who saw any future in the name La Motta.

Rick had a way with me. Sometimes I think he hypnotized me. Maybe he didn't really have that control, I just let him think he had—like with my wives. I let them think they're the boss until I make a decision. Then I put my foot down. "You're the captain," I say, "but I'm the general." If I can't be a man, I might as well kill myself. I'm a very flexible guy—I'm an honest guy and I'm a fair guy. But how many times was I so sure about something and found out I was wrong? I say to myself, I'm 100 percent right—and I'm 100 percent wrong. You just never know. . . . I only hoped Rick was right this time and the book would sell a lot of copies.

Meanwhile Rick was trying to graduate out of the porno business, so he came up with this movie he called *Cauliflower Cupids* about a big time society dame and a bunch of punch drunk hoods. Rick was producer, writer, director and romantic lead. I was one of the hoods along with five other ex-boxers who were out of work at the time—Rocky, of course, Willie Pep, Tony Zale, Pete Scalzo and Paddy DeMarco. The society dame and star of the film was Jane Russell. Rick had a thing about big tits. When it comes to broads, Rick is the near-sighted snake that raped the rope. He always had this fantasy about screwing Jane Russell. I think that's the whole reason he was making the movie.

Rick was taking advantage of the summer weather and was shooting the film on location at this estate in Riverdale that belonged to some lawyer friend of his who helped raise the money for the budget. Judging by what I was getting, I figured most of the money was going to Jane Russell. She got most of the attention. The rest of us were just there to fill in the parts. It was a real hot summer, and during the long breaks between setups we used to hang around the pool and goof off. Rick didn't like it. He was always looking at his watch. "Every second counts. This is my money you bunch of assholes, and I'm not payin' ya to screw around on my time. I need complete attention, even during the breaks!" Rick could be a real pain in the ass when he wanted to be. It was like Erich von Stroheim trying to direct Snow White and the Seven Dwarfs.

I was lying by the pool taking some sun while Rick set up for Jane's next scene, when she walked over to me. She was wearing a short tight skirt and a blouse that hung around her shoulders. Maybe she thought she was still doing *The Outlaw*. She was a sexy looking broad and no question about it, even if she was past forty. I don't know what a dame like her was doing with a bunch of clowns like us. She must have been down on her luck.

"Jake darling, would you do me a big favor and drive me to the supermarket? I have this unbearable headache and no one seems to have any aspirin," she said, running her hand through her long dark hair.

"Sure," I said, "We got time."

Who did she think she was kidding? I knew we were going to the liquor store. She was playing it straight, but I could spot a boozer a mile away. She complained about her headache all the way there. It was a bad one. I parked the car and she got out and walked right past the market and into the liquor store. She got back in the car and showed me a fifth of Jack Daniels.

"How about a swig, Champ?" she said.

"No thanks, not right now."

She opened the bottle, leaving it in the paper bag, and took a healthy belt. I knew then I was right about her. "This is one tough broad," I said to myself.

"How's your headache?" I asked her.

"Worse than ever," she mumbled, taking another swig.

"Well, you're not helpin' it much drinkin' that shit. I could get rid of it for ya, if ya want me to."

"Could you?" she said, turning toward me. "Please, do anything you have to, just do it."

The way she said it, I figured I could have laid her down in the back seat and screwed her right there in the parking lot if I wanted to. I knew she'd be an easy subject to hypnotize.

"All right. Just lean back and close your eyes and listen to my voice. Now start breathin' real deep and slow and even. Just relax and keep breathin' in and out, in and out, real easy now. You're startin' to feel good . . . you feel good all over . . . keep breathin', nice and easy . . . that's a girl . . . easy now. . ."

She was following me like a dream. Her eyes were closed and she was breathing deep and even. I watched her breasts rise and fall, like two round mountains. Then my eyes followed her body down to her long legs. Her knees were spread open slightly. I was starting to breathe heavy myself. I knew if I touched her I wouldn't be able to stop. I figured I'd better pull her out of it before it was too late. You never know with broads. They all want it like crazy, and then when you give it to them, they cry rape or something. I wasn't taking any chances with this one.

"Now when I count to ten, you're gonna wake up and you're gonna feel great. Your headache'll be all gone, and you'll feel relaxed and refreshed. I'm goin' to start countin' now. . . ." She opened her eyes on cue and I could tell it had worked. She looked at me like I was God or something.

"Jake, I don't know what you did, but I feel marvelous. My headache's gone. I can't believe it! You're wonderful. I'm going to take you with me wherever I go."

She moved closer to me and kissed me on the cheek.

"How about having dinner with me in the city tonight? My treat for curing my headache," she said, giving me a wink.

I started the car with a big grin on my face. Maybe she wasn't too happy with her football player husband. I could just see the look on Rick's face when I told him she asked me for a date. Here he was knocking his brains out for her, and I was sure he hadn't gotten to first base with her yet. Sometimes Rick needed reminding that I was the Champ—not him.

When we got back, Rick was waiting for us at the foot of the drive. I could see he was pissed. The Italian blood had hit his head and his face was beet red.

"Where the fuck have you two been? I'm tryin' to shook a fuckin' movie here! We've been shootin' a week and already we're two days behind schedule. What do I look like—Howard Hughes?"

Jane slipped her bottle of booze under the front seat and slid out of the car. She stood in front of Rick, pulling her blouse up over her shoulders like she had all the time in the world.

"Don't flatter yourself, Rick. You couldn't lick Howard Hughes's sweat. I had an excruciating headache. Jake was kind enough to take me to the store for some aspirin. I'm used to having aspirin on the set. I'm surprised you didn't know that."

"All right, forget it," Rick said, backing down. "I'm all set for your next scene, Jane. Let's get this show on the road."

Jane took off to make-up and Rick gave me a look that could kill.

"What did you do—fuck her in the back seat?"

"Stop thinkin' I'm a degenerate. I took her for her bottle of booze and that's all. Except that she wants to buy me dinner to-night," I shrugged.

"You're a miserable fuckin' double-crosser! You know I want that broad and you're cuttin' in!"

"Hey, look, she's got a hard on for me and maybe not you," I told him.

"Listen," he said, calming down. "Maybe I could come along tonight—make it a threesome—like old times, ya know." Rick winked and put his arm on my shoulder. I knew he was thinking of the time we shot that film in Italy together. We must have screwed every broad within a hundered miles of Naples—twice. We'd flip a coin to see who got firsts and who got seconds. It sounded like kid stuff to me now. The last thing I needed was a second-hand fuck.

"Naw, you go ahead and take her out. You're the one with the hard on for her. I really don't give a shit. Besides, she's too old for me," I told him, walking back toward the pool.

"Hey, ya mean it?" he said, surprised. "I owe ya one, Pal!'" he called out, and ran after Jane.

We finished the movie that summer. It ran in a few theaters for a couple of weeks and then petered out. Rick lost a small bundle. He blamed everybody but himself, as usual. "Those fuckin' Jews. They control this business. They're tryin' their best to keep me in porno flicks," he'd say. I guess his mob connections didn't pay off this time. He finally got his date with Jane, though. I always figured it was a hell of a price to pay for a one night stand . . . but maybe I was wrong.

By early October my book hit the bookstores—for better or

worse. Rick was working hard on a movie deal for us, but so far nobody was biting. About the same time, Rocky opened his first pizza joint on Second Avenue. Rick and I were invited to the opening, of course. I thought we might be able to plug the book if some TV cameras showed up, or maybe some sports writers, so I told Rick we owed it to Rocky to be there. Besides, I always liked pizza. I wasn't too sure how we'd do with the book, because I didn't know if people remembered the name La Motta. Everybody knew Rocky, of course, because he had his book out and then the picture with Paul Newman—*Somebody Up There Likes Me.* I didn't know who the hell down here still liked me. I wasn't the easiest guy in the world to get along with, but I was trying my best to change myself for other people to recognize. It wasn't easy.

The place was loaded with all kinds of people—the same old crowd of wiseguys with their society dames and the ex pugs and a lot of jerks that walked in off the street. They was serving wine and beer—no hard booze. There was plenty of pizza, calzones, hero sandwiches and all the other stuff. I'd been dieting all day and I felt a little weak, so I rabbed a glass of red wine and helped myself to the food. I kept looking around for Rick. He was supposed et me with some copies of the book to hand around. I spotted Rocky instead. He walked over to me and gave me a big bear hug.

"Hey, paisan, glad you could make it. What do ya think—some layout, uh?"

"Yeah—the food's not bad," I mumbled with a mouthful of pizza. "Who ever thought you'd end up pushin' pizza. I always said you was too dumb to be a fighter."

The crowd was looking at us like we were two kids back in the Bronx. It was funny how Rocky and I both ended up Middleweight Champs—a couple of Ginzo brawlers from the streets. We were even matched up one time. Right after I won the championship, we were supposed to go at it in Yankee Stadium. It was a big promotion, but it never came off. Rocky broke his hand just before the fight. The fight fans were very disappointed.

Sometimes I think he did it on purpose. Most everybody knew I could beat him hands down; it was no contest. I used to kid him about it. He should have known I wouldn't hurt him. Rocky was like family; we grew up fighting in the same streets together. I was proud of Rocky, and maybe a little jealous, too. He was no dummy like me; he knew how to hold on to his money and his wife.

I finally spotted Rick sitting at a back table with this strange broad. I got myself another glass of wine and walked over.

"Where the fuck were you? The cameras and press split an hour ago. You missed the whole bit," Rick said.

"So what?" I shrugged, staring at the broad. She was a real knockout—like a blond Sophia Loren with the tits to match.

"So what? So you missed a great opportunity to talk about the book, that's so what. That's what we're here for, remember?" Rick was playing wiseguy in front of the broad. He noticed me staring at her so he finally introduced me.

"Jake, meet Petra. Petra, this is Jake La Motta—the middle-weight chump of the world."

"He means champ of the world, but he's uneducated. Some-times he don't know what he's sayin'," I went along, giving Rick a dirty look. "So how are you, you gorgeous, sexy beautiful crea-ture," I said to her, pulling up a chair.

She squirmed in her seat a little and stared back at me. I didn't know if she thought I was a freak or if she was attracted to me.

"I know you," she said to me. "You do that cute air conditioner commercial on TV. I thought you were adorable."

"Oh yeah?" I said. "You should see me in my new movie. You're gonna think I'm beautiful."

"*Your* movie?" Rick jumped in. "I only wrote it, directed it, pro-duced it and financed it—and you call it your movie?"

"Okay, okay, don't get your balls in an uproar. I'm in the movie, ain't I?" I tossed back.

Rick went on to explain how Petra knew his lawyer partner in *Cauliflower Cupids*. It so happened she lived a couple of blocks away from the lawyer's estate in Riverdale where we shot the film. She'd heard a lot about Rick from the lawyer, but this was the first time they'd met. I wondered how well she knew the lawyer. Rick had suspected the guy of stealing money from the film. The next thing I heard, the guy committed suicide; he blew his brains out in his office chair one afternoon not too long ago. I guess he was so afraid of Rick, he shot himself. Maybe Rick killed him—I didn't know. I wasn't about to ask him. I had to find out how interested

Rick was in this broad. I was feeling pretty lonely and I thought I could use some serious female company. Anyway, he owed me one after Jane Russell.

"So this is your first date with this bum, uh?" I said to her. "What's a gorgeous broad like you doin' with an old married guy like him?" I dug.

I could see by the look she gave Rick he hadn't told her he was married. I figured he hadn't. To Rick, another broad was just another notch in his belt. When you've been alone as long as I have, you get more particular. You start looking for companionship instead of just another five-cent fuck.

"Are you married, too?" she asked me straight out.

"I was married three times so far. Right now I'm not married. I'm tryin' to cool it for a while. But ya gotta keep tryin' till ya get it right, I guess," I said, looking her straight in the eyes. "And what about you?" I added. "Are you married, or what?"

"No," she said with a slight smile.

"Hey, maybe this could be the start of somethin' big," I grinned back at her.

"Well, I hope the two of you invite me to the wedding," Rick joked, giving me a stupid look.

"Petra—what kind of a name is that?" I asked her, ignoring Rick. "It sounds foreign or somethin'."

"It's Greek," she said, reaching over and taking a cigarette from my pack on the table. "Do you mind?" she asked, and leaned toward me as I lit it for her. She took a long drag and breathed the smoke slowly in my face. "Both my parents are Greek. I speak Greek fluently."

"Yeah, she won a beauty contest—Miss Greece or somethin', wasn't it?" Rick chimed in.

"No kiddin'," I said, looking at her. "All my wives was beauty contest winners. Every one of 'em."

"Really? How many times did you say you were marrried?" she asked me.

"Look, why don't I just give you my book to read. It'll save a lot of questions and answers. It just came out, and we're workin' on a picture deal next. Eh, gimme one of my books," I said, elbowing Rick.

"Eh, what do ya mean, 'my book'? It's our fuckin' book, Jake, and don't fuckin' forget it! If it weren't for me, you'd be back in Central Park pickin' up paper off the grass!" Rick exploded.

"All right, all right, all right, all right! Just give me the goddam book!" I said.

"You want the fuckin' book? Here, take the fuckin' book!" he shouted, throwing a copy at me across the table.

"OK, Rick, calm down. Stop actin'—just calm down. I was only kiddin' " I said, trying not to get mad.

Petra looked at us like we were both crazy. I took the book and autographed it for her—"To beautiful, gorgeous, sexy . . . How do you spell your name?" I asked her.

She told me and I wrote out ". . . Petra, Good luck, The Champ," handing her the book.

"I'll be sure to read this cover to cover," she said, impressed. "There's something so strong and masculine about a man who fights for a living."

I knew she was pouring it on pretty thick, but I liked hearing it anyway. She got up to go to the ladies' room, giving me a chance to take a good stand-up look at her. She was tall—about five foot eight or nine—with a great body and a beautiful pair of legs. She was wearing a low cut black dress that clung to her body and set off her olive-toned skin—a sexy Greek goddess.

"You want a shot at this one?" Rick asked me.

"Why not?" I said, "If it's okay with you."

"Go ahead. Be my guest. You always were a sucker for the clinging vines. Me, I steer away from the divorcees pushin' forty and lookin' for a husband. I'll make it easy for ya. I'll leave ya alone with her. Tell her I got a call from my wife, or somethin'." Rick got up and slapped me on the back. "Good luck, Pal . . . You're gonna need it," he said, and disappeared.

I was feeling pretty good about Rick's generosity, so I had another glass of wine while I waited for—what's her name, Petra—to get back from the ladies' room. What do broads do in there, anyway? I could get laid three times over in the time they spend trying to make themselves look beautiful. Phony broads, all of them.

"What happened to Rick?" Petra asked me, finally returning. She didn't look much different, but she sure looked good. She smelled good, too.

"Somethin' came up. He had to split," I mumbled.

"Oh, I see," she said, sipping her wine and staring at me over the glass.

She had these big dark almond-shaped eyes and a way of looking at you that made me feel nervous, like she was reading my mind, or something. The place was starting to clear out. I figured she was stuffed with pizza by now and it was going to save me a dinner, so I'd spring for a cab back to her place.

"How about my takin' you home?" I said.

"Oh, do you have a car?" she asked.

"What car? We'll take a cab—what the hell can it cost?"

"Why not?"

It was a long cab ride to Riverdale, so we had a chance to talk a bit.

"Why are you letting me take you home?" I asked her.

"You seem like a nice enough guy," she answered.

"Is it because I'm a fighter, or is it because you like me?"

"I would say a little bit of both."

This broad is straight on, I said to myself. She doesn't pull any punches and she tells it like it is. I liked that in a dame. I met so many phony ones that this was refreshing to me. She crossed her legs, and I couldn't help looking down. I draped my arm behind her over the back seat and moved in a little closer. She started asking me a load of questions about myself. I gave her my stock answer, "It's in the book." She talked a lot and fast like, but somehow I felt comfortable with her. I found out she had been married twice before and now lived alone with her ten-year-old daughter.

"Oh, shit, I just blew the cab fare," I said to myself. Then she said her daughter had her own room, so I felt a little better—in case this broad was going to give in. She told me one of her ex-husbands was paying her child support, and that's how she could afford to live in Riverdale in a nice high rise apartment building. It was beginning to sound like the perfect set up—an all-expense-paid situation. I don't like paying for broads—you never know how it's going to turn out. It's like I never buy a broad flowers, because I know the next day they're gonna die—the flowers, that is. We passed the lawyer's estate where we filmed *Cauliflower Cupids*. I pointed it out to her.

"So you knew Rick's lawyer partner, eh?" I asked her, wondering if she had screwed the guy.

"Yeah, I knew him all right," she said. "I knew him well enough to hate him."

Her voice was suddenly hard and cold, and she looked at me kind of wild like. "What am I gettin' myself into?" I thought.

"He was a total pig," she said. "He told me he could hypnotize me, and like a fool, I trusted him. It was terrifying. He put me under, and then he took advantage of me. He raped me! There was nothing I could do about it," she added, looking up at me wide-eyed.

I didn't know whether to believe her or not. I knew something about hypnotism; Rick had gotten into this religious science stuff once, and he taught me a lot about hypnotism and mind control—"playing checkers" he called it. I always thought you couldn't be forced to do anything you wouldn't want to do. I was just glad as hell I kept my head that time in the car with Jane Russell, or they'd be calling me "Jake the Rake" all over again.

The cab pulled up to this plush high rise building with a wraparound driveway. I paid the cab and the doorman opened the door. We walked through this nice looking lobby with a water fountain in the middle and rode the elevator to her floor. Her apartment was three doors to the right. The hall was carpeted like a hotel and everything was nice and clean. Petra held my book under her arm as she opened the door. I could hear this little dog yapping on the other side. "Mommy's home now, Caesar. Be a good boy now, my precious," she said to this little white poodle as I followed her inside.

It was a fancy looking pad with wall to wall carpeting and expensive modern furniture. "I've got myself a winner here," I said to myself, looking out the big picture window at the view of the Hudson River. I thought of my crappy little studio on the East Side. It was like night and day—mine was night and neon lights and hers was day with sunshine coming through the windows. The little white poodle came up to me and started to lick my hand.

"Oh look, Caesar likes you. He usually doesn't take to strangers," Petra said, looking surprised.

"All dogs love me. Sometime I'll tell ya a story about my little Skippy. He was the ugliest mutt ya ever saw. He was crazy about me. But that was a long time ago. . . ." I said, petting the poodle.

She put my book down on the glass cocktail table and went back down the hall to the bedroom to check on her kid. The kid was fast asleep and she felt good about that. So did I. "I'd like to meet her sometime. What's her name?" I said, being polite.

"Melina—my precious little darling Melina. You can have a peek at her now, if you like. But be very quiet—don't wake her," she said, motioning me toward the kid's room.

I looked into the bedroom, being very quiet about it, and saw this pretty little girl curled up with a doll. She reminded me a little of Lisa at that age. I closed the door gently and walked back to the living room.

"Can I fix you a drink, Jake?" Petra called from the kitchen.

"Yeah, sure, whatever you've got."

She brought two scotches on the rocks and handed one to me. She put some soft music on the stereo and sat down on the couch, crossing those long legs. It felt like an old Joan Crawford movie. I sat down in a chair across from her, and again I couldn't help staring at her gorgeous legs. Maybe I'm a leg man, I don't know, but I'm also a sucker for a beautiful face, and hers was beautiful in an exotic kind of way. I figured she was about Vickie's age—forty-one or so, or maybe a little older. I was used to dating younger broads—they were easier to impress.

I wasn't too sure which one of us was gonna make the next move.

"You ever do any acting? You've sure got the looks for it. I bet you'd look great on camera," I said, wondering how I was going to get from the chair to the couch without scaring her. I sure didn't want her crying rape or something.

"Funny, that's just what your friend, Rick, told me," she said, sipping her scotch and staring at me.

"Aw, forget him. He says that to every broad he meets. But I wouldn't say it if I didn't mean it. I think you're a real knockout—no foolin'," I told her.

"Then why are you sitting way over there? Don't you like me?" she said, like I was some jerk high school kid.

That was all the invitation I needed. I put down my drink, got up and sat next to her. I pulled her to me and kissed her hard on her full sexy mouth. It didn't take her long to respond. While I was still kissing her, she guided my hand to her breast and held it there till I started doing what comes natural. It didn't take me long, either. I yanked open the buttons down the front of her dress and snapped her bra off. I grabbed both her huge bare breasts in my hands and started sucking like crazy on her large pink hard nipples. She was breathing hard and heavy and rubbing her hands through my hair. I knew she was enjoying it like a female cat in heat.

Before I could go any further, she got up off the couch and pulled me after her down the hall to her room, locking the door behind us. The room was dark, but I could make out a ruffled white canopied bed loaded with all kinds of stuffed animals and dolls. If I didn't know better, I'd have thought it was her little girl's room. Whatever turns you on, I thought, and this broad was definitely turning me on. Without saying a word, she peeled off her dress and bra, leaving on her panties, and started unbuttoning my shirt, french kissing me all the while. I got into the kiss and let her undress me. It was nice being on the other end for a change.

We made love until dawn and finally fell out exhausted. I awoke with the late morning sun streaming in my eyes and looked around the strange room. Everything was white—the canopy over the bed, the rug, the furniture, and there were mirrors on every wall. My shorts, pants and shirt were lying on the floor next to her dress and bra and panties. There were stuffed animals and dolls thrown all over the place. It looked like a small hurricane had hit the room. Petra was out cold, and I didn't feel like waking her. You never know how a broad's going to act the morning after the night before. I got into my clothes and slipped out of the room, closing the door behind me. I found the bathroom and took a long hard piss. There were mirrors all over the bathroom, too—even on the ceiling. This broad must love looking at herself, I thought.

I was heading for the door, thinking I'd make a clean getaway, when I heard this little girl's voice behind me.

"Are you a friend of my Mommy's?"

I turned around and saw Petra's ten-year-old daughter standing in the kitchen doorway holding the little poodle and staring up at me. Awake, she looked even more like Lisa than I'd thought before. She was lighter than her mother, with long honey blond hair and big green eyes.

"Are you a friend of my Mommy's?" she repeated.

"Yeah, sure I am. You must be Melina," I said, feeling uncomfortable.

"Yes, and this is Caesar," she said, holding up the little dog.
"What's your name?"

"Uh, you can call me Champ, Melina. Caesar and me already
met. Eh, aren't you supposed to be in school, or somethin'?" I
asked her.

"It's Saturday. I always make coffee for Mommy on Saturdays.
That's when she sleeps late. Would you like some?"

"You got some made? Sure, why not? I take it black—no milk
and no sugar."

"Okay."

She put down the dog and disappeared into the kitchen. I followed her and sat down at the kitchen table, wondering what I was
getting myself into. She brought me the coffee and sat down next
to me, staring hard at my face.

"Why do you have such a funny nose?" she asked.

"That's what you call an occupational hazard. Did you ever
watch the fights on TV?" I asked her.

"Yes, sometimes, with Mommy. But I don't like to see people
get hurt. I get kinda scared."

"Well, darlin', that's part of the fight game, and that's how I got
to be champ."

"Do you still fight?"

"No, sweetheart. Those days are all behind me. . . ." The little
poodle jumped up on my lap.

"Caesar really likes you," Melina laughed.

"That's the story of my life—little dogs and little girls like me the
most," I said, patting Caesar on the head.

"I like you too, Champ," said Melina.

I finished my coffee and said goodbye. As I walked out the door,
Melina had a cute smile on her face. Little girls are lovable, like
little puppy dogs. Too bad they have to grow up. . . .

A couple of weeks later Rick and I were off on a plane to Paris to
promote my book. The publishers were expecting a big sale in
France. I'd never been to Paris before, but I knew the French people had a good feeling about me. They even had a hit song out—
"Jaque, Jaque, Jaque La Motta." The French people were funny
that way. Ever since I beat their national hero, Marcel Cerdan, for
the championship back in 1949, they treated me like I was some

kind of French hero, too. Maybe it was because when I was supposed to fight Cerdan for a rematch three months later, his char-
tered plane crashed on the way to the States and everybody got
killed. The papers made a big thing out of my beating "a one-
armed champ" because Cerdan injured his shoulder when I
knocked him down in the first round, and everybody—especially
the French—were looking forward to the outcome of the rematch.
I don't know, I guess it was Cerdan's karma to get killed, and mine
to stay champ a couple more years. . . .

"So how did you make out with Petra—or did you strike out?"
Rick interrupted my thoughts.

"She's a nice lady. We got along all right," I said, looking out the
window at the clear expanse of blue sky and the bluer ocean below.

"I know, but did you score?" Rick pressed.

I didn't feel like filling in the details for Rick. He had a way of
making any broad look cheap, and that wasn't the way it was with
Petra. I'd seen her a couple more times since that first terrific
night, and I planned on seeing her again. I liked keeping my affairs
private, and telling Rick was like putting it in the headlines of the
Daily News.

"It was nothin'. We had a nice time, that's all," I shrugged,
hoping he would let it go at that.

Rick gave me a suspicious look, then he settled back in his seat
for a snooze.

"Yeah, well just wait'll ya get a load of those hot beauties waitin'
for us in Paris. You'll forget all about those uptight bitches back
home," he said, dozing off.

I knew then I felt more for Petra than for your average broad,
but Rick would just laugh it off. I know it sounds stupid, knowing a
broad for a couple of weeks and thinking you're in love, but who
knows what love is? Like I always say, I can love a ham sandwich,
too.

There was a big reception waiting for us when we hit the Paris
airport. It was drizzling like they say it always does in Paris in late
October, and the sky was cold and gray, but that never stopped a
bunch of headline hungry reporters and photographers. For once I
was glad to see them. This was one time I was using them instead
of them using me.

Jake, The Stand-Up Comic.

As Big Julie (center) in a revival of *Guys & Dolls*.

With Paul Newman in *The Hustler*.

With Lenny Bruce and Milton Berle.

Signing with Rocky
Graziano for the fight that
never came off.
(United Press photo)

With Marcel Cerdan, from whom he won the Middleweight
Championship. (United Press photo)

Losing to another Frenchman, Laurent Dauthuille. (United Press photo)

With Perry Como.

Vickie LaMotta, Wife #2. (AP/Wide World Photos)

Sally LaMotta, Wife #3.

Debbie LaMotta, Wife #5.

With best man Sugar Ray Robinson.

With Theresa LaMotta, Wife #6.

With his daughter, Lisa, during the making of the *Raging Bull* film.

"Hey, get a load of our welcoming committee. It looks like the publishers did the right job," I elbowed Rick.

"Yeah, make real nice for the cameras, Champ. We're lookin' to turn a lot of francs into dollars here, remember?" Rick said, as cameras and microphones flanked us from all sides.

They shot the same old questions at me—some in English and some in French. I had a hard enough time with English.

"Who do you feel was your toughest opponent in the ring, Champ?"

"My toughest opponents were my wives—but I'm only joking. I fought some of the toughest fighters ever. I fought more black fighters than any other white fighter around. But my toughest opponent was always Sugar Ray Robinson. Pound for pound, he was the greatest fighter that ever lived."

"Monsieur La Motta, do you feel that Marcel Cerdan could have beaten you to reclaim the title in a rematch, had he lived?"

"Marcel Cerdan was the greatest fighter to ever come out of Europe. He was a fine gentleman and a great champion. It's hard to say—who knows?"

"What was your greater moment in the ring—winning the championship from Cerdan or defending it from Dauthuille?"

"Winning the championship was the biggest thrill of my career, but I think defending my title against Laurent Dauthuille was the greatest feeling of respect I ever got in the ring."

"Mr. La Motta, how truthful are you about your wives in your book?" a female reporter asked.

"Well, you see, I'm very friendly with all my wives, and I'd like to keep it that way. So draw you own conclusions."

"Is there a future Mrs. La Motta in your life now?"

"How about you? You're a good lookin' broad. You want to get married?" I asked her for laughs.

As we were waiting downstairs for the luggage, somebody tapped me on the shoulder from behind. I turned around and there stood Laurent Dauthuille, big as life. The last time I'd seen him was twenty years ago. He was lying face down on the canvas struggling to get up as the referee counted him out for the final round. If he had stayed on his feet another thirteen seconds, he'd have beat me for the championship and returned to France a national hero. . . .

I was weak from making the weight, as usual, and the fight was close. I knew I had to knock him out in the last round to win the fight and keep my title. I lay low for the first two minutes, conserving my strength, then in the last minute I stunned him with a sudden left hook. I knew I had my opening, and I went at him like a machine, throwing punches left and right. I finally caught him with a mean left hook, and he fell into the ropes and bounced face down onto the canvas. The crowd went crazy, and so did I. Detroit had always been my lucky town, but that night it brought me more than luck. It gave me the respect and dignity I always wanted but never got before—not even when I won the championship . . .

Looking at Dauthuille now, I saw great sadness in his eyes, even though he was grinning at me. He always was a handsome guy, about my size with broad shoulders, but he could have used a shave, and the suit he was wearing had seen better days. It looked like he had lost a lot of weight. Rick just stared at us, wondering who this guy was kissing me. I introduced him to Rick, and while we were waiting for the luggage, we talked a bit. He told us in his broken English about some night club act he had years ago that ended by dramatizing on stage how he had lost to me in the last thirteen seconds of the final round. I couldn't help feeling sorry for the guy. Here I was in Paris promoting my book and all, and here he stood in front of me looking like he was begging for pennies. He'd never believe it, but I was probably as broke as he was. Still, I felt pretty lucky in more ways than one.

"But how did you know I was comin' to Paris?" I asked him.

"Mon Ami," he said, "I still read the newspapers."

When our luggage arrived, he tried to carry it for me.

"Please, allow me, Champ," he said.

"Get out of here—I can carry my own bags," I told him, feeling embarrassed.

When we finally got outside where the limo was waiting, Dauthuille ran ahead of us and opened the door. I knew more than ever that times were bad.

"Do me a favor," I said to Rick. "Slip him a hundred bucks."

"You don't care how you spend my money, do you?" Rick complained, but he gave him the hundred.

Dauthuille refused at first, but I stuffed it into his coat pocket anyway. He kissed me again on both cheeks, and I gave him a manly hug. As we took off in the limo, I looked through the rear window and saw him standing in the rain, looking at the hundred bucks. I couldn't help feeling, "There but for the grace of God . . ." Old fighters don't die—they just wither away, I thought. It made me mad. If all those goddamned wiseguys and promoters that made a fortune off the blood and sweat of us fighters put up a couple of lousy bucks for a decent pension fund, great fighters like Dauthuille wouldn't be left standing in the rain. I never saw him again. . . .

The limo cruised through the heart of Paris, under the famous Arch of Triumph, down the wide tree-lined Champs Élysées, past the large gardens and museums and fancy hotels, and finally turned down a narrow side street to this small hotel that looked more like an old house that might have belonged to Voltaire's grandfather, or something. It wasn't real plush, but it was nice and clean and probably cheap enough. I figured Prentice-Hall didn't have too much money to spend on this caper, but they were taking a chance that a lot of French people would love to read about me and their fellow Frenchmen in the ring. The little old landlady didn't speak much English, but she smiled a lot—especially when I gave her an autographed copy of my book. We were kept busy all that day and the next with radio and TV interviews. I did most of the talking, and Rick did all the lining up of the broads. At night we hit all the clubs, including the Folies Bergère, of course, and the broads flowed around us like champagne. France sure has its share of beautiful women. We must have screwed half of Paris in the five days we were there. The French have a very healthy attitude toward sex. It's as natural as breathing to them. The little old landlady just smiled a little more as we paraded different gorgeous mademoiselles up to our rooms each night. I found out that love is truly an international language. Any other guy in my position would have been on top of the world. Rick thought he had died and gone to heaven. I didn't know what was bothering me, but I kept feeling that something was missing.

"What the hell's wrong with you?" Rick kept asking me. "You're draggin' your ass, and your mind's not on what it's supposed to be."

I couldn't answer him, because I didn't know myself. Everything was more than enough, and I just wasn't happy.

On the flight back I started to think of Petra more than ever. Maybe that was what was bothering me. Sure, the broads in Paris were beautiful, but they were cold and stiff, too. They always had their hand out, like hard-hearted hookers. But then married women can be worse than pros—they won't screw their husbands unless they buy them a dress. Petra was different. She was a straight lady trying to bring up her kid alone. I respected her for that. I'd been living alone for five years now, and the bachelor life was beginning to get boring. She was paying rent, and I was paying rent. I figured, if we got together, it would be a lot cheaper for both of us. She and the kid could move in with me—who the hell wants to live in Riverdale? Then she also had the child support, so it wouldn't really cost me anything more. I liked her, and I think she liked me. I didn't know if it would ever get to a real big love thing, but what the hell, it was worth a try. . . .

When we arrived at Kennedy airport, I handed Rick my baggage tickets and told him I'd be right back.

"Where the hell are you going, ya crazy nut?" he called after me.

I ran to the nearest phone.

"Petra? I just got off the plane. I'm home."

"I thought I'd never hear from you again, Jake."

"Are you crazy? Did you finish the book yet?"

"I sure did."

"Well, what did you think?"

"My first reaction was, I don't believe it."

"Well, okay, forget the book for now. I want to ask you a very serious question."

"What is it?"

"I wanna know one thing—how would you like to get married?"

The phone went dead for a minute, and then she said softly, "Why not?"

It was as simple as that. I guess she was punchy for going for it, and I was punchy for asking her, but I was tired of screwing around with all kinds of broads and getting nowhere. Maybe with Petra I could start a new life with a built-in family and even a little poodle who liked me. . . .

Twelve

"Oh Jake, look! Look! That poor little bird—it'll be killed! Get the bird, Jakie, oh please, go get the bird! Hurry, Jakie!"

"All right, all right. Don't get excited. I'll get the goddam bird. Just calm down, Baby."

Petra was pulling me by the arm and screeching hysterically as she pointed at this bird lying in the middle of the street with the cars whizzing by from all directions and narrowly missing it. It was late afternoon in Chicago and the rush hour traffic on Michigan Avenue wasn't about to stop for any injured bird. Petra and I had been married about two weeks now, and I took her along as my new wife on this last promotional tour for the book. Rick was pissed as hell that I took Petra instead of him, but what did he want me to do—marry him, too? They were putting us up in style at the classy Drake Hotel in downtown Chicago, and I figured, why pass up an all-expense-paid honeymoon?

I knew Petra well enough by now to know how she loved animals, but I was beginning to notice how she loved making a scene and drawing attention to herself too. She had a phobia for every invention known to man. I had to get her plastered and coax her like a baby to get her on the plane to Chicago, then she suddenly developed claustrophobia and refused to get in the elevator at the hotel. I was beginning to wonder if I'd married a hypochondriac or Tallulah Bankhead. Now she wanted me to run in front of a load of speeding cars and rescue some dumb loon that missed the lake and landed in the middle of Michigan Avenue. One of us was loonier than the loon.

131

"Jake, don't just stand there. Go get the bird before he's run over. Oh Jakie, please—I can't stand it!" Petra screamed, digging her long red fingernails into my arm.

Michigan Avenue had to be the widest avenue in Chicago. It made Fifth Avenue look like a side street. I took a deep breath and walked into the street, holding my arms up against the oncoming cars like an asshole traffic cop. I made my way to the middle of the street, dodging cars screeching their brakes all around me, and grabbed for the loon. The dumb bird tried to fly away and I missed, falling onto my knee and ripping my pants. "What the hell am I doing—I gotta be nuts!" I said to myself. I made another grab for the bird and caught it. I stuffed it under my jacket and made a run for it back to the sidewalk. "Here's your goddam bird—now stop squawkin'!" I said between breaths, handing Petra the stupid thing. "Aw shit!" I added, looking down at my torn pants. The whole front of my jacket was covered in bird shit.

Petra was cooing and ahing at the bird like it was her first born. She didn't give a shit about me. I only risked my life saving the damn thing. How soon they forget, I thought.

"Oh look, Jakie, I think it has a broken wing, poor little thing. Let's take it to the cute little pet shop down the street," Petra said.

It was the middle of November, and the wind blowing off Lake Michigan was beginning to penetrate through my suit jacket. Petra started down the sidewalk wrapped in her full-length fox coat and matching fur hat, talking to the bird and strutting like a Hollywood star. She was playing the role of Mrs. Jake La Motta to the hilt. She hadn't wasted any time setting up the wedding. Within a week of my asking her, she'd told her family and friends and the social column of *The New York Times,* and before I knew it, I was saying "I do" to the judge for the fourth time around. My old pal in the jewelry business, Abe Margolis, came through for me again and gave me a great deal on a diamond ring, like he did when I married Sally.

"Jake, I always keep a spare on hand for you in the back room," he told me. He even sprang for the reception at Les Champs—I called it "The Champs"—this fancy French restaurant on Thirty-ninth between Park and Madison that must've cost a bundle. It was a good thing, too, because if it was up to me, there'd be no reception. I was running through the advance on the book like there was no tomorrow, and if the book didn't sell, I'd be in the shithouse all over again. If Petra knew what I had in the bank, she'd grab the first cab back to Riverdale. I'd already figured out, if it wasn't for her ex-husband's child support, she'd be mooching off her mother and father and older sister.

I met them at the reception. Her parents ran a small beauty parlor in Brooklyn. They were a nice old Greek couple—nothing special. Her sister didn't have Petra's looks, but she got all the brains. She worked on Wall Street, and looked pretty successful. Melina was all in pink and looked like a little dream. None of my family showed up. "Marrying a girl you hardly know—you're making a mockery of marriage," my mother said. I guess my sisters and brothers felt the same way. I don't know why they couldn't understand me. They all had families and a home life, and here I was, the oldest, living all alone. Why couldn't they just be happy for me for once? Rick was my best man, as usual. He just kept grinning at me and shaking his head. "I always knew you had more guts than brains, Pal," he said.

We left the bird with the lady at the pet shop. "Be sure you feed him enough. I think he likes fish," Petra told the woman as I dragged her out of the place.

The following morning I had an early interview with a local TV station. I wanted to take Petra with me to show her off, but she said she had one of her migraine headaches and wouldn't get out of bed. I told her to meet me at the Polo Room at the Ambassador East at twelve o'clock for a luncheon with some of the Chicago salesmen, and left her with her head buried under the pillow. Broads . . . every time you count on them for something, they come up with some stupid excuse. If it's not a headache, then they got their period or a run in their stockings or something. I was beginning to wish I'd taken Rick with me after all. No man would ever pull this shit.

I made it through the interview okay and got to the Ambassador East a few minutes late. It was a small but elegant hotel on North State Street a few blocks down from the Drake, famous for the celebrities who hung out at the little piano bar in the Pump Room. I remembered being in the Pump Room with Vickie the last time I was in Chicago back in 1951, when I fought Sugar Ray for that final round. I stopped for a minute by the closed glass doors just inside

the lobby to the left and looked inside. I could see booth number
one that was always reserved for top dogs like Sinatra and Bob
Hope where I sat with Vickie that night, and the grand piano and
the small stage where Hildegarde, the chanteuse from Milwaukee,
was singing about Paris in her long white gloves, and the blonde
cigarette girls in their short black skirts and fishnet stockings, and
all the tables lit with candles. . . . I could still hear the music and
Hildegarde's sultry voice and the talking and the laughter . . . but
it was all dark and empty now. . . .

I turned away and walked across the lobby to the Polo Room.
The place was packed with well-suited businessmen, but Petra was
nowhere in sight. It figures, I thought. The hostess led me to a
back table where four or five sales guys were waiting. They all
stood up and shook my hand. I sat down, folded my hands on the
table, and waited for them to shoot the first question. By the way
they were looking at me, all shifty-eyed and squirming in their
seats, I could tell they were expecting me to live up to my anti-
social reputation—"savage, brutal and sordid" the press was calling
the book.

"Eh, look guys," I said for openers, "I know you read a lot of bad
things about me, but don't believe everything you read. I'm really
a very lovable guy—just ask my wives."

There was dead silence.

"Yeah, sure, Champ. We were hoping to meet the latest Mrs. La
Motta. Will she be here?" one of them asked me.

"Who knows? You know how broads are. She's probably out
shoppin'," I shrugged.

I struggled through the meeting as best I could, wondering
where the hell Petra was the whole time. I wished more than ever
that Rick was with me. Sure, I knew how to handle reporters—I
just gave 'em my stock one liners, like in my act. But when it
comes to business and politics, Rick was a genius compared to me.
I choked down the roast beef as fast as I could and got the hell out
of there.

Walking the few blocks back to the Drake Hotel, I was getting
more and more pissed at Petra for not showing up. I knew I didn't
make too good an impression with those sales guys. She should
have been with me. The one thing I asked her to do for me on this
trip and she disappointed me. I should listen to Rick more often.

He told me she was flaky and not to count on her too much. Broads
. . . just because they've got a slit between their legs, they think
they have it made. All they think they gotta do is lay there and
some jerk will kiss their ass and pay all their bills. Vickie was the
same way—I couldn't trust her as far as I could throw her. I used to
tap her bedroom phone from the bar downstairs in our house on
Pelham Parkway in the Bronx. I never found anything, so I figured
it was just my suspicions. After all, I'm Sicilian. But I caught her
one time at the Shorehaven pool with this young wiseguy from
Harlem—a button guy for the mob. I grabbed him and took him off
to the side. I was gonna beat his head in, but he begged me not to
hit him in the head because he had a plate in his skull, so I started
choking him instead. The mob knew I almost killed the guy, but
they also knew you don't fool around with a paisan's wife and get
away with it. Broads, they'll get ya into trouble every time.

I got to the hotel and made it up to the room as fast as I could. I
started to reach for the key in my pocket, then I remembered I left
it with Petra. I started banging on the door, but nobody answered.
Where the fuck was she? She couldn't still be sleeping, I thought. I
took the elevator back down to the lobby and went up to the desk
clerk.

"Hey buddy, did you see my wife go out this morning?" I asked.

"No, Mr. La Motta, I've been on all morning and I haven't seen
her. Would you like me to ring the room for you?" he said.

"Naw, just give me another key."

I grabbed the key and went back up to the room. She'd better
have a goddam good excuse for not answering the door, I thought.
Maybe she's got some creep in the room with her, or maybe she
met some guy in the hall and she's up in his room right now. . . . I
turned the key in the lock and threw open the door. The room was
empty and the bed was made. She must have been gone for hours,
I figured. What was she trying to pull? Migraine headache my ass!
Boy, was she gonna get a beating!

"Oh Jakie darling, you're back. You won't believe what a sexy
little nightgown I bought. You're going to love it."

I turned around and saw Petra standing in the doorway with an
armful of packages.

"Where the fuck have you been? Why the hell didn't you meet
me like you was supposed to?" I shouted at her.

"Jakie darling, don't be mad at me," she cooed, kissing me on the cheek as she brushed past me into the room. "I had to get some air to help my headache, and while I was out I passed the cutest little shops and I just couldn't resist. Besides, you didn't really need me, did you?" she asked sweetly, dropping the packages and her fur coat onto the chair and kicking off her high heels. "My feet are just killing me. I walked everywhere, you know," she sighed, and fell backwards onto the bed.

"You selfish Greek bitch! You make me look like an asshole in front of all those guys," I yelled, slamming the door shut behind me and walking over to her. "Just for that, you're gonna get a spankin'!"

I had to teach this Greek-American princess a lesson—what I say goes. I grabbed her and rolled her over on the bed. I pulled up her dress and yanked down her panties and started smacking her on her bare bottom.

"Jake, what are you doing? Stop it—stop it, Jake! Ouch—you're hurting me!" she screamed as I spanked away.

I learned one thing about women. You give them a black eye, and the next morning it's all over the papers. A spanking on their bare butt they'll never talk about.

Back in New York, things began to get a little rough. My book wasn't selling too good, and it didn't look like the publishers were going to break even on it. Even Rick stopped saying we had a best-seller and started working on different screenplays, hoping to sell the rights to a motion picture company. I had just about run through my share of the advance money, and I was starting to worry about next month's rent. Then Petra's ex-husband pulled a fast one and stopped the child support payments. That was five hundred bucks a month less we could count on. Petra had given up her apartment in Riverdale, and we were all living in my small furnished studio on East 56th Street—me, Petra, Melina and Caesar. I was so used to living alone, I forgot what it was like having a woman, a kid and a dog sharing your bathroom and taking over your closets. Petra kept saying she was a good cook, but I ended up doing all the cooking. She wasn't much of a housekeeper, either—and I thought I was bad! She must've been used to having a maid. The dishes and the laundry and the newspapers kept piling up. The place looked like a squirrel's nest most of the time. When it came to walking the dog, I put my foot down. If she thought I was going to be seen with a toy French poodle sporting a phony diamond collar, she had another guess coming. Petra started sleeping a lot during the day—again with the migraine headaches—while Melina was at school. To top it off, with the kid sleeping on the couch at night in the same room, we couldn't get it on like we used to. The honeymoon was definitely over.

I was sitting alone in the apartment watching something stupid on TV and hoping the phone would ring with some good news from somebody, when I got a phone call from Vickie.

"Jake, it's me. Your son Joey's been in a bad car accident. I need some money for the hospital right away."

My face dropped. I hadn't heard from Vickie in over five years, and now she hits me with this.

"How bad is the kid?" I asked her.

"Pretty bad. He has a concussion. His head is swollen twice its size. The doctors want to operate. Jake, you know I wouldn't bother you if it wasn't an emergency. You've got to help me. He's your son too."

Vickie's low, sensuous voice was as persuasive as ever, in spite of the strain and long distance.

"How much do you need? I'm pretty busted myself right now," I said, knowing better than to ask.

"How much have you got? The operation is pretty expensive."

"I got about $1500 in the bank, and that's it," I told her.

"It'll have to do. Send it to me right away. And Jake, thanks . . . . I won't forget."

She hung up the phone and I sat there thinking for a while. Vickie . . . Vickie . . . Vickie . . . Just hearing her voice was enough to get me going all over again. I hadn't seen her in years. She'd married this nightclub singer in Miami, Tony Foster, a couple of years after our divorce. They had a son, Harry, that she was crazy about. Joey was eighteen now, and had moved out of the house I left Vickie in Miami where our kids, Jackie, Joey and Christie, grew up. Joey was always kind of wild and cocky, like me. I hoped to God he hadn't screwed himself up too bad.

I was in Miami several years back doing a commercial for Fedders air conditioners when I ran into Tony Foster at the Harbor Club buying some broad a drink at the bar. We called the house together and I talked to the kids, but Vickie wouldn't get on the phone. The next night she met me for dinner with our old friend, the fight trainer and manager Angelo Dundee, and his wife. Vickie drove me to the airport. On the way she told me that she never would have married Tony if I had stepped in at the time. Stepped in?—somebody'd already been in. I figured it was a little too late. She wouldn't even let me kiss her good-bye at the airport. Tony was fucking around on her even then, but if I knew Vickie, she made him that way. I remembered that round bed we had in Miami before the divorce where we both slept naked. She wouldn't let me touch her. I tried forcing her at first, but after a while I gave up and looked elsewhere. It was a matter of pride. If Vickie had shown me any love and affection then, I wouldn't have fooled around. We might still be together today. . . .

Petra was out at a doctor's appointment. She was always seeing some Park Avenue doctor about something or other. I was glad she was out. It saved me a lot of explaining. I grabbed my jacket and left. It was a cold gray December day, and I walked the few blocks to the bank as fast as I could. I drew out what cash I had left and closed out the checking account. It was the last bank account I ever had. Then I walked a few more blocks to the Western Union office and wired Vickie my last 1500 bucks. I pocketed the less than 200 bucks I had left and headed home. If I was going to be broke, I might as well help out my kid while I still could, I figured. Then I thought about how I was going to break the news to Petra that the money was gone.

When I got back to the apartment, Petra was standing in front of the full-length mirror in the black nightgown she bought in Chicago, with a glass of scotch in her hand. She hardly ever took a drink by herself. Her make-up was smeared down her face, and she was crying. What now, I thought to myself.

"Hey, what's the matter with you?" I said. "Get dressed. The kid'll be home from school any minute."

She didn't say a word. She just stood there staring into the mirror with the tears streaming down her face.

"Okay, so we're broke. So what? There's no sense cryin' about it. I've been broke before. We'll make it," I tried to comfort her.

She still didn't say anything.

"So what do you want from me?" I shouted. "Can I help it if that lousy ex-husband of yours cut off the child support? Maybe you oughtta go back to your fancy Riverdale pad and have him support you. I'm tapped out! Here—here!" I threw my last few bucks onto the table. "That's all there is—go ahead, take it—buy yourself a new dress—maybe you'll feel better!" I yelled, feeling like a real loser.

She looked up at me with those dark mysterious eyes.

"Sit down, Jake. I want to talk to you," she said, dead serious.

I sat down on the edge of the bed and waited.

"Jake, it isn't working. I know you've tried, God knows you've tried, but it just isn't going to work. It isn't just us. I have a daughter to consider. I can't allow her to grow up like this, with no security, no future. I've thought a lot about it, and I want a divorce."

I could tell she meant it. Petra was never one for pulling punches. In a way I felt relieved. I was sick and tired of all the worry and problems. Maybe she was doing me a favor.

"You want a divorce? You go and get it," I said quietly.

I got up and walked out.

I borrowed a few bucks from Rick and moved down the street to the Sutton Hotel—another crap house. I left Petra the apartment and wished her luck. She got her divorce almost four months to the day after we got married. I felt like a victim of a hit and run driver. I never even got her second name. The leftover wedding cake was still in the freezer. It lasted longer than the marriage.

Thirteen

☞ "Put your pants on, Baby, it's time to go home. I gotta go to work," I told the nineteen-year-old blonde in my bed.

"Whatta ya, a fag or somethin'? I been here all night and ya didn't even touch me. Whatsa matter, grandpa, can't get it up any more?" she smacked in her Brooklyn accent.

"Get out of bed, get your clothes on, and get the hell out of here before I give ya a spankin', ya little snot nose!" I shouted on my way out. "Just slam the door behind your ass," I said, and headed out the door.

There was nothing more than a bed, a chest of drawers and a used TV in my cell of a studio, so who cared? The blonde was a new waitress at the Mardi Gras. I'd already forgotten her name. After two years of being up to your ears in tits and ass, screwing gets to be more of a habit than anything else. My fiftieth birthday was coming up, and I was still living like a juvenile delinquent. Every broad I knew was young enough to be my daughter. I was starting to feel like a dirty old man.

Topless go-go bars were as big as ever on Broadway in the early 70's, and Robbie's Mardi Gras at the corner of 49th and Broadway was the biggest of them all. There were 12 cashiers and 30 girls to a shift dancing to the rhythm section in nothing but bikini bottoms before a bunch of horny guys in the center of this dark smoky room as big as a barn. Robbie, gave me a job as bouncer after Petra and I split—$250 a week under the table and as much as 100 bucks a day in tips. I was no Jack Dempsey, but at least I was making a living. I saved enough to move out of that stinking little hole in the Sutton

140

Hotel and into another studio apartment on East 81st Street. It wasn't much bigger, but when I'm alone, I don't take up too much room. I'd probably be just as happy in a jail cell. Petra got evicted from the apartment not too long after I left, and she and the kid moved in with me for a little while. I had nothing against her, but it just wasn't the same. I was glad when they moved on. Petra still stopped by the Mardi Gras once in a while, and I'd buy her dinner and give her a few bucks, and maybe we'd get laid for old times' sake.

There were two shifts at the Mardi Gras around the clock, seven days a week. I had the day shift from noon to eight, and I'd walk every day from my East side apartment to the West side. I enjoyed the half hour or so of exercise and being out in the streets and sunshine, especially on a warm, sunny summer day in early July like today was. I preferred the day shift. It left my nights free, and the regular hours gave me some sense of working a normal job like everybody else. The ex-heavyweight contender, Nino Valdez, had the night shift. He was a big black Cuban about six foot six and 250 pounds. Hey, but I always reminded him that I knocked out heavyweight Bob Satterfield, who knocked him out. "What kind of a fighter are you?" I'd tease him.

Between us, we kept the Mardi Gras one of the cleanest and most respected joints on Broadway. We were like big brothers to the girls. I had my pick of the prettiest, but I preferred the waitresses—the dancers were too commercial and stuck up. They thought they were hot shit. To me they were just sucker bait. Creeps of all kinds came in at all hours of the day. The ugliest guys would walk in off the street and imagine they could get the prettiest girls. A lot of money is made in this world playing to guys' fantasies—especially some of the lonely sick desperate losers that wandered in for a couple of bucks worth of dreams.

Rick stopped by once in a while, and I'd get him a drink on the house. He was still making the porno flicks, but he hadn't given up on the idea of selling the screenplay of *Raging Bull*. Some top actors would come into the bar sometimes—guys like Ben Gazzara, Al Pacino, James Caan, Peter Falk, and Dustin Hoffman. I'd give them each a copy of my book for free, hoping something would happen. They all said they'd read it, but none of them called me. I guess Rick and I were just dreaming.

It was a routine day. The same old drunks stumbled in and started bothering the girls and had to be thrown out. A couple of guys who had too much to drink got into a fight over one of the dancers, and I had to break it up. One guy refused to pay his bill, till I took him outside and convinced him that it was a lot cheaper than the hospital bill he was going to have if he didn't pay up. Two of the waitresses had a dispute over a tip, and I settled it by telling them to split it, or I'd give them both a spanking. It was the same old bullshit that used to go on in my club in Miami Beach, except then I was the boss instead of a hired muscle. I still did my own dirty work then, though. Some jerk walked up behind Vickie in the club once and put his hands on her bare shoulders, asking her for an autograph. I came up and told him, "Take your hands off my wife or I'll break every bone in your body." He backed off, apologizing. In my room over the club, I had a look-out for the cash register through a hole in the medicine cabinet—like George Macready in *Gilda*. I even had an escape hatch through the closet door—just in case. I was always looking to survive, even if I acted like I had a death wish. If I ever thought of committing suicide, I'd rather rob all the racketeers and let them kill me. Then, if I got away with it, so much the better. You've got to be crooked in this world to get rich. I always thought hoods were like Robin Hoods: they rob from the rich and give to the poor—themselves. But at least they spread it around.

By seven I took my first double scotch like I always did toward the end of my shift. The cute blonde I took home the night before showed up for the night shift. She looked better than I remembered she did lying in my bed this morning. I thought of asking her to switch shifts and come home with me again tonight, but it's bad policy to play favorites with the girls. Besides, who wants to eat cold spaghetti two nights in a row? I downed a few more scotches, ordered my usual steak and fries from the kitchen, and hung out awhile, then I started on my walk home. I figured I'd get a good night's sleep for a change.

Broadway was alive and crawling with the usual variety of nighttime hustlers, misfits, prostitutes, pimps, druggies, drunks and bums that gave the Times Square area its reputation as the noisy, colorful, smelly cesspool of humanity it was. I headed across town on 50th Street, leaving the carnival lights and sounds behind me, toward the quieter, saner East Side. It was a hot, still muggy night, the kind that gets you woozy just trying to breathe. I got to the corner of Third Avenue and was thinking of checking out the action at P.J. Clark's when I noticed this tall, good-looking chick standing in the shadows and crying her eyes out. I walked up to her and asked her what was the matter. She told me she had a fight with her boyfriend, and he'd left her there on the street. I told her to come with me; I'd buy her a drink.

"Why not, sugar," she said. We walked down the street to-gether. About halfway down the block, I pushed her into a dark-ened doorway and started kissing her. The door gave way, and she fell backwards into this dim, deserted hallway, I stepped in after her, pressed her up close against the wall with my body, and made a grab for her crotch, going for the end result. My hand froze in mid-action. I was holding a handful of cock! I reeled backwards against the wall, stumbled out the door, and ran down the street like the hounds of hell were on my heels. I didn't slow down till I'd put as much distance as I could between me and that son of a bitch bastard, whoever it was. It wasn't so much that she had a cock that bothered me, as the fact that I was fooled so easy. I wasn't that drunk that I didn't know what I was doing. What kind of a man was I that I could go for a guy in woman's clothes like a blind dog in heat? I was disgusted with myself—disgusted with my whole stink-ing pointless existence.

When I got up to my apartment, I went to the bathroom and washed out my mouth. I took a hot bath and scrubbed my body till it hurt. I sat on the bed and poured myself a tall one, hoping to wash away the whole stinking memory, but I couldn't get rid of the rotten taste in my mouth. I felt like throwing up. I was sick to death of too much booze, too much sex, and too little love. Nothing turned me on anymore—not booze, not women, not even money. As long as I was eating and paying the rent, what did I care? Maybe that was it—I didn't give a good fuck about anything or anyone, and no one gave a good fuck about me. They say it's more blessed to give than to receive, but I had nothing to give. My whole life added up to one big fat zero. Fuck it! Leave it there. . . .

I was sitting on the edge of the bed getting drunk and feeling sorry for myself when the phone rang.

"Yeah, who is it?" I mumbled into the receiver.

"Jakie Bird, it's me, Sally. Did I wake you?"

"Sally . . . my little Sally Bird! How've ya been, Baby?"

"Oh, I'm okay. Jake, you don't sound too good. Are you all right?"

"Yeah, yeah . . . just a little tired, that's all. What's all that noise? Sounds like you're at a dog pound or somethin'."

"I'm still at my poodle shop. You know, my dog grooming business."

"Oh yeah, yeah . . . So what's happening?"

"I called to wish you happy birthday, Jake."

"Birthday? Oh yeah, yeah . . . my birthday. I forgot. So how come you remembered?"

"I remember a lot of things, Jake. Since I've found God in my heart, I want to make peace between us . . . . I want you to forgive me, Jake."

"Forgive you? Who am I to forgive you? You should forgive me."

"I have forgiven you, Jake, with all my heart. I know and God knows, Jake, that deep inside you're a good person. We're all God's children, Jake. My life has changed since I let God into my heart. I was no angel, either."

"Sally, Sally . . . You are an angel. You've . . . you've got somethin' I want . . . . I want what you have. You have peace of mind. I need that. I don't know what's wrong with me, Sally. Nothin' turns me on anymore—nothin' matters anymore. I keep lookin' for somethin', but I don't know what it is. . . ."

"You need God, Jake. Let God into your heart, and He will help you. Pray with me, Jake . . . Ask God to come into your heart . . ."

"I used to pray. I was an altar boy once—would ya believe it? But I forgot how, Sally. I wouldn't know what to do. You pray for me, okay Sally Bird?"

"All right, Jake, I will . . . just like I pray for Lisa."

"Lisa—how's she doin? How's my favorite girl?"

"I've been very worried about her, Jake. She's getting too wild. I don't know, maybe it's this crazy Miami weather. She skips school; she hangs out with this tough motorcycle crowd; she stays out all night. I just can't control her. She needs a father. She needs you, Jake. You two were always so close. She misses you."

"Yeah, I miss her, too. What the hell's wrong with her? If I was there, I'd straighten her out in a minute, the cocky little bitch."

"I was hoping to talk to you about this, Jake. I think Lisa should come up and stay with you for a while. She could go to school in New York and get away from this bad crowd. I've prayed a lot about this, Jake, and I think it would be the best thing for her."

"Stay with me? You mean live here? I don't know, Sally . . . I only got a small studio here, and I go to work all day, and, I don't know, maybe the kid wouldn't like it here . . ."

"Jake, I've never asked you for a favor before, but I'm asking you now. Please, do this for me. If you love Lisa, you'll help her. She needs you."

"All right, all right. . . . Let me think about it. . . ."

"God bless you, Jake. . . ."

It was my day off, and I was cooking myself something to eat—sausage and peppers like my father used to cook. You heat the pan with a little olive oil on a low flame. Then you toss in the sliced peppers—no onions, that's Neapolitan, not Sicilian. You let the peppers sizzle a while, then ya take 'em out and ya throw in the sweet sausage. And when it's good and browned, ya throw the peppers back in, with just a touch of sugar—that takes the acid out. Then ya gouge out the middle of a fresh loaf of Italian bread with your hands and slap the whole thing together. What a great Italian meal!

I just took my first bite when there was a knock at the door.

"Who is it?" I called with a mouthful of food.

"Hey, open up, man. It's me, Lisa!" somebody yelled through the door.

I choked on the food. It can't be, I thought. Sally said she wouldn't be here till next week. I put down my sandwich, got up, and opened the door to a pair of dirty long-haired creeps. I sort of recognized one of them as my daughter. She looked fifteen going on thirty, and I could bet she was no virgin.

"Hiya, Pops, we made it. We rode all the way. Boy, is my ass sore! Bet ya didn't count on gettin' stuck with me again, did ya?" she greeted me as they walked in with their bulging backpacks and dropped them on the floor. . .

"Que pasa, man. Smells good. Tengo hambre. What you got to eat, chucho?" the other one said.

This young punk who thought he was Che Guevera with the hat and the boots and the leather jacket and the motorcycle chains was strutting around the room like he owned the joint. I wanted to take his chain and wrap it around his neck.

"Yeah, Pop, I'm thirsty as hell. Ya got any beer?" Lisa said, plopping herself down on my bed.

I stared at her long tangled hair and dirty jeans and ripped Hell's Angel T-shirt. She was a total stranger. I thought of the pretty little girl riding on my shoulders in the park . . . "Daddy, I wanna ice cream. . . ." She always liked ice cream. . . . What the hell happened?

"Hey, whatta ya think this is—the Plaza? And who the hell are you?" I said, pointing my finger at this punk she walked in with.

"Cual es tu problema, man? I'm Paco—the pride of Little Cuba. And Lisa, she's my old lady. So you're the Champ—El Campeon eh? . . . Lisa, she wouldn't shut up about ya all the way from Miami. Ya look like ya could still go a few rounds, eh Pop? Pero viejo, I expected a better layout than this. Where's the bedroom?" he rattled off in a heavy Spanish accent.

"You listen to me now, creep. Pick up your bag and get the hell out of here!" I growled, opening the door for this animal.

"Hey Pop, if he goes, I go. Paco's my old man," Lisa chimed in.

"Right now I'm your old man, kid—and you're goin' nowhere," I said to her.

I glared at the animal, picked up his bag and tossed it into the hall.

"Follow that bag out of here, punk, or I'll bust every Cuban bone in your body!" I shouted.

The kid tensed, and I thought I was going to have to belt him one, when Lisa jumped up and stood between us.

"Cool it, Paco. It's okay. Let me talk to him. Wait for me outside, okay?" she said to this bastard.

He pulled her to him and kissed her on the forehead.

"Si, si mi amor . . . si tu me lo pides. I'll go check on the bike. But don't be too long—no te tardes," he said to her. He flashed me a last angry look and sauntered out the door.

Lisa and I stood there staring at each other for a few minutes, then she broke the silence.

"Look, Pop, I know this wasn't your idea—and it wasn't mine either. Mom's got it in her head that I need parental authority or somethin', and you've been elected for the job. Let us just crash here for tonight, and we'll get out of your hair in the morning."

"Lisa, you're not going anywhere. I promised your mother I'd take care of ya, and you're stayin' right here with me where I can keep an eye on ya. Now go down and tell that little creep that's the story and get your ass back up here—alone," I told her.

"Same old shit—you're all heart, Pop. Thanks, but no thanks. Paco and me'll make it on our own. We'll sleep in the park, if we have to," she said, grabbing her bag and heading towards the door. She turned and gave me a defiant look. "Remember the park, Pop?" she said over her shoulder, then she walked out, slamming the door behind her.

I stood there staring at the door, not knowing if I should go after her or not. Like a jerk, I let her go. Kids . . . you bring them into this world and bust your chops caring for them, then they grow up and come back to give you a kick in the ass. I fed her, I gave her baths, I changed her diapers and wiped her ass, I carried her everywhere on my shoulders, and now she comes back with this cocky little bastard and spits in my face. What the hell's the use in trying? I walked back to my forgotten sandwich. It was cold and greasy and all dried up. I took one look at it and threw it in the garbage. I'd lost my appetite.

I was lying in bed watching the late show that night—*Body and Soul* with John Garfield, one of my favorites. I always watched it for the last line, when Garfield meets the wiseguys coming out of the ring. He didn't throw the fight, and they said he was a dead man. "Everybody dies," he told them. I wish I'd said that . . . . I switched off the set and grabbed my solitaire deck. I was trying not to think about Lisa and where she'd gone. I was hoping to God Sally didn't call. I wouldn't know what to tell her. Then I heard a light knock on the door. I cracked it open, and there stood Lisa. She was alone. Her face was smudged and her eyes were red, like she had been crying.

"Hello, Daddy, can I come in?" she said in a small voice.

I opened the door wider.

"Sure, kid, come on in," I said, trying not to let on how happy I was to see her.

She stepped inside and stood holding her bag, looking down at her feet.

"Why don't ya throw that over there," I said.

She walked over and dropped her bag in the corner.

"We had a fight. . . Paco split on his bike . . ." she mumbled, looking miserable.

"You're a young kid, Lisa. You've got a long way to go and a lot to learn. You'll find out they all take off, sooner or later," I said.

"I told him you had a lot of bread. I didn't know. . . . He thought I lied to him . . . ." she shrugged, looking around the empty room.

"I don't want to hear about it. You're here now, and that's all that matters," I cut her short. "There's a cot in the closet, some sheets and a pillow on the shelf. Get it out and get yourself set up. You can sleep over there," I told her, pointing to the small alcove area.

She went to the closet and started pulling things out. I'll have to get a bigger place, she's gonna need her own room, I thought, watching her.

"Hey, ya hungry?" I asked. "I am. I'm starvin'. Tell ya what, I got two loaves of bread left—some more sausage and peppers. I'll cook ya the greatest Italian hero ya ever had. . . ."

By the end of September, Lisa and I had it pretty well worked out. She'd get home at about four from the local high school I had got her enrolled in, start on her homework and straighten up the place a little. Then I'd come home from work and we'd have dinner together. Either I'd cook us something, or we'd go out for a pizza or to a neighborhood restaurant. She used to love Chinese food. Then we'd go home and watch some TV or play a few hands of gin. She got pretty good and would beat the pants off me, the shrewd little bitch. On weekends we'd take long walks to the park like we used to when she was little. She still got a kick out of people recognizing me and calling me Champ. "And I'm Lisa," she'd always chime in. "Yeah, that's my daughter," I'd say, feeling proud. We were getting to be known as a regular couple around town again.

My social life wasn't what it used to be, but I didn't mind too much. It was nice coming home to someone who needed me. And Lisa needed a lot of straightening out. She must have gotten away with murder with Sally. I got her to quit cursing so much. I never liked cursing, especially in women. She was sounding like a truck driver, I told her. She would smoke a little pot in front of me, but that was no big deal. "Come on, Pop, have a toke—let's get high," she'd joke. But that crap's not for me. I'm strictly a boozer. It's when I saw the tattoo on her arm that I blew my stack.

"Whatta ya want to brand yourself like a little tramp for?" I told her. That's when I found the stash of pills on her cot—uppers, downers, you name it. I flushed them down the toilet and told her if I ever caught her with any of that crap again, I'd spank her till she was black and blue. No daughter of mine was gonna turn into a junkie in front of me. I'd lost Christie to Vickie years ago. Maybe with Lisa there was still time. She pitched a fit at first, but after a while she calmed down. Kids know when you're just bullshitting and when you really care about them. I think she was starting to learn some respect.

It was slow at the Mardi Gras, even for a Monday, so I cut out early and headed home. I figured I'd surprise the kid and take her to dinner at the Gold Coin, this fancy Chink restaurant on Second Avenue. I got to the apartment and put my key in the lock, but it was open. What the hell's wrong with her, I thought. I told her to always lock the door when she was home alone. I pushed open the door and stepped into a nightmare in progress. Lisa was crouched in the corner like a frightened wild rat, clutching a long kitchen knife in both hands. That lousy Cuban punk, Paco, was standing over her. He was shaking and looked white as a ghost.

"Hey, what's going on here—what the hell are you doin?" I shouted at him, the blood shootin' to my head like a fire hose. He turned and looked at me, his eyes big and frightened. "I don' know what happen. She's crazy—she trying to kill me!" he stammered.

"What the hell did ya give her, you crazy bastard. I'll kill ya, ya son of a bitch!"

I grabbed him and threw him across the room. He hit the wall hard, his knees buckling.

"We smoking angel dust. Creeme, man, nunca happen before.

Si vol vio loca de repente. She crazy—esta loca—quiera matarme—me quiera matar—she want kill me!" he sputtered in broken Spanish.

I turned to Lisa. She was frozen in her corner like a terrified animal, still holding the knife. Her eyes were wild, the pupils like two large black holes. She was breathing hard and heavy, hyperventilating like crazy. She stared at Paco, ready to spring across the room and attack him. She looked possessed by the devil himself. I knew she couldn't see or hear me.

"Get out! Get the hell out of here! If I ever see you near her again, I swear I'll kill ya!" I shouted at Paco.

"Is not my fault, man. Your daughter, she crazy—para el carajo!" he mumbled and ran out the door.

I turned back to Lisa and walked over to her slowly.

"It's all right, Lisa baby—he's gone now. This is me talkin'. Daddy's here; you're safe now. Everything's gonna be okay," I said to her, keeping my voice low and calm.

I knelt down next to her and held out my hand.

"Let me have that now. . . . Give Daddy the knife, sweetheart," I said, trying to loosen her grip on the knife handle.

She grabbed on tighter than before.

"No, no! Get away. Get away from me! she cried, trying to fight me off.

"Lisa, I mean it! Give me the knife! Stop it, now Lisa!" I said, grabbing both her wrists and wrestling with her.

I couldn't believe the strength in her arms. The dope and adrenaline in her body must've given her superhuman power. It was all I could do to hold her down and try to pry her fingers from the knife butt. In the struggle, the knife slipped, cutting me across my arm. The sight of the blood distracted her for a moment, and I grabbed the knife and threw it across the floor. She screamed and tried to go after it, but I straddled her and pinned her arms down. She was kicking and screaming like a madwoman. I slapped her hard across the face, hoping to snap her out of it. All at once, she stopped struggling and her body went limp. I pulled her up to a sitting position. Her eyes were glazed and she looked dazed, like she was in some sort of hypnotic trance. She started talking in this far off little girl's voice. She sounded like she was six years old.

". . . Where are we going? It's dark in here. I don't like it in here

. . . I'm cold. I want to go home. Where's my Mommy? . . . Don't touch me . . . Stop, you're hurting me . . . Don't . . . Don't do that . . . I want my Mommy . . . Mommy, Daddy, where are you? . . . He's hurting me . . . Stop that . . . Please don't touch me . . . Don't let him touch me anymore . . ."

As I listened to her sad little voice, a chill ran through me. My whole body started to tremble. That time she was lost. . . .

She was six years old and Sally had moved with the kids to Staten Island. Sally called me that afternoon, frantic. Lisa was missing from the playground. I took a cab over the Verrazano and got there as fast as I could. She'd called the cops, and they were searching the whole area. It was getting dark, and there was no sign of her. Sally and I were going crazy. Then two cops showed up at the door with Lisa in their arms. She was scared, but she looked all right. They said they found her wandering in the neighborhood alone . . . but they were lying. They must have been lying. . . . They found her with some sick bastard who put his dirty hands on her, and they were afraid to tell me. They knew I'd go out and find the son of a bitch and kill him! Those lousy bastards! They never said a word. All this time and I never knew . . . they never said a word. . . .

Lisa was crying like a newborn baby. She had finally let it all out, and now she was sobbing in my arms like a prisoner just released from solitary.

"Go ahead and cry, Baby. . . . It's all over now. Go ahead and cry," I said softly. I rocked her back and forth till she fell asleep in my arms. . . .

Lisa slept late the next morning. I had put her in my bed and took the cot for myself. I didn't have the heart to wake her. I figured she could use a day off from school. I fixed her a big breakfast and took it to her in bed. We ate together, neither one of us saying much. She stared across the room at my bandaged arm.

"Did I do that?" she asked quietly.

"Aw, it's nothin'—just a scratch. Ya almost had me down for the count, kiddo. Lucky thing ya didn't punch me in the nose. Look at this nose," I joked with her.

She gave me a little smile. I smiled back, and another day started. I'd already decided to take her to work with me. After yesterday, I was scared to leave her alone. It had been drizzling all morning, and looked like it wasn't letting up, so I skipped my walk and sprang for a cab for the two of us. I'd never taken Lisa to the Mardi Gras before. I told her I sort of managed this restaurant on the West Side. I wasn't too happy about taking her there, but I figured a few bare tits had to be better than Paco and his angel dust.

The place was jumping with the early shift when we got there. Showtime started at 8 A.M., and the joint was filled with a lot of bums looking to get out of the rain and get themselves a cheap thrill at the same time. The girls were bleary-eyed, most of them still up from the night before, going automatically through their tired routines to the off-beat music. The rainy gray sky outside was bright compared to the dark cave inside, the dampness filling your nostrils with the dank smell of last night's booze and sweat and vomit. Lisa's eyes got big as she looked around the smoky room.

"Wow—far out. . . . Neat place, Pop," was all she said.

I introduced her around to the crew.

"Hey, I didn't know you had a daughter, Jake. I guess you're human after all," cracked Al, one of the bartenders.

"What's a nice girl like you doin' in a joint like this—don't answer that, honey," quipped Nancy, one of the waitresses. "Ya know, you've got a real sweetheart there for a father," she winked. "She's a doll, Jake. I didn't know you had it in you."

I took up my station near the door and sat Lisa down at a nearby table where I could keep my eye on her. Nancy brought her a soda, and she sat sipping it and staring at everything around her like Alice in Wonderland. She'll be okay, I thought. She's a good kid; she's just had a few bad breaks. But a few breaks never stopped a La Motta. She's a survivor. I taught her that much anyway. She always had a good fighting spirit, even as a little kid. It's what I liked about her most.

By late afternoon, I'd given a couple of drunks the bum's rush and straightened out this fag from Kansas who thought the dancers was female impersonators, but mostly it was a pretty quiet day. Lisa watched my every move like a hawk.

"Gee, Dad, you're a pretty smooth operator. Did ya ever have to really belt a guy?" she asked.

"Naw, I just give 'em a kick in the ass and they move on. Nobody ever messes with me—they know better. Besides, if I ever punched a guy, they could say I was usin' my fists as deadly weapons," I told her.

I was thinking of heading home early with Lisa when Petra swung through the revolving door.

"Hello, Jake. How are you?" she said, giving me a peck on the cheek. "Have you got a minute? I need to talk to you."

"Yeah, sure, but first there's somebody I want ya to meet," I said, taking her by the hand and leading her over to Lisa.

"Petra, meet my kid, Lisa."

"So you're Lisa. I've heard all about you. You're the same age as my Stephanie. Are you living in New York now, dear?" Petra said, giving me a look.

"I'm living with Daddy now," Lisa said.

"Oh? How nice. Do you think it's wise bringing her here, Jake?" Petra said, arching an eyebrow.

"I had to. It's a long story," I said, steering Petra over to a corner. "So what is it you wanted to talk about?" I asked her.

"I'm behind in my rent, Jake. They say they're going to evict us this time if I don't give them some money this month. If I could just pay them half, I could stall them for the rest. . ."

"How much?" I said.

"About three hundred should do it . . . just until I get back on my feet . . ."

I reached into my pocket and drew out a handful of bills. I counted out three hundreds and handed them to Petra.

"That's it for this month. I got a kid I'm responsible for now," I said.

"Thanks," she said, slipping the money into her bag. "I'm glad to hear you're responsible for someone, Jake" she added.

"Go sit down with Lisa. I'll get ya a drink and order you and the kid some dinner," I told her.

I was busy at the door checking the ID's of a bunch of kids that looked like they belonged in high school when I noticed out of the corner of my eye this hulk of a guy standing over Lisa and Petra. They were trying to ignore him and go on eating their dinner, but he was drunk and wouldn't take no for an answer. I waited a few minutes, then I walked over to their table.

"All right fella, that's enough. Beat it," I told the guy.

He was a big Irish goon—about six feet and 200 pounds, but he was sloppy, and by the whiskey on his breath and the way he was swaying, I knew he was in no condition to put up a fight.

"Ya wanna make me, tough guy?" he slurred back.

"Look, buster, leave the girls alone, or I'll throw ya out of here on your ass," I said a little louder.

"I think the girls want me to stay, don't ya, honey," he slobbered, leaning over the table to Petra.

Petra leaned away from him in disgust.

"Get out of here, ya lousy creep!" Lisa yelled.

"Who asked you, ya little cunt!" the drunk snarled back at her.

I grabbed the bastard by his collar, pinned his arm behind his back, and waltzed him to the door. I pushed him through the revolving panels and followed him outside.

"Get out and stay out, ya son of a bitch! I ever catch ya back here, I'll break every bone in your body!" I shouted at him.

"Ya lousy wop pug. Come over here—I'll punch ya out, ya no good dirty bastard!" he slobbered back, staggering toward me.

It was dark out, and the rain was still coming down in a steady drizzle. The multi-colored neon lights of Broadway were flashing off and on, reflecting off the wet sidewalk and streets. A small crowd was beginning to gather around the two of us, like we was a couple of gunslingers facing off in the Old West. Some of the help from the Mardi Gras came outside to watch the action. Petra and Lisa were pressed up against the glass windows inside, looking at me with frightened eyes. I felt like Gary Cooper in *High Noon.*

"Come on, ya lousy coward, I'll kick the shit out of ya!" the drunk slobbered again, coming at me with both fists up.

I stood there with my feet planted wide and my fists at my side, waiting for him to make a move. I knew there was no use trying to talk him out of it; this mean Mick wanted a fight. I don't know if he knew who I was, but I don't think it would have made any difference. He telegraphed a heavy right punch to my jaw. I blocked him with my left, gave him a right to the stomach, and a left punch to the head. He went down like a ton of bricks, his head hitting the curb with a loud crack. He lay there with his head in the gutter, out cold. I couldn't tell if he was dead or alive. I heard the screech of sirens and the red flashing lights of the cops and the ambulance blinked in my eyes. I stood there staring at the guy's still body, not knowing what to do. Then I saw Nino Valdez, the night bouncer, pushing toward me though the crowd.

"Jake, what the fuck happened here?" he said to me.

I couldn't answer him. Nino knelt down next to the unconcious guy and lifted up his head. There was no response. Nino turned and looked up at me.

"Run, Jake! Get the hell out of here! Run, man, now!" he said.

I looked around me at the strange leering faces. I could see Lisa through the door, trying to get out and Petra holding her back. The cops were coming toward me through the crowd.

"My kid and Petra are in there—take care of 'em," I told Nino, then I broke through the crowd behind me and ran into the rain and the night.

PART IV

High Times

Fourteen

Jake maneuvered his way through the suited men to the back of the crowded elevator and placed his broad back against the wall. His eyes were focused blankly in front of him and both hands were clasped behind him as he waited out the jerky descent to the lobby of Plaza 400 on East 56th Street, where he had been visiting his brother, Joey, and Joey's new wife, Margaritte. Jake had dropped several pounds of soggy flesh in the past few months, and his natty sports jacket, a remnant from his days at the Mardi Gras, hung loosely on his hard square frame. Jake had no particular destination on this particularly pleasant afternoon in May, and he was thinking of nothing in particular when a pretty blonde bearing a striking resemblance to Bridget Bardot stepped gingerly into the midst of the closely packed elevator. Jake's expressionless eyes lit up at the sight of the attractive young woman standing in front of him.

"How's come you're so beautiful?" he asked her with a rhetorical grin.

She smiled self-consciously and tried to ignore him.

"Ya know, you're the kind of girl I like, but ya should see the kind of girls I get," he cracked.

She laughed nervously along with the elevator full of bemused men. The doors opened onto the first floor and the suddenly released passengers dispersed into the lobby. Jake followed the attractive blonde out onto the sidewalk and started walking beside her.

"Hey, slow down you beautiful, lovely, gorgeous creature. I'm Jake La Motta. Where have ya been all my life? What's your name, anyway?" he pitched.

"Debbie . . . Why are you following me?" she asked as she kept on walking.

"You're a good-lookin' broad. I thought I'd like to get to know ya. What's that—you a model or somethin'?" Jake asked, looking down at the large black portfolio she was carrying.

"No, it's Mitchell's composite—my son. I'm trying to place him with a good agent here in New York. He models, acts. He's only ten, but he's very good," she said, turning the corner and heading toward 57th Street.

"Your son? Aw, you're married, uh," Jake said disappointedly.

"I was. I just got divorced last year," she said.

"Oh yeah? So you live around here or what?" Jake asked, encouraged.

"My mother lives in that building right over there," she answered, pointing to the high rise Excelsior House on 57th and Third.

"So ya got money, too, uh," Jake commented, impressed.

"Look, I've got to go now," she said, stopping at the corner. "It was nice talking to you, uh, Jake, is it?"

"Jake La Motta—Middleweight Champ," Jake said, handing her his card with his photo of an early fighting pose printed on one side. "Why don't ya give me your number? I'd like to take ya out sometime."

"I don't go out that much. I've only been in New York a few months now. I don't know Manhattan very well. It frightens me," she evaded.

"Aw, whatta ya scared of? I'll take care of ya. Whatsa matter— don't ya trust me? Look at this face. Now is that a honest face, or what? Come on, give me your phone number," Jake insisted.

"All right, but this doesn't mean I'll go out with you," she relented, scribbling her number on a piece of paper and handing it to him.

Jake read the number and stuffed it in his pocket. "Debbie . . . beautiful gorgeous Debbie . . . I'm gonna call ya now, sweetheart," he called after her as she disappeared into the Excelsior lobby.

Jake headed home to his Yorkshire House studio on 81st Street wearing a cocky grin. What a knockout! She's a classy broad with a sexy body and a pouty little face that looks so innocent with those wide baby blue eyes—what a score! he thought, congratulating himself.

Jake entered his barren-as-ever bachelor studio, grabbed a beer from the refrigerator and stood looking out the window at the rush hour traffic in the street below. He'd had his L-shaped room all to himself for the past nine months, ever since Lisa left and returned to her mother in Miami. After the incident at the Mardi Gras, Sally had changed her mind about Jake's being the ideal guardian for their wayward daughter. Jake had put Lisa on the bus bound for Miami with a mixture of relief and regret. "Be good, Daddy. Don't do anything I wouldn't do," Lisa said with a forlorn smile as she waved goodbye.

The drunken customer Jake had knocked out had recovered and no charges were filed, but by consensus of opinion Jake was let go from his bouncer position at the Mardi Gras. It was a blessing in thin disguise. The Mardi Gras was not the sort of environment that tended to bring out Jake's better nature. Another year on the Broadway beat, and he might have sunk beneath the muck and mire forever. These past months in "solitary" collecting unemployment had proved a recuperative period that wrought a definite improvement in Jake's state of mind and body. He had knocked his drinking down to practically nil, as his trimmer form and leaner face attested. His long therapeutic walks around town revived some of the lost discipline of his Spartan training days. His self-imposed fast from women and booze had a tonic effect on his personality as well. The old paranoia and suspicion that dominated his every relationship had retreated to the back of his mind, allowing his natural wit and humor to come forth. It was as if he had received a personal invitation to rejoin the human race.

He was seeing more of his estranged family again. His brother Joey and wife Margaritte invited him to dinner more and more often. At the same time, he was seeing less and less of Rick. Involved with his own film production and business hassles, Rick had faded from the daily scene of Jake's bohemian existence, the dream of "Raging Bull" ever becoming a film apparently forgotten.

Jake finished off his beer and took the number Debbie had given him from his pocket. What if she had given him a phony number just to get rid of him? he thought. He went to the phone and dialed the scribbled digits.

"Allo," a woman's voice answered in an Italian accent.

"Uh, is Debbie there?" he asked.

"No, she's out visiting her mother now. Who is calling please?"

"Uh, this is Jake La Motta, a friend of hers. I got a book I want to deliver to her. What's the address there—I forgot."

"It's 400 East 56th Street, Apartment 7K, Mr. La Motta."

"Thanks. Oh, yeah, how do you spell her last name again?"

"That would be Hade—H-a-d-e—Deborah Florsheim Hade."

"Florsheim? Ya mean the shoe?"

"Yes, the same spelling."

"Thanks lady, ya been a big help."

Jake smiled to himself as he hung up the phone. So she was on the level after all. And she lived right in Joey's building, too. How about that. Who was that Italian broad that answered the phone, he wondered. Maybe the maid, or something. He figured she came from a wealthy family. She had that well-groomed, pampered look about her—a real Jewish-American princess. Could it be the same Florsheim? he wondered. She must be loaded, he thought. Jake opened another can of beer, switched on the television, and lay back on the bed to watch the evening news. . . .

The following morning Jake was out early, heading jauntily down First Avenue toward 56th Street with a copy of his book under one arm and visions of delectable Debbie dancing in his head. He entered the familiar lobby at Plaza 400 and greeted the doorman heartily.

"Hiya, pal. Ring 7K for me, and let me have the phone."

Jake took the receiver and listened expectantly to the repeated rings, his breath coming in short, heavy sighs.

"Debbie? It's me, Jake. I brought ya somethin'—somethin' special."

"Jake? Jake who?" came the sleepy reply.

"Jake who? Jake La Motta—that's who! I met ya in the elevator yesterday. You remember?"

There was a long pause.

"You mean you're here? You're here right now?" she asked in dismay.

"Yeah . . . Can I come up? I got somethin' for ya."

"No—no, don't do that. . . . I'll come down. Give me a minute to throw something on. I'll meet you by the service elevator, okay?"

Jake paced doggedly by the rear elevator for a good twenty minutes before Debbie finally appeared in a long white terrycloth robe, her long blond hair flowing over her shoulders. She wore little make-up, and looked younger than Jake remembered from their first meeting.

"Eh, how long does it take to come down seven floors? Hey, look at you! Ya look like a juvenile delinquent. How old are ya anyway—twenty-five, twenty-six?" Jake greeted her.

"No, but thanks for the compliment. I'm thirty-two," Debbie answered.

"No kiddin'! Ya sure don't look it. Here, I brought ya my book, *Raging Bull*. I autographed it for ya, inside there," Jake said, handing her the book and opening it to the page where he had scrawled "To beautiful darling Debbie—The Champ."

"Oh, that's very nice . . . thank you," Debbie said, dutifully reading the inscription.

"Ya know, you won't like me if you read this," Jake added.

"Then why are you giving it to me?" she asked.

"Well, 'cause I just want ya to know who the Champ is. Eh, how 'bout comin' out for a drink with me—right now."

"But it's still morning, and besides, I'm not dressed."

"All the better. No, seriously, let's go for a cup of coffee or somethin'."

"No, maybe some other time. I've got to go now. Thanks for the book," she said, stepping into the elevator.

"Aw come on, just around the corner . . ." Jake persisted.

"I'm sorry; I can't. I have to go," she said as the elevator doors closed shut in Jake's doleful face.

Debbie stared in bewilderment at Jake's imposing form standing in the corner phone booth on the street below her apartment window as she tapped her fingernails nervously on the receiver in her hand and pondered an answer to Jake's latest demand that she go out with him. He had called her religiously for the past three weeks, and his dogged persistence was beginning to wear down her natural resistance. There was something vulnerable and disarming beneath his gruff, beaten exterior that lent a little boy charm to his intimidating presence in spite of himself, she thought. She had finally read his *Raging Bull* autobiography, dismissing it as largely a work of fantastic fiction. Still, she sensed a sinister strength and power within him that both repulsed and attracted her. . . .

Since her divorce from Jerry Hade, the handsome neighborhood Jewish boy she had married when she was barely fifteen, Debbie had had no lack of suitors sending their chauffeured Rolls-Royces and private planes to pick her up and whisk her off to their Long Island mansions and Southampton yachts, but she was bored sick with all the Gatsby boys and their custom silk shirts and Gucci loafers and polite smiles and manicured nails, stuffed full of lobster, money and themselves. They were the kind of eligible men her mother approved of—highly credentialed and eminently marriageable. Lillian Florsheim, beautiful socialite, five-time widow and mother of six, had raised her five daughters to be the proper wives to the men of means who could support them in the style and comfort to which Lillian was determined they remain accustomed. Debbie had grown up in the isolated, pampered milieu of private parochial North Carolina schools and Long Island girls' academies that bred a thirst for adventure and a hunger for the world at large in their captive young boarders. Debbie's premature marriage had been an attempted escape from her mother's restrictive world of mouton coats and polished white shoes, an escape that dead-ended fifteen years of suburban housewifery and two children later in a Mexican divorce. She had left Jerry the North Miami Beach house and custody of their older son, Rick, and moved to Manhattan with eight-year-old Mitchell, a modest cash settlement, and $500 a month alimony.

Money had never been a problem for Debbie, as long as she had the stock dividends from her stepfather's generous investments on her behalf. Louis Florsheim, a well-respected Wall Street underwriter and cousin to the Chicago Florsheim shoe family, had been a close father to Debbie, his little "princess," since he married her mother when Debbie was twelve. But the recession of 1969 and the unexpected failure of AES technology systems left Louis Florsheim, Chairman of the Board of the long established Stanley Heller brokerage firm, under serious financial stress.

Debbie knew something was very wrong when her stepfather returned to kiss her good-bye a second time at the Miami airport that final day, his face all gray and drawn. He died of a heart attack sitting at his Manhattan office desk a few days later, leaving little more than a respected name, fond memories and a portfolio of rapidly declining stocks. Debbie arrived at the Walter B. Cook funeral home on Third Avenue feeling as bereft as a lost child. Her own father had died of cancer when she was very young. She only briefly remembered Uncle Joe, Uncle Frank and Uncle Sal from her mother's three subsequent marriages. Mr. Florsheim had been the strong, kind gentle giant in her life, and now there was no one to replace him. Perhaps in Jake's confident, guttural tones she heard the echo of the powerful, protective patriarch she could no longer lean upon. . . .

"Okay, that's it—I can take a hint. I'll be waitin' for ya at the bar at Hobeau's. If ya don't show up in an hour—I'll never call ya again."

Jake hung up the phone with an air of finality and strode away with both hands shoved in his pockets and his eyes focused determinedly ahead. Debbie gazed at his retreating form from her window above and felt an inexplicable sense of loss.

"So go. Go out with the man. Have one drink with him. What could he do in a public place—molest you?" Annette broke into Debbie's thoughts matter-of-factly.

Annette Pollini, an old friend of Lillian Florsheim's from Naples, Italy, had taken Debbie under her wing upon Debbie's arrival in New York, becoming her full-time confidante and part-time chaperone in matters of the heart.

"Okay, I'll do it. I'll meet him for one drink—but only if you come with me, Annette. I don't want to be alone with him. Promise me you won't leave me alone," Debbie pleaded.

"I promise, I promise, cara mia. Oh, what your mother would say if she knew!" Annette said, rolling her dark eyes with a mischievous twinkle.

"My God, my debutante daughter being seen with that pugilist pig!" Debbie mimicked her mother as they both laughed.

Jake was seated alone at the far end of the bar at the popular Second Avenue restaurant sipping his fourth scotch when Debbie and Annette finally arrived.

"Where was you? I've been sittin' here an hour and a half like a jerk. I figured you wasn't goin' to show up," Jake greeted them gruffly.

"Jake, this is my friend, Annette," Debbie said, ignoring his remark.

"Who's she, your bodyguard?" Jake retorted.

"Yes, you might call it that," Annette laughed. "We've met before—on the phone—Mr. La Motta."

"Oh yeah. You're the broad that's always tellin' me she ain't in. Well, come on, sit down—have a drink," Jake offered grudgingly. "How do ya like that. I knock my brains out for a month tryin' to get a date with ya, and ya finally show up with a chaperone. What's the matter—don't ya trust me?" Jake said to Debbie as she sat down next to him.

"No. Should I?" Debbie replied.

"Naw, I guess maybe ya shouldn't at that," Jake muttered, eyeing her voluptuous body.

They struggled through an awkward three-way conversation over a couple of rounds, Jake desperately dishing out his usual schtick, until Debbie excused herself for the ladies' room. Jake got up after her and followed her up the long narrow flight of stairs. As they reached the top and Debbie started to round the corner of the small alcove, Jake suddenly grabbed her by the arm and pulled her to him, kissing her forcibly on the mouth. Caught off balance in her high heels, Debbie tried to pull away from Jake's grasp. She tripped in the process, breaking her heel, and slid helplessly on her bottom down the full flight of stairs. More embarrassed than hurt, Debbie sat on the bottom step in a daze as Jake ran down to her, broken shoe and heart in hand.

"Debbie, are you okay? I'm sorry. I didn't mean to do that. Jesus Christ, you looked like a bouncing ball!" Jake exclaimed.

He gently handed her the broken shoe. Debbie looked up pitifully at Jake. As their eyes met, they both burst into laughter.

Jake walked Debbie and Annette the few blocks to the apartment and waited outside for Debbie to change her shoes. Watching Jake from her apartment window, pacing up and down the sidewalk like a bull in heat, Debbie had second thoughts. "I don't know, Annette . . . Maybe you should go down and send him away. He's so . . . so different. He's not like any man I've ever known. He's weird," Debbie said, confused by her own emotions.

"I admit, he's quite clumsy, and his manners certainly need polishing, but I don't think he's such a bad person. It's up to you, cara mia. Do as your heart tells you," said Annette.

Debbie gave a final shrug and walked out the door.

They walked in silence in the direction of Jake's apartment. It was a warm June evening, and a gentle breeze whispered through the trees that lined First Avenue, rippling the checkered table cloths of the busy outdoor cafes filled with chattering couples.

"When we get to my place, I'm gonna show ya my scrapbook. It's like a picture history of my fightin' career. Then we'll order up some Chinese food, or somethin'. How's that, Debbie darlin'?" Jake said, breaking the awkward silence.

"Okay," Debbie answered meekly, wondering what to expect.

Debbie stifled a gasp as Jake switched on the overhead light, illuminating his barren studio in the harsh glare of the naked ceiling bulb. She looked around in dismay at the bare walls, the dull wood floor, the unmade bed next to the old chest of drawers with the finger-smudged television on top. Two iron chairs stood stiffly at a small round table in the far corner on which lay a large black dusty scrapbook. It was the only personal object in view.

"You live here?" Debbie asked incredulously.

"Sure—where else? Let's have a drink," Jake replied, going to the tiny kitchen and taking down a bottle of scotch and two plastic tumblers.

"You want ice?" he called to her.

She nodded, standing uncomfortably in the middle of the nearly empty room. Jake busted out the last remaining cubes noisily from the battered ice tray, throwing it carelessly into the dirty sink. He tossed a couple of cubes into one glass and poured both tumblers half-full of scotch, taking his neat.

"Here, drink this. You want more, I got more," Jake said unceremoniously as he handed her the glass.

Debbie stared dubiously at the over-sized tumbler in her hand. She took a timid swallow, choking involuntarily on the harsh straight booze.

"Guess you're not used to takin' it straight, uh. Boy, have I got a lot to teach you. You're just a baby, an innocent babe in the woods. Lucky thing ya ran into me when ya did. The bastards in this town'll eat you up and spit you out. They're not all like me," Jake said. "Come over here. I wanna show ya somethin'."

He grabbed Debbie by the hand and pulled her across the room, sitting her down on the edge of the bed. Then he walked over to the small table and returned carrying the heavy scrapbook—the last battered vestige of his lost days of glory—and placed it on Debbie's lap, sitting down next to her.

"Eh, whatta ya think about this, uh," he said proudly as he opened the book to the faded patchwork of photos and clippings that chronicled the best decade of his life—from 1941 when he went professional in the ring, to 1951 when he lost the coveted championship to his nemesis, Sugar Ray Robinson. All the rest was but a faint flicker of those brief shining moments, dimly reflected in Jake's sunken eyes. Debbie dutifully surveyed the rough terrain of Jake's violent past, properly impressed by the tattered testimony to an aging warrior's forgotten exploits.

"Who's she?" Debbie asked, pointing to a late forties photograph of a beautiful, sultry blonde standing regally beside an adoring young Jake.

"That's my wife, Vickie. That's her there, too, with our three kids. What a beauty. I married her when she was fifteen. We was happy then. . . . Now I call her a barracuda," Jake said, turning the page abruptly. "Aw, now that's what I wanted ya to see—that's the night I won the championship. That's Joe Louis standin' behind me—the great heavyweight champ. What a night that was—the greatest night of my life. Nothin' every compared to that— nothin' . . ." he said, his voice trailing off bitterly.

"That's enough of that," he said, suddenly snapping shut the book and removing it from Debbie's lap. "Hey, I need a refill. How 'bout you?" he asked her, getting up and heading towards the kitchen.

"No thanks. I'm fine," Debbie said, rising and walking over to the dingy sixth-floor window overlooking a narrow section of First Avenue.

Jake emerged from the kitchen with a full tumbler and walked over to the door, switching off the glaring ceiling light.

"What's that for?" Debbie asked in alarm, her soft silhouette traced against the window in the dim light streaming from the street lamps below and the nearly full moon above.

"I hate that light. This is more romantic," Jake said, walking toward her.

"Not much of a view, is it?" Debbie said nervously, looking intently out the window.

"That depends on what you're lookin' at," Jake rasped seductively, his eyes undressing her.

He stood close behind her, put both hands on her shoulders, and turned her slowly toward him.

"You're comin' to bed with me now, darlin', or I'll throw you right out that window," he said evenly, looking her right between the eyes.

Overwhelmed by his powerful presence, Debbie stared at Jake in astonishment, not knowing whether to believe him or not. Jake took her in his arms and kissed her passionately; Debbie responded with an intensity she didn't know she possessed.

They spent the entire summer in bed.

"So you're finally goin' to meet the old lady, uh," Rick said to Jake as they strolled across 57th Street toward the Excelsior apartments, enjoying the brisk Fall weather and the late afternoon sun.

"Sure. I'm marryin' the girl, ain't I?" Jake responded happily.

Rick shook his head in disbelief.

"Ya know, you're a crazy fuck. Ya oughtta know by now, Jake—you're not the marryin' type. You love everybody, but somehow or other they all end up hating you."

"Whatta ya talkin' about. All my wives still love me—even Vickie in a way," Jake responded defensively.

"You're too goddam jealous, ya dumb son of a bitch—and jealous guys don't make good husbands. They don't even make good lovers. Why this dizzy broad wants to marry you, I'll never know."

"That's just 'cause you're jealous. You're jealous of me 'cause I got this beautiful young broad who loves me, and her son, Mitch, he likes me, too. He's just at the age my boys were when I left. I missed all the growin' up years. I'd kinda like to experience that kinda thing in my life. . . ."

"Are ya gonna marry the kid or the broad?"

"Aw, I can't talk to you. Everything's a joke with you. Look I never met her mother before. I think she's some kind of high society dame or somethin'. Don't screw it up for me. I want to make a good impression," Jake said, straightening the tie Debbie had bought for him.

"I always make a good impression. It's you we gotta worry about, pal. Wipe your mouth—you got food or somethin' on it. And why don't ya get rid of the stupid mustache; it makes ya look like some dumb wop who just got off the banana boat."

"What, and be a bald-faced pussy sucker like you? Besides, Debbie likes it. She says it makes me look distinguished," Jake said as they entered the decorous lobby.

"A Mr. La Motta and a Mr. Rosselli to see you, Madame," the stiff doorman announced over the house phone. "You may go up, gentlemen—apartment 20A," he pronounced in nasal tones.

"Now I mean it, Rick—don't pull any of your dumb capers. I gotta watch ya like a hawk, or the first thing I know, you'll be shootin' porno flicks in the old lady's apartment like ya did with Debbie that time I was away. Her place was a mess. I had to bribe the kid Mitch a fortune to keep his mouth shut about it," Jake grumbled on their way up in the elevator.

"I remember that. We shot some great stuff that day. Her pad was perfect for the office seduction scene. Debbie was a pretty good sport about it, too," Rick grinned.

"Yeah, well I won't be a good sport if ya pull anything like that again," Jake growled as they reached the apartment.

Debbie flung open the door, greeting Jake and Rick with unaccustomed restraint, and introduced them self-consciously to her leery mother. Lillian Florsheim acknowledged their presence with polite coolness, offering them a drink they readily accepted. Noticing the expensive decor and antique furnishings in the spacious apartment, Rick immediately turned his attention to the still attractive older woman, charming her with a smooth stream of false compliments and affected solicitations. Jake sat stolidly in one of the rarer antique chairs and devoured Debbie with his eyes. It didn't take Rick long to convince Lillian to show him her closet full of furs and original collection of Harry Winston designed jewelry as he cheerfully cased the apartment and its valuable contents.

Returning to the living room from his grand tour with Lillian,

Rick blurted out, "Ya know, Lillian, if ya wanted to make a fast buck, I could show ya how to do it."

Jake and Debbie exchanged worried glances.

"A fast buck?" Lillian echoed. "I'm afraid I don't understand."

"Well, I imagine you're pretty heavily insured for all this stuff, right?" Rick pressed.

"Of course. My husband insured everything," Lillian replied.

"That's what I figured. So here's what we do—we pull a little caper. You take off to Florida or wherever for the weekend, leavin' me the keys. When you return, you discover you've been robbed—only you really haven't been—I'll stash the furs and jewelry somewhere temporarily, see? I'll even break the lock to make it look good. You report the robbery, collect on the insurance; I give you back the loot, and we split the insurance money—simple as that," Rick concluded triumphantly.

Lillian stared at Rick in astonishment as Jake and Debbie sunk into their seats with chagrin.

"Oh no, I couldn't do that—it wouldn't be right. Besides, I'm a very poor liar—they'd be certain to find out. No, no—it's out of the question," Lillian said firmly, walking away from Rick.

"It was just a suggestion. It was worth a shot," Rick shrugged as Jake and Debbie glared hotly at him.

"Don't you have to go now, Rick?" Debbie hinted, standing up abruptly.

"Yeah, yeah. Let's get outta here," Jake muttered, rising heavily from his seat.

As Jake stood up, he leaned into the delicate arm of the expensive antique chair, breaking it with a loud crack. Debbie stared in horror, first at Jake, then at her purse-lipped mother, who glared at Debbie in silent anger.

"Aw gee, sorry about that. Guess these chairs are kinda flimsy, uh," Jake mumbled.

"Come on, ya clumsy jerk. Let's get outta here before ya destroy the joint," Rick cracked, pushing Jake toward the door.

"Hey Debbie, ya comin' or not," Jake said on his way out.

"No, not now. I'll see you later, okay?" Debbie replied in a strained voice from across the room.

"Okay, have it your way," Jake shrugged. "Nice meetin' ya, Lillian," he called as Rick ushered him out the door.

"Rick, ya know I hardly ever curse. I only curse when I get mad—and you got me mad now. How the fuck do you have the goddam nerve to say what you did to Debbie's mother?" Jake yelled at Rick as they reached the lobby. "Are you crazy or what?"

"I was only lookin' out for your ass," Rick replied coolly. "Look, if the lady had gone for the caper, then we'd know she was busted, but now we know she doesn't need the money—capice, stupid?"

"Yeah, but I could've found out some other way. God knows what the woman thinks of me now . . ." Jake lamented.

"It had nothin' to do with you—it was my idea. You were too busy makin' ga-ga eyes at her daughter."

"Jesus, Debbie's gonna be mad. . . . You're supposed to be my friend, and ya make me look like a fuckin' low life!"

"Then take care of your own ass! I'm tired of playin' wet nurse for you all the time!" Rick shouted angrily. "And ya know what—you can't even sit in a fuckin' chair without bustin' it into pieces, ya dumb son of a bitch!"

"Aw, who the hell cares. Debbie and me is gettin' married, no matter who likes it or not!" Jake insisted as they headed down the street.

In spite of widespread skepticism and her mother's strong disapproval, Debbie and Jake were married in a suite at the Commodore Hotel next to Grand Central Station just before Christmas. Earl Wilson's column in the *Daily News* read: "Florsheim's daughter marries Jake La Motta. . . . It was a small private affair, all the de's dem's and do's guys were there . . ."

The same judge who had recently married Joey and Margaritte performed the simple ceremony before a motley gathering dominated by Jake's family and Rick's show business friends. Debbie's mother and older sister, Arlene, looked on with young Mitchell in subdued silence as Debbie, looking all of sixteen in her pink empire gown, a simple wreath of pink flowers in her long blond hair, stood shyly beside a beaming, brown-suited Jake, flanked by her maid of honor friend and Jake's perennial best man Rick, and murmured the fateful "I do." Jake placed the ring he had again promoted from his buddy Abe on Debbie's trembling finger, pronouncing fervently, "This'll never end, Debbie darlin'. This'll never end. . . ."

Fifteen

Debbie hung up the phone and returned to the lukewarm cup of coffee she left on the small kitchen table where Arlene sat contemplating her younger sister, a frown of concentration knitting her intelligent brow.

"Was that him again? Honestly, Debbie, I don't know how you stand it. The man never leaves you alone— Debbie darlin', Debbie darlin' all day long. It's enough to drive you crazy!" she said crossly, stubbing out her cigarette and lighting another. "I know all men are basically children, but Jake is a screaming infant when it comes to you. He can't let you out of his sight for a minute. Is he that insecure, or is it that he doesn't trust you? Sicilian men are notoriously jealous, you know," she said with a sidelong glance.

"No, it's nothing like that. He just wants to share things with me," Debbie replied between sips of coffee. "He was calling from Toots Shor's. They just gave him a big liquor order for this month, and he's all excited. Standard Foods had lost the account, and he just revived it for them. He's worked so hard at this job, Arlene. He's like a little boy on his first paper route—up early every morning and making his rounds all day—and he's doing very well at it. He got fifty new accounts in his first month. You know, Charlie Norkis—that ex-heavyweight, or middleweight, or something who got him the job—said a liquor salesman can make a lot of money with the right accounts. We're both very excited about it."

"Well, I just hope it lasts, for your sake. But I'd keep my eye on him, if I were you. He's got the perfect setup for cheating. He can

171

reach you, but you can't reach him. Men are only nice to their wives when they feel guilty," Arlene said bitterly.

"Oh Arlene, you're just down on all men because of Steve," Debbie said, knowing her sister was going through a bitter divorce after eighteen years of marriage. "Jake and I are very happy—and we're going to stay that way," she said confidently, glancing at her watch. "Oh shit, is it that late already? I've got to run out for a few things for dinner. You want to stay? Jake is making eggplant parmesan tonight."

"No thanks, I wouldn't dream of intruding on your little love nest," Arlene declined, getting up and slipping on her designer coat. "I told Mother I'd drop by. I'll tell her how deliriously happy you are, but she won't believe me. She gave you two weeks after the wedding before you came running home in terror. Who ever dreamed a year later you'd still be the bubbling bride? Don't mind me, darling. I'm just a jealous bitch. Stay happy, baby. I'll call you," she said and headed out the door.

Debbie smiled thoughtfully after her sister, idly petting Kisha's thick, silky coat. The handsome yearling husky had been Jake's present to Mitch when they first moved into the odd-shaped penthouse apartment on the twentieth floor of the Yorkshire House. Jake had cared devotedly for the puppy himself from the beginning, walking him every morning and patiently teaching him tricks. He had a way with dogs and kids, showing a gentle tolerance he rarely extended to adults. Mitch had taken easily to "Uncle Jake," much to Debbie's relief, and a growing fondness and respect had developed between the man and the ten-year-old boy. Jake took an active interest in Mitch's schoolboy scrapes, becoming his personal boxing instructor and staunch protector.

Debbie smiled to herself, recalling the time Jake had gone running out into the snow in his boxer shorts after a couple of older kids who had chased Mitch home for throwing snowballs. She surveyed the comfortable room around her approvingly. Debbie and Jake had come to love the unconventional sprawling apartment with its wrap-around terrace and exhilarating view of the East River. When they had learned that the apartment on the top floor of Jake's building was available, they had jumped at the chance to take it. Debbie converted one of the small extra rooms into a bedroom for Mitch, and the new family settled happily into their feathered nest, high on the promise of auspicious beginnings.

Jake's liquor salesman job had come just in time, staving off the old financial pressure that always seemed to loom on his uncertain horizon. If there was one thing that Jake knew from hard experience, it was bars and booze, and here was an opportunity to profit with the best of them. His route included some of the most prestigious saloons in Manhattan, from the "21 Club" to Sardi's and Backstage where the theatre and sports elite generally hung out. With his guaranteed salary plus commission, his borrowing days would soon be over.

Jake tackled the job with a renewed self-esteem that lent him an enthusiasm for life he hadn't felt in a very long time. Each Sunday he would invite a crew of family, friends and found strangers up to the apartment for a full course Italian feast featuring nine or ten of his special dishes. He would start cooking early in the morning, happily content in his resurrected role of family head and chief chef. Jake had remained as affectionate and devoted to Debbie as the day they were married, and if at times his manners were lacking, or on occasion he would embarrass her with a jealous outburst in public, Debbie would shrug it off as being just Jake's way. Content in the knowledge that she was loved and protected, Debbie wrapped herself in the cozy cocoon of their intimate penthouse in the sky.

"Come on, Kisha boy, let's go shopping," Debbie called to the obedient dog as she rose expectantly in preparation for the imminent arrival home of the two "men" in her life. Entering the empty elevator, Debbie and Kisha descended gaily to the madding crowd in the streets below.

"Aw, come on, Charlie, ya didn't order enough this month. I'll make ya on offer ya can't refuse—and give us two more brandies, me and my wife," Jake ordered loudly to the head bartender at the "21 Club".

"All right Champ, but hold it down, okay? You're gettin' too loud. You've had three and this makes four—I'm goin' to have to cut you off, pal," Charlie said as he free poured two more shots into the large brandy snifters set before Jake and Debbie at the far end of the long, dark polished wood bar.

"Hey, ya lookin' for a beatin', or what!" Jake said with a false grin as Debbie kicked him warningly beneath the bar.

Hey, what's that for? He knows I'm only kiddin'," Jake retorted, giving Debbie an annoyed look.

Debbie followed Jake in angry silence out of the dimly lit club into the glaring afternoon sunlight.

"Jake, what the hell is wrong with you. You can't talk to those people that way. You sound like some cheap hoodlum from Al Capone's day. You're going to blow the whole goddam thing!" Debbie yelled at Jake as they reached the sidewalk.

"Whatta ya talkin' about, ya dumb broad. They know I'm only foolin' around. Whatta ya think, they take me seriously?" Jake answered back.

"I've been talkin' to Charlie Norkis, Jake, and he says they do take you seriously. Look at yourself, Jake—how do they know you don't mean it? And another thing, you've drinking too much. You know how you get when you're had too much to drink. What the hell are you trying to do?" Debbie cried.

"Occupational hazards," Jake mumbled under his breath. "And what does Charlie know anyway, He's punch drunk. They're lyin', Debbie, when they tell you these things. Believe me, they're lyin'! I'm always the underdog. I don't know why. I'm only tryin' to do my job. They're usin' me. Everybody uses me. They all use me!" Jake protested, strutting angrily ahead of her.

Debbie shook her head sadly as she watched Jake sway his way down the street. She might have known the past two years were too good to last.

"Where do we go from here?" she sighed to herself.

Jake was fired two months later on a cold wet day in early November. Thanksgiving dinner, usually an occasion of much family feasting and revelry at Jake and Debbie's penthouse, was a less than festive affair. Debbie stared at Jake across the table in silent resentment, deepening his already keen sense of guilt and failure. Jake sought solace in the familiar brandy bottle, a remedy that only increased his stubborn sullenness and the growing tension between them. There wasn't a whole lot to be thankful for.

As Jake sank deeper by the day into his private depression, his relationship with Mitch began to deteriorate, and Debbie found herself caught more and more in a tug of war between them for her undivided attention. Mitch retreated into his schoolboy world of growing adolescence, and Debbie felt herself losing control of her increasingly rebellious son. Jake's unemployment checks barely covered the rent, leaving little for such luxuries as Mitch's private school tuition. The child support payments were needed to supplement their daily living expenses.

When Christmas came and went with little improvement in sight, Debbie reluctantly agreed to allow Mitch to return to his father and older brother in Miami. Kisha, left tied on the terrace alone and neglected, began to claw and bite at the terrace floor. He became increasingly uncontrollable, and finally had to be given away.

Debbie took a temporary receptionist job at a large law firm while Jake occupied his empty days making the rounds of his old barroom haunts. It seemed like old times. . . . Debbie's wounded pride prevented her from confiding any of her difficulties to her mother or sister. She simply couldn't face the litany of "I told you so's."

"If we can survive this winter, when Spring comes, it might be better," she kept telling herself.

"Hey, come on, you guys. Are ya goin' to by us a drink, or not?" Jake shouted across to the next table where a group of P.J. Clark's regular customers sat with their evening cocktails. Jake grabbed the passing waiter by the arm.

"Give me and my wife another round. It's on that table," he ordered gruffly, pointing to the party of nameless faces in three-piece suits.

The waiter gave Jake and Debbie a dubious look, collected their empty glasses, and moved quickly on. They had become an all too familiar and unwelcome sight at P.J.'s these past months. Jake's obnoxious habit of passing his tab onto the nearest table was becoming an embarrassment for the management and a growing annoyance to the paying customers. Debbie had long since become immune to the disdainful looks and snide remarks. Pride was a luxury she could no longer afford. Jake's unemployment insurance had run out months ago, and her job had not lasted long enough to qualify her for benefits. They hadn't paid April or May's rent, and now June's was overdue. They had become a lonely pair of aimless outcasts, reduced to begging and borrowing from what few friends they had left. Even Rick, fed up with the endless handouts, had shunned them. Now they couldn't even get a five-dollar loan.

The waiter returned with the promoted drinks. Jake took a large swig of the straight bar scotch and looked around at the packed room for a familiar face among the after-work singles crowd of advertising and TV execs, Seventh Avenue manufacturers, secretaries, models, and high class hookers on the make. It was too early for most of the wiseguys and show bizzers that were usually good for a couple of laughs and a round or two. He was about to rouse Debbie from her despondent stupor and stagger around the corner to Johnny Squire's where the old gang of ex pugs and sports celebrities hung out, when he spotted Charlie Buttons coming towards their table. Short, dark and wiry with a hard-bitten face that betrayed his sinister occupation, Charlie, an old colleague of Rick's, was known, among other things, for his well-tailored suits and fancy dress buttons.

"Hey, goomba, how are ya," Charlie said, putting his hand on Jake's shoulder. "Did you guys ever find a guy to play you, Jake—in the movie, I mean."

"We're still lookin'," Jake mumbled into his glass.

"Well, take it for what it's worth, but I just heard this guy— what' his name—De Niro, you know, the guy that just now won the supportin' award for Godfather II—he's in town now. He's stayin' over at the Sherry Netherland. Why don't ya give it a shot? Call him. Whatta ya got to lose—nothin', right? So give it a shot," Charlie urged.

"Yeah, Jake, why don't we give him a call. What can he say—no, right?" Debbie chimed in, coming suddenly alive.

Jake shrugged his shoulders noncommittally as Debbie rummaged through her over-sized purse for a stray coin.

"Jake, ya got a dime?" she asked as Jake stared blankly back at her.

"For Chrissakes—here—here's a dime—here's two of 'em," Charlie said impatiently, tossing the coins on the table. "Geez— ain't the two of you got a dime between ya?"

Debbie picked up the dimes and walked over to the phone booth, closing the folding doors behind her. She emerged a few minutes later and returned to the table.

"The line was busy, so I left a message at the desk," she explained to Jake.

"Aw, come on, let's get outta here. He'll never call back—you're dreamin'," Jake said as he stood up abruptly, ready to leave.

"No, Jake, let's wait a few minutes. Wait'll I finish my drink," Debbie urged.

Jake sat back down moodily. Ten minutes later the waiter came up to their table.

"There's a phone call for you, Mr. La Motta. You can take it at the end of the bar," he said to Jake.

"Yes . . . yes, this is Jake La Motta," he said into the phone. "Would you be interested in doing my story—*Raging Bull*?" he asked.

"Yes, I would. I'm very interested in playing the fighter," Robert De Niro answered.

As he ran excitedly back to the table to get Debbie, Jake said to himself, "This guy's gonna save our lives. . . ."

Sixteen

"Holy shit, baby, we made it! This is really gonna be big time. I'm gonna buy ya a fur coat—maybe two—and no more cryin' about the rent. I'm gonna pay it up six months in advance. . . . We're loaded, Debbie darlin', and this is just the beginnin'. This could mean millions—millions! Boy, are they all gonna be jealous, all those creeps that wouldn't even lend us five bucks. . . ."

Jake strutted down 57th Street with his arm slung around Debbie and an advance check from film producers Chartoff-Winkler for $78,000 shoved in his pocket.

"Ya know what it means havin' all this money again? It's like bein' champ all over again. Ya see, you come into my life and look what happens. I'm gonna make it all up to ya. You're gonna be the happiest girl in the world. . . ." Jake said, giving Debbie a hard squeeze.

"Jake, let's go somewhere—get away from New York for a while. Why don't we go to Miami and surprise Mitch and Lisa?" Debbie asked, her face flushed with excitement. "We haven't seen the kids in months."

"Yeah, why not? We don't pack a goddam thing. We'll buy all new stuff. We both need all new stuff anyway," Jake said, lighting up a cigarette. "To hell with this, too," he said, suddenly tossing the pack of cigarettes into the street, "I'm gonna get myself some good expensive cigars. . . ."

It had been two long frustrating years of waiting since their first meeting with Robert De Niro in Rick's office the day after that fortuitous phone call in P.J. Clark's. On the strength of De Niro's interest in playing Jake in a film version of *Raging Bull*, Rick had quickly secured a $25,000 advance from producer Dino De Laurentiis. De Niro, busy completing his current film *Taxi Driver*, rejected the De Laurentiis option, electing his own team of producers Chartoff-Winkler and director Martin Scorsese. The advance was returned to De Laurentiis and the project awaited De Niro's availability through three more films. When De Niro called from Bangkok during the filming of *The Dear Hunter* to apologize for yet another delay, Debbie had cried in exasperation, "Please Bobby, we need the money!" De Niro finally agreed to a production date for *Raging Bull*, and the advance money was released just in time for Christmas of 1977, not a day too soon for Jake and Debbie. It had not been an easy vigil. Their half of the first advance hadn't gone far before it had to be returned, and they had continued to borrow and promote heavily on the promise of better days soon to come. Maybe now it would all be worth it.

From that first hot summer day that De Niro came up to their penthouse apartment to interview Jake, things began to get out of hand. Debbie had felt a twinge of excitement mixed with a vague anxiety as she stood on their narrow terrace and watched the wiry, long-haired, blue-jeaned actor running across Gracie Mansion Park, his small tape recorder mounted on his belt. It was supposed to have been a quiet meeting just between the three of them, with nobody else around. Jake hadn't even told Rick about De Niro's coming over, but Debbie had sensed that somehow he would find out and show up to dominate the scene.

Rick had come booming back into their lives since De Niro's interest in the movie, and Debbie wasn't so sure she liked his constant overbearing presence and Svengali-like influence on Jake. It had been different before when there was nothing much to win or lose and she and Jake had been left alone to play their own luckless hand. Now the money was in the pot, and the ante was going up, and everybody wanted to be in the game. Not ten minutes after De Niro had arrived, there was a loud knock on the door, and Rick strode in wearing his Cheshire Cat's grin and polyester plaid sport coat, his over-sized hand extended ingratiatingly to the silent De Niro. Tension filled the room as the spotlight shifted from its natural focus to ringmaster Rick, leaving Jake to sweep up the side ring with a resigned Emmett Kelly frown. Debbie sat on the sidelines and watched the three-ring circus with mounting concern and an ominous sense of impending disaster.

"Hey Jake, tell Bobby about that time you raped that broad in the back seat of the car. What a dramatic scene," Rick leered. "Ya gotta hear this, Bobby—we put it in the book, but we cleaned it up a little for the publisher. It'd be great stuff for the movie."

Debbie stared wide-eyed at Jake.

"Jake, tell Bobby that's not true. You told me all those scenes in the book were made up by you and Rick. You never raped anybody in your life. Tell him, Jake, for heaven's sake tell him!" Debbie protested in alarm.

Jake looked exasperated from Debbie to Rick to the confused De Niro and sank back in his seat with a heavy sigh. "I don't remember," he mumbled, gazing stubbornly into the floor, "but if it's good for the movie, use it," he shrugged.

Debbie stood up and glared at Jake, then she stomped out of the room, slamming the bedroom door resoundingly behind her. What the hell was wrong with Jake? Didn't he care about the truth—or had he been lying to her all this time? she thought as she threw herself onto the bed, biting back the tears that came so suddenly those first weeks after her miscarriage. Jake hadn't wanted the baby in the first place, she knew. It wasn't exactly the best timing for added responsibility in their lives, and Jake's possessiveness had shadowed even Mitchell's presence with a pervasive jealousy. Still she couldn't help the depressing sense of loss and regret that often overwhelmed her without the slightest warning.

In the old days, when the movie was just wishful thinking, Jake would have been as tender and solicitious toward her as a mother hen, but now his attentions were increasingly distracted from his private life to his public image, and Debbie had felt more and more left out of the decisions that affected both their lives. The closer the film came to reality, the further she felt from Jake.

While De Niro was becoming the fighter, faithfully rendering Jake's mannerisms, gestures, habits and voice, Jake was becoming the star, playing the role of celebrity to the hilt. If she had a choice, she preferred the humble had-been champ to the strutting, cigar-brandishing big shot that Rick was leading around like a dancing bear. In a rare moment of privacy, when they weren't surrounded by the perpetual entourage of family and friends who had shunned them for years and who now dropped in at all hours hoping to catch a glimpse of De Niro, Debbie had looked across the dining room table at Jake and told him with a firmness that surprised even her that she was leaving him if things continued the way they were. She could no longer ignore the persistent inner voice that warned her of disaster yet to come.

Jake had stared at her in shock, hearing her for perhaps the first time in months, then he had suddenly burst into sobs, crying with an intensity and abandonment she had never seen before. Overwhelmed by his unprecedented display of emotion, Debbie had gone to Jake and cradled her sobbing husband in her arms, reassuring him that she would stay no matter what. She had immersed herself into the growing show business milieu around them with renewed conviction, determined to hang on through the bumpy roller coaster ride that had just begun to take over their lives. . . .

Debbie looked up petulantly at Jake from the bed of their Newport Hotel room in Miami Beach where she was stretched out comfortably in her jeans, her unpainted lips pouting.

"Jake, do we have to go? I'm so tired from shopping all day. I don't feel like getting all dressed up. Why can't she just come over to the hotel and have dinner with us here? What's the big deal, anyway? I thought you said she was a barracuda and you didn't want me to have anything to do with her. Now we have to go all the way to Fort Lauderdale to meet her at some fancy restaurant. I need to wash my hair and I feel lousy. Besides, we haven't even see the kids yet. I thought we could have Mitch and Lisa over tonight. Can't you call her and tell her we'll meet her tomorrow or something. Please, honey?" Debbie entreated.

Jake frowned back at her as he fastened the belt to his new trousers and reached for one of the several designer polo shirts they had purchased on their afternoon shopping spree. "Naw, she's expectin' us. Ya don't have to dress up—ya look fine. Just go as ya are—you're not goin' to a beauty contest. Vickie said it was just a neighborhood joint. She's not dressin' up. Whatta ya worried about anyway—ya got fifteen years on her—she's an old lady now. Get your ass up and let's go. We're gonna be late," Jake said, dousing himself generously with a new bottle of cologne.

Debbie gave her long blond mane a quick toss in the mirror as she followed Jake out the door. To hell with getting made up, she thought. Who did she have to impress anyway? She wouldn't even be going, but she was curious to meet Vickie in spite of herself. Ever since Vickie had suddenly started calling her in New York after the miscarriage, inviting her to recoup by the pool at Vickie's Miami home, Debbie had wondered what the woman behind the cool, sultry, seductive voice was really like. Jake had frowned and shaken his head negatively when he arrived home that one afternoon and discovered her on the phone with Vickie. There was something strange about the way Jake hadn't wanted her to become friendly with Vickie, and something even stranger about the way Vickie had seemed to want to befriend her, repeatedly urging her to come down alone to Miami. Why would this woman from Jake's stormy past, whom Jake rarely mentioned except with bitter undertones of regret, suddenly come into their lives now, just when everything was going so well? Then, too, Vickie had recently divorced her second husband, Tony Foster, and re-taken her first married name of La Motta—some twenty years after she divorced Jake! Curiouser and curiouser, thought Debbie as she rode beside Jake in the hotel elevator and tried to ignore the fluttering butterflies in her stomach.

Debbie gave Jake a dirty look, feeling suddenly naked in her worn jeans and simple white blouse, as the hotel limo pulled up the long circular drive to the elegant *Pier 66* restaurant off Fort Lauderdale's main drag.

"Jake, this is a little neighborhood joint? Why didn't you tell me where we were going? I look ridiculous," Debbie cried, looking forlornly down at her scuffed sneakers.

"Aw, who cares? You're with me, aren't ya?" Jake said carelessly as he tossed the limo driver a $100 bill. "Here pal, keep the change. And don't bother waitin'. We got a ride back."

Debbie followed Jake meekly out onto the wide covered veranda entrance to the sprawling, glitzy restaurant where a stunning blonde posed before a group of photographers, surrounded by an entourage of family members. Jake walked directly over to the intimate grouping and slipped his arm possessively around his well-preserved ex-wife, stepping naturally into the scene to complete the family portrait. Debbie stood awkwardly alone on the sidelines and stared open-mouthed at the glamorous, serenely smiling Vickie. She was fashion plate perfection, decked out in the latest velvet knickers over high leather boots, a plunging pink sweater with short capped sleeves that revealed her deep golden tan and firm, voluptuous curves cunningly eclipsed by a long open suede coat. Her golden curls were piled carefully above her professionally made-up face to complete the grand illusion of the Hollywood femme fatale. Vickie gazed coolly across the veranda at Debbie, their eyes meeting in a tense moment of mutual recognition. It was hate at first sight.

Debbie looked nervously away as Vickie focused her brilliantly flashing smile on the suddenly beaming Jake, who seemed instantly transported into a past world far beyond Debbie's reach. As the evening progressed, with Vickie presiding over the carefully arranged table, strategically seated between Jake and their three grown children, the beckoning web of the past combined with the freely poured spirits to cast a spell of intoxication over Jake. He couldn't take his eyes off Vickie.

While Jake posed endlessly with Vickie and their children before the pre-arranged newspaper photographers anxious to capture the resurrected Raging Bull with his suddenly reinstated photogenic wife and family, Debbie grew increasingly jealous. Her hurt and anger smoldered into an outraged sense of betrayal as she watched her husband publicly claim a woman he was supposed to hate as his beloved wife while silently denying her very existence. She could barely maintain her composure as Jake repeatedly ignored her demands to leave, dismissing her injured feelings with a careless wave of his hand. At last they all filed out of the closing restaurant and piled into Vickie's waiting Cadillac. Jake jumped into the front seat next to Vickie as Debbie was shoved into the back like a recalcitrant child. The pent up emotions finally burst forth from Debbie's tightly compressed lips. In the glare of the neon street lights, she could see for the first time the meticulously hidden lines and thick cake of heavy make-up over Vickie's picture-perfect lifted face.

"What's going on, Jake? Why are you sitting up in the front seat with Grandma. Don't you want to be back here with us kiddies?" Debbie dug.

"Hey, who you callin' grandma? Show some respect, or I'll give ya a beatin'," Jake slurred in defense of Vickie.

"Ignore her, Jake. She's just a stupid little jerk. What the hell would she know about anything," Vickie shot back.

"At least I know a phony bitch when I see one!" Debbie retorted.

"That's enough out of you. I mean it, keep your mouth shut," Jake growled, turning and glaring back at Debbie.

By the time they reached the Newport Hotel, they had all lapsed into a tense silence. Debbie squeezed out of the back seat as Jake leaned over and kissed Vickie on her coyly proffered cheek. The car sped off and Jake and Debbie proceeded in stiff silence up to their room. More hurt than angry, Debbie silently implored Jake across the room, tears swimming in her eyes. Jake, continuing to ignore her in stony silence, climbed into the far bed, pulled the covers over his head, and began snoring loudly. Debbie slipped miserably alone into the remaining bed and stared at Jake's back. In the four years they had been married, Jake had never allowed an argument to separate them through the night. He had always made up with her before going to sleep. This Vickie was more powerful then she had ever imagined, Debbie thought to herself as she lay awake and shuddered in the darkened room.

Debbie rose early the next morning after her sleepless night and crept out of the room without awakening the still snoring Jake. She walked aimlessly down the wide commercial boulevard along Collins Avenue toward the glittering row of North Miami Beach hotels and shopping malls. She wandered through the posh boutiques, lost in a stupor of shock and confusion over Jake's overnight transformation from faithful husband to hostile stranger. She felt herself growing smaller and smaller by the minute, utterly powerless to alter or control the sudden turn of events that seemed to be propelling her headlong down a bottomless rabbit hole.

Several hours passed before she returned to the hotel, her travelers checks unspent, and opened the door to their room, her heavily rehearsed "how dare you" speech to Jake on the tip of her tongue. The room was empty. Debbie's heart sank in renewed panic as she wondered where Jake might have gone. There was no note in sight. She called down to the lobby, but he had left no message for her. Maybe he had gone down to the hotel bar for a drink and would call her shortly to join him, she thought. Two more hours passed as she changed the polish on her nails from "pink innocence" to "raging red," painted her toe nails to match, flipped idly through some outdated magazines, and tried not to stare at the stubbornly silent phone. A shrill ring shattered the silence and Debbie jumped involuntarily, spilling the bottle of crimson polish onto the maroon carpeting as she made a dive for the receiver.

"Yes. Jake, is this you?" she said breathlessly into the phone.

"No, this is me, Rick. Debbie? Ya sound like ya just saw a ghost or somethin'. Are you okay, kid?"

"Oh, Rick, it's you. I thought you were Jake. How did you know where to find us? Where are you, anyway?"

"I'm here in Miami. Where the hell did you think I was? Where's Jake?"

"How the hell should I know. I don't know anything any more. When I got back to the room, he was gone—and that was hours ago."

"Did you try Vickie's?"

"Vickie's? No . . . What makes you think he'd be there?"

"Hey, come on, kid—wise up. Everytime he sees that broad he goes berserk. This has been a long time thing with him."

"I thought you were my friend, Rick. What the hell are you trying to tell me?"

"I think you're a fool, Debbie. I hate to say it, but I think you're a fool. Jake can't love anybody but Vickie."

"He's my husband."

"So what? You didn't know what you were getting yourself into."

"Rick, are you crazy, too? What are you trying to do to my mind? I thought I married a man I loved and he loved me. All this has become total insanity. Tell me what to do, Rick. I don't know what to do.

"Jake's hard on for Vickie will always be there. Remember what I'm telling you. If you can put up with his shit, then put up with it. If not, get on the next plane back to New York and say to yourself, I made a big mistake. He's a bastard, and you know it. Leave the son of a bitch—forget you ever knew him. Give it up, kid—go home."

"I thought I knew who I was and where I came from, but Jake's making me feel like I'm as much trash as this Vickie is. I'm not a whore, Rick, believe me, I'm not a whore. Maybe that's what he's been used to all his life, but I'm not that kind of person. I come from a pretty good family and I'm proud of it. I'll always be proud of it. Why is he doing this to me?"

"Look, kid, all I can tell ya is he's probably at Vickie's with everybody for Christmas Eve dinner. If you don't believe me, call him there."

"Yeah, I'll try that. Thanks . . . and Rick, Merry Christmas, uh?"

Debbie hung up the phone, choking back the sobs that suddenly filled her throat. She searched blindly through her bag for her address book and dialed Vickie's number, wiping the tears from her cheeks with the back of her trembling hand.

"Yes," came the cool, hard voice over the phone.

"Vickie, this is Debbie. Is Jake there?"

"Why, yes, as a matter of fact he is."

"Well, can I speak to him?"

"I'm afraid he can't come to the phone just now. He's drunk and he's sleeping it off on the couch."

"You just tell him I'm leaving. I'm on my way to the airport, and if he wants me, he can meet me there!"

"I'll give him the message, if he wakes up," Vickie replied.

Debbie slammed down the phone, beside herself with anger and frustration. Rick was right—he is an animal—a no good selfish bastard, she told herself. How could he do this to her? What had she done to deserve this? It wasn't fair, it just wasn't any fair at all, she sobbed inwardly. Refusing to give in to her tears, Debbie took down her suitcase and began packing her belongings with grim determination. Tossing the room key on the bed, she picked up her bags and slammed out the door without looking back. She rode down the elevator, marched through the lobby, and hopped into a waiting cab in front of the hotel. Arriving at Miami's International airport, Debbie booked herself on the next flight to New York, then she walked over to the large bank of pay phones and dialed Vickie's number.

"Yeah," a gruff male voice answered the phone.

"Let me speak to Jake, please," Debbie said testily, recognizing Jake's son Joey's voice from the other evening.

"Jake? Just a minute, I'll see if he's here," Joey replied brusquely.

Debbie tapped her foot nervously as she waited on the phone and listened to the cacophony of voices and laughter in the background.

"Hello? Who's this? Who's calling?" a strange female voice came on the line.

"This is Debbie La Motta. I want to speak to Jake. Where is he?" Debbie said, exasperated.

"Oh . . . Hold on—I'll see if I can find him," the stranger said, putting down the phone.

Debbie held her breath as she hung on the line, resisting the impulse to hang up. What the hell was this, Grand Central Station? Where was Jake? she screamed to herself.

"Hello? Jake isn't here. I think he went out with Rick to get some more beer or something," Vickie's voice came over the phone.

Rick? He was there, too? What was going on? Were they all in some kind of conspiracy against her? Debbie thought wildly. "Look, Vickie, I don't know what the hell you're up to. Just tell Jake I'm at the airport and he'd better call me if he ever wants to see me again. I'll be at this number for another hour, then I'm flying back to New York."

Debbie repeated the number of the pay phone to Vickie and hung up the receiver for the final time. That's the last call I'm making. If he doesn't care enough to return a phone call, then what the hell am I doing? she asked herself. The past 24 hours had been one endless nightmare. Was she ever going to wake up?

Debbie paced back and forth before the phone, desperately willing it to ring, as two more flights went by. The last flight to New York was announced; the phone remained silent. Debbie heaved a heavy sigh and called her surprised sister, Arlene, in New York, asking her to meet her at La Guardia airport on the late night flight from Miami. Then she boarded the near-empty plane and sat numbly alone in a vacant window seat, the tears rolling down her face as she gazed past her unhappy reflection into the thick black night.

"I wouldn't leave the bastard a pot to piss in, if I were you, Debbie. After what he's done to you, he's lucky you don't sue him for every dime he ever makes," Arlene said as she helped Debbie pack the heirloom silver and china into cardboard boxes. "I still can't believe he just left you there at the airport like a total stranger while he cavorted with that fuckin' Vickie—and on Christmas Eve, too! The son of a bitch ought to be shot!"

Debbie continued packing in resigned silence, too tired and heartsick to answer her indignant sister. It was a hell of a way to spend Christmas morning, she thought wryly—dismantling her home and packing her life neatly away into cardboard boxes. She looked around the penthouse apartment that had once so delighted her, taking mental inventory of her personal valuables. She would leave him most of the furniture and his clothes, of course. The antique pieces and all the art she had brought from her old apartment she would store at Arlene's. She stared at the heavy old oak desk with the secret compartment where she and Jake had hidden the remaining $40,000 advance check when they had taken off for Miami so carefree just three days before. It seemed like a million years ago. Let Vickie make it up to him, she thought, smiling mischievously to herself.

"That should do it for now, Arlene. I'll pick up the rest of the things later. Let's get out of here—this place gives me the creeps," Debbie said, grabbing her overstuffed Gucci bag and heading out the door.

"I don't see any problem in cashing your husband's check, Mrs. La Motta. But I'm afraid you'll have to wait while we courier the money from our downtown branch. We aren't normally equipped to handle cash transactions of this size, you understand," the well-composed young bank officer said as he studied the doubly endorsed check for $40,000 that Debbie had handed him.

"Oh, I don't mind waiting. Is it all right if I just sit here at your desk?" Debbie replied, smiling sweetly.

"That would be perfectly all right. Now, if you'll excuse me for a moment, I'll make the necessary arrangements," the dark-suited bank executive smiled back, leaving Debbie to herself to ponder her next move.

An hour and a half later, Debbie calmly made her way out of the bank, her large Gucci bag bulging at the seams with $40,000 in crisp 100-dollar bills. It had taken half an hour just to count out the

money. Wow, I never knew how heavy $40,000 could be! Debbie
said to herself as she hailed a cab and headed directly for the airport. Jake, wherever you are—go fuck yourself! she thought as she
leaned back in the seat and closed her eyes, spent and exhausted
by her emotions.

"That dirty little bitch! You mean she had the balls to forge your
signature and take off with the whole bit? I gotta hand it to her—
she's got more guts than I ever gave her credit for. But 40,000
bucks—that's serious money, pal! I told ya never trust any broad.
You think when they say 'I do' they mean it? Put the little cunt in
jail—teach her a lesson she'll never forget!" Rick fumed at Jake as
he stomped around the disarrayed penthouse apartment slamming
open drawers and cabinets while Jake sat slumped on the couch
staring morosely at his torn and tattered scrap book thrown carelessly on the floor.

"But why? Why'd she do such a crazy thing? Look what she did
here. She tore all of Vickie's pictures out of my book. She's gotta be
nuts. What I do—what I do wrong?" Jake repeated in sad confusion.

"What wrong? When a broad gets a hair up her ass, ya never
know what she's gonna pull. 'Hell hath no wrath . . .' and all the
that crap," Rick said sourly. "Look at this—she even took the
fuckin' silverware. Have her arrested and put her ass in jail. That's
all—end of story."

"She'll be back, I know she'll be back. I know Debbie, and when
she cools off, she'll get scared and come runnin' back home. Ya
gotta understand—Debbie's like a child in a woman's body. Ya
gotta treat her like a little kid. When I find out where she is, I'll get
her back fast enough. She knows better than to pull this crap with
me," Jake muttered darkly.

"Go ahead, be a sucker—take her back. Why you want this pain
in the ass back I'll never know, but that's your headache. It's the
other barracuda you gotta worry about, pal. She's trouble lookin'
for a place to land. Vickie made chopped meat out of your precious
Debbie. I know what she's up to—'Mrs. Raging Bull.' And I can
tell ya somethin' else—she's not gonna make chopped meat out of
me. I won't put up with her crap—or yours either," Rick said
hotly.

"Whatta ya talkin' about?" Jake growled back.

"I'll tell ya what I'm talkin' about. I busted my ass puttin' up with your shit all these years. I got the goddam book published. I set up the movie deal—or did you forget? And no stupid broad's gonna fuck it up for me now. You do it every time, Jake. Every time it gets down to the nitty gritty, you let some broad throw in a monkey wrench. It's fucked up you whole life—broads and booze. Why do you think that phony bitch Vickie is all over you again after twenty years? Did ya forget how she walked out on ya when your ass was in jail? You think she wants you, ya dumb slob? Look in the mirror, pal—just look in the mirror! She wants a piece of your ass. She's lookin' for a cut of the movie—and she's been talkin' to De Niro. God knows what she's been feedin' him. I'm tellin' ya right now, you let Vickie get too close and she'll screw up the whole damn thing for both of us. She's a shrewd bitch. Look how she had you eatin' out of her paw from the minute you laid eyes on her."

"Whatta ya talkin' about? I just got a little drunk, that's all. And who you callin' a slob? I'm the Champ—you're nothin'. I'm the guy you wanna be. I'm the guy you wish you was. You'd give up every dime ya ever made to see your name in lights. You're punchy!"

"I'm punchy? You're the moron that stayed bombed out of his gourd the whole week in Miami. If ya hadn't let your cock rule your head, maybe ya wouldn't have a wife run out on ya with forty grand!"

"Aw, women—they're all jealous bitches. . . ."

"Yeah, well I'm gonna tell ya how to get rid of 'em once and for all. Vickie wants to make *Raging Bull* her baby, right? So we use a little applied psychology."

"Whatta ya mean?"

"I got this actor friend of mine—he owes me one. I'll get him to come up to my office and make like a United Artists exec—one of those crew cut assholes that are always shovin' papers under your nose. We'll bring up Vickie. We'll sit her down. In walks my buddy, and he explains to her very professional like how she has to sign this general release on the movie."

"Naw, she'll never go for it. Whatta ya think—she's a jerk? Why would she sign a release now?"

"She wants to be in the movie, doesn't she? 'And in this corner we have the one, the only, Mrs. Jake La Motta!' If she doesn't sign, then we tell her we'll find a Mrs. La Motta who will—and there are plenty of 'em around. She's written out of the script—simple as that."

"Are you crazy? We'll never pull it off. Vickie's too smart to fall for a bullshit scheme like that. She's gotta know De Niro's calling the shots on the screenplay."

"She doesn't gotta know nothin' if you keep your big Sicilian mouth shut. Let me do it."

"Aw shit . . ."

"Look, I gotta get home. It's New Year's Eve, for Chrissakes. Are you comin' over for the party, or what?"

"Naw, I don't feel like it."

"Suit yourself, pal. Just remember what I told ya. Get rid of the broads, and your troubles are over."

Rick left Jake slumped alone on the couch in the empty apartment. The setting sun was reflected in the windows of the neighboring buildings, casting long shadows across the darkening room. Jake sat still and sullen for a few long moments, then he roused himself from his torpor and made his way to the kitchen, pouring himself a tall scotch. He headed back to the living room and gazed dully at the torn scrap book and the crumpled pages of Vickie's faded image strewn across the floor. Even now, the slightest glimpse of her quickened his pulse and sent chills of desire running through him. Why the hell couldn't he shake this hopeless obsession with a woman who had betrayed him more often than he cared to know? If he thought there was even half a chance that Vickie would take him back, he knew he would run to her side without thinking twice.

That's just the way it was, and there was no use trying to change it. He couldn't really expect any woman to understand it, especially a spoiled child like Debbie. Okay, so he stayed too long at the fair, but did she have to make such a big deal out of it, pulling this disappearing act with the money and all. He wasn't worried about the money—he knew he'd get it back one way or another—but now he knew he couldn't trust her, and that made all the difference. Broads were so stupid! She'd stuck it out through all the shit years, and now when things were getting good, she let's her dumb pride fuck up her whole future. How stupid can you get? She's gotta come back sooner or later, and what did she prove? That she's a flaky broad that can't be trusted. Why couldn't she just have sat tight and waited for him? He'd have been back soon enough. If she hadn't acted like such a spoiled brat with Vickie, she could have come along and had a good time. But no, she had to get a hair up her ass and take off like a stuck-up bitch. And that wasn't like Debbie—most of the time she was a pretty good sport. She put up with a lot of shit without complaining. She cashed in her own pre-paid ticket that time to buy him a new suit so he could attend that bash for Muhammad Ali in California. Not a lot of broads would have done that. And she always stuck up for him in a pinch, too. That was one thing about Debbie, she was very loyal to her own. When she loved, she loved all the way, and he knew she loved him. He never knew why, but he knew she did. Did she still love him now? Maybe he'd lost that, too.

Vickie had loved him once, but he'd fucked that up a long time ago. He knew Rick was probably right—all she wanted was a piece of the action, but somehow that didn't matter. Just having her around him again was enough. But he needed Debbie, too. He didn't want to lose her. Where the hell did she go? If he could just talk to her and make her come back. He missed her pretty pouting face and clear blue eyes and soft, white yielding body. He'd taught her everything, and he had to admit, these few years in bed with her were the best sex he'd ever known. Suddenly, he missed her like crazy. . . .

The winter sun sank smoothly beneath the jagged city skyline, plunging Jake deeper into the gathering shadows as he stood, drink in hand, contemplating his dubious fate. Some long moments pass-ed before he heard the familiar sound of a key turning in the lock. As he faced the door, his hand gripped tightly around his glass, Debbie stood meekly before him, both hands clutched around her Gucci bag, still-bulging with the unspent 40,000 dollars. Tears of remorse ran down her face. Jake gulped his unfinished drink, then he walked slowly over and took her in his arms, holding her like he would never let her go.

"It's okay, Debbie darlin', I forgive you. You're home now; everything's gonna be okay," he whispered hoarsely as Debbie, dropping her heavy bag, wept gently on his shoulder.

Seventeen

Augie Tumminia, president and sole member of the Jake La Motta Fan Club, stood looking up in wonder from the bottom of the steep, splintered steps leading from Fourteenth Street to the dilapidated neighborhood Gramercy Gym, a large faithfully compiled scrap book under each arm and an expression of utter disbelief on his youthful Sicilian face.

"I can't believe it. Here I am. I'm finally gonna meet him—the Bronx Bull, the Champ, Jake La Motta himself! How nice . . . how nice . . ." Augie repeated to himself as he trekked up the stairs to the shabby, smelly, raw boxing gym that had served as a tough haven for the down and out and the up and coming alike for more than fifty years.

Augie tensed with excitement as he sensed the presence of the boxing greats who had had their humble beginnings within those sweat-stained walls—Rocky Marciano, Floyd Patterson, Jose Torres, Muhammad Ali—and now he was about to meet the toughest of them all—The Raging Bull himself. It was enough to make a guy want to cry.

August John Tumminia was a skinny, shy stuttering twelve-year-old hiding from the shock of his revered widowed father's courtship of a strange new woman when he had projected his intense fatherly devotion onto the image of the indefatigable Jake La Motta, forging a fierce identity with the tough Bronx fighter. Augie had followed Jake's career religiously from his first fight with Tommy Bell in 1946 to his last losing round with Billy Kilgore in 1954. He remembered every round of the infamous Fox fight, suffering the shame

193

and defeat of his fallen champion as if he were there in the ring with him. He understood the perverse pride that kept Jake vertical in spite of the forced dive, and Augie alone was able to forgive his chosen god for his mortal weakness in the face of title-hungry torment. He had written Jake countless letters, sent endless numbers of clippings and photos that he had catalogued over the years with the persistence and meticulousness of a master researcher, all without the satisfaction of a single reply from his hero. But then Jake was Jake—the Middleweight Champion of the World—and Augie was just a little Italian guy who fought his daily battles on the gang-infested Queens playgrounds where he served as a city park attendant, modestly supporting his wife, Marie, and four kids in their small, heavily-mortgaged Lindenhurst, Long Island, home of twenty years. How could he possibly know that all the strength and power and beauty he beheld in his distant idol was but the dim reflection of his own humble soul?

Augie stood self-consciously in the doorway of the stuffy, battered gym, the afternoon sunlight filtering hazily through the large unwashed windows into the near-empty room as all eyes centered suspiciously on him.

"Hey, Al, I thought you locked the doors. I told you, I don't want anybody around while I'm training," Robert De Niro addressed the gym-owning partner quietly.

"Yeah, I know, Bobby, but this is Augie—the guy I was telling you about, Jake. This guy is your fan club. He's been dyin' to meet ya," Al Gavin explained quickly.

Jake glared across the hazy gym at Augie. "Wait a minute, Bobby, He's here to see me—not you. Let me talk to him," Jake said.

Al motioned Augie over, and he made his way gingerly across the room toward the far end of the gym where Jake stood with De Niro by a sadly worn punching bag. Rick was leaning against a nearby wall puffing importantly on an Italian paroti; Jake's brother Joey sat in the corner reading a copy of *Ring Magazine*. As Augie approached, Jake scowled in concentration. He'd seen that face somewhere before, but where? Those eyes—he remembered those sad cocker spaniel eyes. That was the little guy—the little Italian guy who stood alone crying behind the fence at the airport that lousy afternoon in the rain when he returned from the

Kefauver mess and everyone was shouting "Jake the Fake"! That was almost twenty years ago, but those were the same eyes. What the hell was he doing here now? Who was this guy? Jake asked himself.

"Gee, Champ, Augie Tumminia here. I don't know how to tell ya how much this means to me—finally gettin' to meet ya here like this! Gee, well whatta ya know, the Champ himself, in person. I can't believe I'm here!"

Augie spluttered as he tried to shift the heavy scrapbooks from under his arm and shake Jake's hand simultaneously.

"Yeah, nice meetin' ya. Ain't I seen you someplace before?" Jake asked warily.

"Me? Naw . . . I've seen you plenty of times in the ring and all, but you never woulda seen me—manacha. I can't believe it. I'm here with you—the Champ himself! Look, look here. I brought ya my books. These are all your fights from 1946 all the way through. I thought maybe you could use 'em, for the movie and all," Augie said excitedly as he opened the large books for Jake's inspection.

Jake flipped quickly through the well-ordered pages, pleased and impressed with the extensive documentation of his career.

"Stop punchin' that bag, Bobby. Come here. I want ya to meet a real man. Show him your scrapbooks," Jake said.

De Niro walked over in his baggy trunks and leather punching gloves and dutifully looked through the books as Augie proudly turned the pages and Rick moved in, eyeing the pictures over Jake's shoulder.

"That's nice; that's very nice," De Niro remarked softly, returning to his punching bag.

"You're a real nice guy, Augie—a true fan and a friend," Rick boomed, laying his large hand on Augie's shoulder.

"This is great! We've got De Niro, Jake, the gym, the president of Jake's fan club and all the pictures right here!"

Rick commented obviously.

"Hey, Augie, come over here. There's somebody ya oughtta meet," Al called from across the room.

Augie walked reluctantly away from his Champ toward his old friend from the parks department. Big, tough, six-foot-two Al Gavin had known Augie through their mutual jobs as city park attendants for over fifteen years, just about the same amount of time

since Al and Bob Jackson, a sergeant in the city corrections department, had taken over the failing landmark boxing gym for one dollar and other valuable considerations from Cus D'Amato, the manager and trainer of heavyweight champion Floyd Patterson. Al and
Bob had run the Gramercy Gym their own way—with no handouts
and no bullshit, acting as surrogate fathers to the giant stew of
street kids who found daily refuge from irate fathers, mothers,
wives, girlfriends, landlords and cops within the spartan sanctuary
where respect could be earned, but never bought. It was a labor of
love, with no salary and no pension attached, only the personal satisfaction of knowing that twelve good rounds, three minutes a
round with a minute in between, could make all the difference between a back alley mugger and a champion human being.

De Niro had chosen the neighborhood gym as much for conven-
ience to his Fourteenth Street loft as for the raw, realistic atmosphere that he so earnestly pursued, anxious to prove he was a regular guy who could take his licks with the best of them. Having hired
the gym for his and Jake's exclusive use between the hours of one
and three, five days a week for one year, giving strict instructions
that he was to receive no special treatment during his training, De
Niro had his work cut out for him.

"Augie, this is Frank Topham—Toppy—the guy who trained
Jake," Al said, introducing Augie to a tough, wizened little man
drawing heavily on the stub of a cigarette.

"Who are you?" Toppy asked unceremoniously.

"Jake is my idol. I have these scrapbooks and all— Toppy, geez,
I can't believe it. There's a million questions I want to ask ya—
about Jake with the weight . . ." Augie started in.

"Aw, the guy lost eight million pounds—it's all true," Toppy said
in a gravel voice.

"On the night of Robinson's fight—I've been eatin' my heart out
since I was thirteen—now I'm 48—I gotta hear it from the horse's
mouth. The night of the fight—the night before—six pounds, five
pounds?" Augie queried.

"He was five and a half pounds overweight the night before the
fight. The man was a robot—the greatest fighter in the world—
right here," Toppy confirmed.

"I know it. I love the fight game, but I don't have too many idols.
Jake is my idol because, that's a man. I consider myself a man, but

if I match up in the same room with Jake, it's pathetic. I don't even come up like a nail!" Augie testified.

"The man had the stamina of a bulldozer. The only thing was the weight," Toppy repeated.

"But he went thirteen rounds with Robinson!" Augie protested.

"After the second round, he started to spit. I knew he lost the fight in the second round, 'cause he started to throw up. When a fighter starts doin' that . . . He wasn't eatin'—the beef blood and water for three days . . . He's gotta be 100 percent. Robinson went nine years without losin' a fight till Jake beat him in '43. When he fought him in '49, Jake was almost through then. Sure, ya go into the sweat baths and lose five, six pounds in six hours, but ya come out and you're all petered out. Ya don't have nothin', even Jake that's a bull," Toppy confided.

"Ya know, for the longest time, when I was a kid, if I would've seen Robinson in the street, I would've shot him. He used to run like a deer, the son of a bitch! And Jake havin' to go from 200 pounds down to 160 in eight weeks—'Don't worry, I'll do it'—but it was an ordeal. He was always fightin' the weight, and after 80 fights—wars with that big Irish brawler Bob Murphy! . . . The day after the fight, Jake was takin' oxygen, and he says through his mask to Robinson, 'I'll fight ya again, but this time I'll come in at 168 pounds, and I don't give a shit what weight you have.' Robinson looked at him like he was crazy! I have clippings on this. Is it true?" Augie asked anxiously.

"You're a fan . . . Yeah, he told 'em that," Toppy replied flatly.

"Ya see? It's why I get pissed off—It's not a fair son of a bitchin' thing—It's not fair! Ya know what it was? Jake would go into the ring purposely not lookin' too good, so the Frankie Carbo's and the Blinky Palermo's would think he was finished and finally give him a shot—the lousy bastards! There's only one Jake La Motta, and there'll only be one. He was a fighter—a real great fighter!" Augie said earnestly as he gazed across at Jake in his trunks and boxing shoes giving instructions to a skinny, pale, unimpressive De Niro.

"Hey, Toppy, tell me something. Is this scrawny little guy really gonna play Jake in the ring? I mean, look at him—there's no comparison. How's he gonna be the Raging Bull?" Augie questioned.

"That's show biz. The guy seems to be takin' his job pretty seriously. Time'll tell if he's willing to take his licks. Stick around. Maybe you'll see somethin','' Toppy shrugged and walked off to his own business.

Augie noticed a short, muscular, fashionably tanned man adorned in heavy gold chains and prominent diamond rings. He had greying curls and the unmistakably broad La Motta head and nose, and was poring intently over his books. Augie ambled amiably over to his side. "You're Jake's brother, Joey, right? I'm Augie—these are my books. Boy, your brother was really somethin', uh?" Augie volunteered.

"These books are really somethin'. They're real nice. But tell me somethin', Why do you do all this? Nobody likes Jake. I'm his brother and I don't even like him. Whatta ya want out of this?" Joey asked suspiciously.

"Me? I don't want nothin'. I just thought Jake would like to see my books . . . Jake is . . . Well, Jake has been my idol since I was a kid. I just wanted to meet him, ya know, in person and all."

"Yeah? I was a fighter, too, ya know," Joey said defensively.

"Yeah, sure, sure I know. But Jake . . . I remember—the Park Arena, 1946. You was fightin' Jesse Flores. Boy, did he knock the shit out of you—closed both your eyes. The referee wouldn't stop the fight, and I remember Jake jumped into the ring and started beatin' the shit out of Flores with his bare hands. What a night! You remember that, Joey?" Augie asked innocently.

"Yeah, Jake was always a crazy fuck," Joey replied sullenly. "Hey, do you mind if I keep these books for a while? I'd like to go over them."

"Sure, sure, of course. Keep 'em as long as you like. I got plenty more at home," Augie said, looking admirably over at Jake.

Augie walked timidly over to where Jake was resting alone with a beer after his training session with De Niro.

"Hey, Champ, I'm uh gonna have to go now—get back to the wife in Lindenhurst and all—but uh, do ya think it'd be all right if I came back tomorrow? I wouldn't get in your way or anything. I'd just like to kinda be around—see how these things are done and all," Augie rasped hoarsely.

"Yeah, sure, why not? I guess you're entitled. I meant to tell ya— I know you've been sendin' a lot of stuff to the house. From now on, send it down to my wife, Vickie, in Miami. She takes care of all those things. Me and Debbie ain't gettin' along so good lately," Jake confided.

"Oh sure, sure, Champ. Whatever you say. No problem. I'll just mail everything to her, like you say," Augie said quickly, embarrassed by the sudden glimpse into his idol's personal life. "So uh, I'll see ya tomorrow, uh Champ?" Augie said hopefully and descended the long steep stairs as if he were walking on air.

Jake sat alone sipping his beer, suddenly depressed by his own last remark. When some things are going so great, something else has to go so wrong, he thought glumly. Ever since Debbie had returned with the money, they had both tried hard to pretend that nothing had happened, but things just hadn't been the same. They had lost that easy companionship and trust they had taken for granted, and now a self-conscious tension stretched constantly between them, injecting the slightest smile or sidelong glance with a heavy dose of suspicion and resentment, sparking hot, sudden arguments over nothing in particular.

Hoping to escape from the scene of their recent past, they had moved into a brand new, large two-bedroom apartment on the corner of 57th Street and First Avenue, sparing no expense on new carpeting and furniture. But the change of scenery had done little to dispel the persistent ghosts of Christmas past. They had tried to forgive, but they could never forget. Out of a desperate need to fill the vacuum between them, they had allowed their personal lives to be invaded by every kind of intrusion these past months.

De Niro had become a daily guest, probing, prodding and inspecting every nuance of their private affairs with the relentless thoroughness of a dedicated scientist. Rick was always around, bathing vicariously in Jake's spotlight as he leered eagerly from every corner, making a suggestion here, coming up with the right angle there, ever anxious to control and direct the real-life actors in his private movie.

Then Vickie had begun to appear on the scene, making frequent trips to New York, where she was sure to flash her gleaming smile at photographers and reporters, generously giving ample interviews while perched coyly on Jake's willing knee and gushing forth on the forthcoming film documenting their well-publicized married years together. Vickie knew what she wanted, and she didn't miss a trick. She spent long hours talking to De Niro in her hotel room, intimating publicly and privately her willingness to seduce the young actor so faithfully portraying her legendary husband.

A kind of undeclared war raged on between Vickie and Debbie as each vied for the undisputed title of "Mrs. Raging Bull," each insisting that she be portrayed as the true leading lady in the final version of the already controversial film. At one point, the FBI was called in to investigate a pair of threatening letters sent to De Niro and Scorsese, which stated in an odd jumble of pasted cut-out letters that something would happen to their wives and families if they went through with the film because Jake was a rat. It was a hell of a way to make a movie.

In the midst of it all, Debbie had begun to seek refuge from the daily battles of will in a subtle but growing fascination with gambling. She presided over weekly poker games held at their apartment and eagerly pocketed the house cut. Losing rapidly on the home front, Debbie believed she'd finally found a game she could win. Jake had gone along with her harmless preoccupation at first, but when she started playing her own hand, losing as much as a few grand a night, he realized too late the monster he had created. It was as if they had been set on a collision course at high speed, with no brake to pull and no emergency hatch to open.

Jake's frown deepened, his eyes narrowing in sudden anger, as he recalled the disastrous scenario of his and Debbie's first night together in their new apartment. Celebrating with a forced carefreeness they were far from feeling, he and Debbie had met at their old watering hole, P. J. Clark's, where a couple of handsome, well-dressed young men from California who had something to do with United Artists had joined them. After several jovial rounds, they had all migrated to Jimmy Weston's, yet another East side hangout preferred by hard-drinking businessmen and tough ex-cops. Seated intimately around a small table in a dark corner of the dimly lit bar, the foursome had continued their non-stop drinking into the night as Debbie, obviously enjoying the company of the two young gentlemen, had become increasingly familiar. Jake, obviously disapproving of the spontaneous friendship between his pretty youthful-looking wife and two handsome young strangers, had become increasingly jealous. His mounting anger and frustration heightened by the considerable amount of liquor he had consumed, Jake had finally reached out at Debbie, pinning her into the tiny corner with his small but powerful hand.

"Get your coat. We're leaving—now," he'd growled menacingly. Outraged by Jake's sudden, unprecedented violence toward her, Debbie had promptly thrown her drink into Jake's face, and he had promptly thrown his drink back into hers. Her hair dripping with stale beer, Debbie had scrambled up from the table, leaving her new fox fur hanging on the back of her chair, and run blindly to the ladies' room, locking the door behind her, as the two astounded nameless young men stared blankly at Jake. Debbie refused to leave the sanctuary of the ladies' room, having called her faithful sister from the pay phone inside for reinforcements, until Jake had left the premises.

When Jake arrived back at their new apartment a couple of hours and several drinks later, Debbie had at first refused to open the door, then relented as Jake's highly vocal threats became louder. She had already called the police, following her sister's strong advice. Two burly Irish cops showed up at the door some twenty minutes later, informing a surprised Jake standing innocently in his shorts that he would have to spend the night elsewhere. Too tired and incredulous to put up a fight, Jake had allowed the bemused officers to escort him out of his apartment, and so he had spent what was to have been the first night in his new apartment on his brother Joey's couch. It had been the beginning of the end, Jake realized sadly as he crushed his empty beer can and tossed it carelessly into the large garbage can in the corner of the grimy gym.

"I don't know—something's gotta be wrong. His line's been busy for the past two hours. It's not like Jake to miss dinner. Maybe you'd better go over and see if he's all right, Joey," Margaritte addressed her husband in worried tones as she hung up the phone in their plush, modern apartment on the seventeenth floor of the well appointed pre-war building diagonally across the street from Jake and Debbie's.

"He'll show up. Jake never missed a free meal in his life. I'm tired of runnin' after his ass," Joey replied from his favorite leather chair in the corner of the white carpeted room.

"Yeah, sure—sure—he's all right. Don't worry, Margaritte. He's probably just sleepin' or somethin'," Augie chimed in reassuringly. "Ya should see what this guy goes through every day. That De Niro—he's terrific! He knows how to bob and weave and throw a left hook—everything. I never would've believed it. In six months the guy's become a real fighter. Jake tells him, 'Tag me with everything you've got. I want ya to know how it feels to tag somebody.' And boy, De Niro gives him a mean left hook, and then a right to the body, and another left. And Jake takes it. He's what, fifty-five or fifty-six now?—with no gear or nothin', just like he was trainin' to fight Robinson. And De Niro, he takes off his head gear, too, and, boy, they really go at it!" Augie related effusively.

"Yeah, they're both nuts. De Niro's costin' us a fortune in insurance already. If they find out he's boxing Jake without his gear, they'll double the premiums on us," Rick complained from the low black leather couch. "But let's face it, I'd be surprised if they let Jake back into the gym after yesterday's little fiasco. I thought he was going to flatten that fag choreographer. Jake just can't get it through his thick head that they're making a movie. Whatta they care how many times he really hit the guy? They want what looks good on camera. They're payin' this fancy dan Hollywood choreographer a hell of a fee. Ya think they're gonna let Jake get up there and tell the guy what to do? Bullshit!"

"Yeah, Rick, but Jake is right. They got De Niro hittin' the other guy with seven, eight body punches in a row. Nobody fights like that—they'd be left wide open! Jake was tryin' to tell 'em. It was a left, and a right, and another left—but they didn't want to listen. Ya mean, Rick, that because of that they don't want Jake to train Bobby anymore?" Augie asked anxiously.

"I mean they're talkin' about payin' him off his lousy 500 bucks a week for the rest of the year and keepin' him the hell away for good. He did his job anyway. He made a fighter out of De Niro—a hell of a good one. Now he's just a goddam pain in the ass to have around," Rick remarked with a philosophical shrug.

"Hey, if they're talkin' about payin' off Jake, how about talkin' to somebody up there about settling up with me? I put in just as many hours as Jake in that dirty sweat box. They owe me. I thought you were supposed to be the big shot co-producer or somethin'," Joey challenged Rick.

"What the hell do I know? Those West coast Jew bastards stick together like glue. Ya think they're gonna tell me anything? I went to the trouble of setting up a private viewing of my movies for them to prove I could produce a film as well as they could, and they acted like I farted in their fuckin' faces!" Rick fumed.

"Rick, do you really think it was wise showing your porno flicks to the United Artists executives and their wives?" Margaritte remarked archly.

"Those holier-than-thou assholes. They were gettin' off on it—I could see it in their faces. Who do they think they're kiddin'? I've read the latest screenplay—'CLOSE-UP on La Motta's erection as he pours ice water over it prior to the fight.' If that's not porno, I don't know what is!" Rick rejoined.

"Yeah, well maybe Jake doesn't give a fuck if they make him look like a cockroach. All he ever wanted to know was how much and if they spelled his name right. But they didn't get any release from me. They'd better be goddam careful what they say about me, or they'll wind up payin' plenty for it!" Joey said hotly.

"Eh, camo, camo, what're you guys worried about? They're makin' a movie of the Champ's life. It's a great thing. Isn't it a great thing? Come on, you guys, you should be happy. What money? You guys don't need the money. Just let 'em make a good movie about the Champ," Augie appeased.

"I wonder if Jake was bringing Debbie. I told him to invite her, but he acted like he didn't know if she'd come. I wish she'd make up her mind to leave him or not. Jake always looks so lost when I mention her—like a beaten stray dog," Margaritte mused aloud as she set the glass and chrome dining table.

"He should have put that bitch in jail when he had the chance. Now she's gambled away everything but his balls. And he's helping her do it! He'll be flat broke again before the movie's even finished, the dumb bastard," Rick muttered.

"Hey, I'm gettin' hungry. Are we gonna eat or what? Let me go over there and find out what the hell happened. He probably killed Debbie and stuffed her in the closet," Joey joked darkly as he headed for the door.

He swung open the door to find Jake standing silently before him in his grimy sweat suit, an expression of utter misery on his unshaven face. He was breathing in short, heavy gasps, and large drops of perspiration beaded his furrowed forehead. His right eye was bruised and swollen.

"Where the hell have you been? Ya look like hell!" Joey exclaimed as Jake walked woodenly into the room and sat down heavily at the table, his lackluster eyes staring blankly ahead. The wheezing of his labored breathing filled the silent room as all eyes focused in alarm on Jake's pathetic form. Margaritte broke the uncomfortable silence.

"Jake, you look terrible. Are you all right?"

"Bobby gave me a couple of shots in the ribs. I don't feel so good," Jake mumbled between painful gasps.

"But Jake, De Niro did this to you? Boy, I guess you taught him too well, uh?" Augie said in astonishment.

"I don't like the sound of that wheezing. I'd better get you to a doctor, pal. Come on, I'll drive ya right now," Rick said soberly.

"I don't want no doctor. All they do is take your money," Jake mumbled.

"What money. Your ass is insured. Let them pay for it. Just get yourself fixed up, ya bullheaded fuck," Rick boomed back.

"I don't want no doctor. I know my body—I can heal myself," Jake repeated stubbornly.

"Don't hand me that religious science bullcrap, Jake. This is me you're talkin' to, remember?" Rick bellowed." Ya can't paint over a shadow and think it's gonna disappear, pal. It'll always be there!"

"I said I don't want no doctor," Jake grunted back.

Rick threw up his hands in exasperation as Joey and Margaritte exchanged long-suffering glances and Augie looked on in nervous concern.

"So, Jake, I guess this proves it. You really did it. De Niro's really that good now," Augie interjected.

"He could go a good ten rounder. He'd rank in the top twenty. Bobby could fight professional right now," Jake snorted.

"You'd better forget De Niro and worry about yourself, Jake. Where's Debbie? Why isn't she taking care of you?" Margaritte asked pointedly.

"Aw, women. Ya can't live with 'em and ya can't live without 'em. I can't figure that broad out. I buy her a seven thousand dollar diamond ring and what does she do? She throws it back in my face.

And I didn't even finish payin' for it yet. She's gotta be crazy . . .
Maybe I'm crazy . . . I don't know . . ." Jake wheezed dully as the
dinner commenced in grim silence. "Gimme some of that
squash. . . ."

Jake and Debbie sat hunched over their cards, their elbows
pressed deeply into the padded leather border of the blackjack table as they swayed precariously on their high gambling stools.
"The Bridge Club," a plush, illegal after hours gambling parlor ca-
tering to the serious high roller, sequestered discreetly near the
foot of the 59th Street Bridge in a disarmingly respectable Manhattan townhouse, had become an habitual hangout for Jake and
Debbie these last desperate months before the final completion of
Raging Bull.

"Hit me again," Jake muttered to the attractive brunette dealer
as he grabbed another shot of blackberry brandy and tossed a generous handful of chips onto the tray of booze smilingly proffered by
a long-legged blonde.

"Twenty-one," Jake announced with a cocky grin as he greedily pulled his latest winnings into the large pile of 100-dollar
chips stcked before him. The inscrutable dealer silently slipped
the next round of shiny cards face down before the poker-faced
players.

"Come on, Jake. Give me some of your chips. You've been winning big all night, and I'm practically tapped out," Debbie complained crossly.

"Whatta ya mean give you some chips? You'll only lose 'em like
ya did everything else. You're a born loser. Leave me alone—I'm
on a streak," Jake slurred gruffly.

"Well, then, give Harry some chips. You owe him five grand,
and he's been losing bad tonight. Give him some of what you owe
him, Jake," Debbie persisted.

Jake scowled over at a small, unobtrusive Wally Cox character
perched nervously on the edge of the next seat, his pale watery
eyes darting feverishly over the table from behind thick glasses as
he sucked deeply on the stub of a cigarette.

"Why should I give my chips to a lousy loser. That's his problem.
I need what I got," Jake muttered as he peeked at his inside three
and shoved a large stack of chips onto the playing area. "Hit me,"

he said to the dealer as she smoothly laid the one-eyed jack of spades over his hidden three of clubs.

"But that's not fair, Jake. Harry lent you the money when you needed it, and now you won't even give him back a few chips. That's not right, Jake. Come on, give Harry some chips," Debbie pestered loudly.

"What are you—his mother or somethin'? My own wife—jealous that I'm winnin'. Leave me alone. You'll jinx me," Jake growled, quickly deliberating the odds of his getting an 8 or below on his next card. "Hit me again," he said, shoving another large stack of chips onto the betting area.

The dealer quietly placed the queen of hearts over Jake's one-eyed jack.

"Now look what ya did. Ya made me go bust. Ya broke my winning streak, ya dumb bitch," Jake snapped at Debbie as the dealer retrieved Jake's losing cards and efficiently swept his lost chips into the house bank.

"It's your own fault. If you'd paid back Harry, your luck wouldn't have turned on you. You have to pay, Jake. Sooner or later you pay for everything—just like you'll pay someday for what you did to me," Debbie said bitterly.

"What I did to you. I didn't do nothin' to you ya didn't do to yourself. Look at ya. You're an old lady already," Jake said, absently running his hands through his still ample pile of chips.

"You dirty son of a bitch! I know what you're trying to do to my mind—but I won't let you!" Debbie cried, her eyes registering her pain and anger. "You can't just kill somebody, Jake, and say 'I'm sorry, I made a mistake.' I'm a loyal person. I don't need anybody that badly to sell my soul, my body, my family, my friends—like you did for Vickie. You're both a pair of selfish, two-faced whores!"

Debbie scooped up two handfuls of Jake's chips, throwing them on the table in front of Harry.

"Happy birthday, Harry!" she shouted in half-drunken abandonment to the stunned little man, glaring defiantly back at Jake.

"What the hell do ya think you're doin'. Keep your hands off my goddam chips!" Jake yelled in sudden rage.

"Why should I? Vickie got away with a lot more than that!"

"You couldn't lick Vickie's ass," Jake snarled back.

Debbie picked up her full glass of wine and threw her drink into Jake's face. Instinctively, Jake's right arm lashed out at Debbie, knocking her backwards off the stool. The last thing Debbie saw was the look of shock and horror on the gaping faces above her before she passed out on the floor.

Eighteen

Jake stood stiffly in his new tuxedo, scotch in hand, gazing reflectively out into the crisp, clear mid-November evening through the dirty windows of his studio apartment. He was waiting for Vickie to pick him up on the way to the much anticipated New York premiere of *Raging Bull*. Looking directly west by northwest, Jake had a clear view into the familiar corner apartment across First Avenue where Debbie sat desperately dealing to her high rolling gambling clients. "The blackjack queen of 57th Street. . . . Look at her, and look at me," Jake mused.

The movie was finally over—the outtakes were on the editing room floor, the final cut was in the can, and the credits were ready to roll. Only who was left to take the bows? Jake asked himself as the jumbled events of the past two years lurched before his mind.

It had been a long, bloody war with more casualties than survivors. Rick had retreated from the scene of battle in bitter defeat, having suffered a severe double blow to his large, vulnerable ego midway through the winter campaign. The first came in the form of a letter from Chartoff-Winkler's attorneys offering him an extra three points of the producers' share in exchange for kindly removing his less than kosher name from the list of producers credits. It was an offer he couldn't refuse. The second came in the form of a brand new screenplay rewritten by De Niro and Scorsese during a last-minute retreat to the Bahamas in which Rick discovered his co-starring role completely written out and replaced by the character of Jake's brother, Joey. It seemed that Vickie, seething over Rick's botched attempt to trick her into signing a release, had made a point of informing De Niro of the fact that Rick had been conspicuously absent serving an extended prison term for armed robbery during most of Jake's fighting career, the book and its contrived Becket theme notwithstanding. Confronted with the truth, Jake had finally sided with Vickie, leaving Rick to fend unsuccessfully for himself. His dreams of movie stardom crushed beneath the wheels of executive production decisions, Rick had reluctantly played his compensatory bit gangster role and walked broken-hearted off the set.

Unable to arrive at acceptable monetary compensation for his release on the supporting character in the final version of the screenplay, Joey had initiated legal proceedings against one and all, naming everyone from United Artists to his brother, Jake, in a handsome libel suit.

Demoralized past belief, her once fierce pride trampled beyond recognition, her lost innocence buried beneath the layers of her lonely, frenzied existence, Debbie had been the saddest casualty of all. A sudden shudder ran through Jake as he flashed back to that first day on the elevator when Debbie had stepped unwittingly into his life with her bright, blue eyes and fresh, young innocent smile. Could this be the same girl? he asked himself as he watched his frenetic, obsessed, estranged wife wink and joke and laugh too loudly with the sinister customers of her dubious trade. Had he loved her too much or not enough? Haunting strains of an anonymous poem drifted into Jake's mind as he stood lost in his reverie. . .

"Out of the dark that covers me, deep as a pit from pole to pole, I thank whatever gods may be for my unconquerable soul. . . . It matters not how straight the gate, how charged with punishment the scroll, I am the master of my fate; I am the captain of my soul. . . ."

A sharp ring from the doorman's buzzer jolted Jake back to reality. Giving his listing bow tie a final tug, he turned on his heel and headed springily out the door, full of hopeful anticipation at the thought of having the triumphantly smiling Vickie on his arm once again.

Regally attired in a full-length white fox fur and a matching hat that framed her flawlessly painted face, Vickie strutted down 57th Street toward the Sutton Theater in her high white leather boots. She was proudly supported on the arms of Jake and their tall and handsome eldest son, Jake Jr. It was Vickie's moment of triumph for which she had fought, plotted, schemed and manipulated from the day three years before when she had taken back the La Motta name and vowed to make *Raging Bull* her baby. Her efforts had paid off. She alone had survived the tempest of warring egos that threatened to engulf the entire film project in a tidal wave of destructive emotions, and it was she alone whose sultry blonde image would grace the relentlessly brutal black and white montage of Jake's controversial fighting career. Vickie's lips curled into a well-pleased smile as the family threesome approached the brightly lit theater marquee boldly proclaiming RAGING BULL in giant red letters. A milling crowd of working press, privileged ticket holders and gawking spectators thronged the theater entrance, hoping to catch a glimpse into the coveted lives of the currently rich and famous.

The scene seemed to unfold in slow motion before Jake's bleary eyes as an eager group of reporters and TV cameramen broke from the excited crowd and ran halfway down the block to meet the real Raging Bull and his prized beauty. The blinding lights flashed around them in a confusion of blurred images and sounds. Surrounded by their entourage of news cameras, the trio made their way past the buzzing crowd into the glittering theater lobby. As they passed through the padded doors into the cool darkness of the inner theater, Jake noticed out of the corner of his eye a sullen Rick leaning against the wall in the crowded lobby, inhaling deeply on his Italian Cerrutti as he watched them pass, a smile of bitter irony on his handsome Calabrian face.

Following Vickie and Jake Jr. down the sloping aisle to their reserved seats in the first rows, Jake quickly surveyed the intimate theater for a familiar face among the well-dressed strangers, half-expecting a standing ovation from the still scattered audience. No one seemed to notice as they slid into the comfortable velvet cushioned chairs bearing their names. Jake found himself elbow to elbow with his brother Joey, who was seated stoically next to Margaritte; both stared stonily ahead at the blank screen in deliberate silence. Co-stars Joe Pesci and Cathy Moriarty were seated in the row ahead. The seats designated for Robert De Niro and Martin Scorsese were conspicuously empty. Jake stole a secret glance at Vickie's chiseled profile, hoping for some small sign of reassurance, but her cool gaze remained fixed ahead as she wriggled out of her luxurious fur coat. Jake sat impatiently twiddling his thumbs as the theater gradually filled, his anticipation mounting at the prospect of seeing what he was about to see for the very first time.

The house lights dimmed to black, the whispering crowd fell into hushed silence, and the blank screen came suddenly alive as the opening credits rolled over the image of a hooded leopard-robed figure dancing alone in an empty ring to the haunting strains of Mascagni's Sicilian opera. From the first moment De Niro appeared on screen, a bloated, besotted, battered hulk of a man reciting lines mechanically to himself in a broken down backstage dressing room, Jake's mouth dropped open with the shock of painful recognition. Riveted to his seat, he stared at the screen with a mixture of horror and fascination, mesmerized by De Niro's portrayal of his violent past as his mercilessly exposed life unfolded before him. The heavily sound-effected boxing sequences were more dramatically and sensually effective than real, but Jake could appreciate De Niro's attempt to recreate his devastating power in the ring. It was the cruel portrait of his destructive force outside the ring that Jake found hard to swallow. At the stark scene depicting their inevitable divorce, Jake reached tentatively for Vickie's cold hand, gulping back the tears that squeezed past his eyes. As the last line of credits faded from the screen to the cinema verité soundtrack of background nightclub noise, Jake turned to Vickie and asked, "Was I really that bad?" Vickie looked at him with her cold eyes and answered icily, "You were worse."

The theater emptied in stunned silence, the audience bludgeoned into a stupor by the stark, barren landscape of the soul depicted so fiercely by De Niro's performance. He had spent four months stuffing himself with vitamins and pasta to gain 60 pounds, substantially extending the production schedule and budget of the film, in order to effectively portray Jake's physical, moral and spiritual decline in the final devastating scene. It had worked. De Niro had succeeded in creating on celluloid one of the most repugnant characters in the history of movies.

Jake numbly followed Vickie and his silent son out of the empty theater onto the deserted sidewalk. A lone cocky reporter shouted "What did ya think, Jake?"

Jake stopped and answered in sad bewilderment, "I looked like a real SOB. I guess I was. . . ."

If the critics were quick to point out the weaknesses in plot, theme and conventional characterization in Scorsese's *Raging Bull*, most were sure to agree that De Niro had earned an Academy Award nomination for best actor in his unsparing portrait of a wretched, damaged survivor whose deepest wounds were self-inflicted. Audiences around the world stood in line to witness De Niro's foul-mouthed anti-hero, some coming to praise the work while damning the man, others strongly identifying with the much maligned and misunderstood gladiator. United Artists, having sunk over 30 million into what was originally a modest three-million-dollar film budget, were certain of one thing: they had a hit on their hands.

Inhaling philosophically on his medium-sized Havana cigar, his arm slipped possessively around Vickie's trim waist, Jake endured the first of countless interviews with the insatiably curious press, bestowing generous praise on De Niro's performance while calmly disclaiming any current resemblance to the character of his ex-humed past. When asked inevitably if *Raging Bull* was a true picture of himself, he would respond thoughtfully, "That was how I was then, but not now. I'm sure I've mellowed a lot. You learn from your mistakes. When it comes to emotional feelings, I'm really a softie." Then he would smile contentedly at Vickie as she posed agreeably by his side for the ever-present cameras.

Sent on a salaried all-expense-paid promotional tour of Europe by United Artists, Jake found himself in Milan, Italy, with his son Jake Jr. acting as his personal manager while Vickie cavorted in Paris with Cathy Moriarty, the young Hollywood newcomer who had effectively portrayed Vickie as the steamy Bronx blonde who had driven the young bullish Jake to total distraction. Given strict orders by his doting mother to keep close tabs on his notorious father's behavior, Jake Jr., an eligible bachelor of thirty-three with Jake's nose before it was broken six times and Vickie's soft brow and flashing brown eyes, stuck like glue to Jake, carefully ordering

a single bottle of expensive wine with dinner while discreetly cur-
tailing his father's erstwhile drinking habits. A touching mutual respect arose between the two men as father and son became re-
acquainted after their prolonged separation. Jake Jr. had been a serious, sad-eyed twelve-year-old prematurely succeeding to the
position of the man of the household when Jake had said goodbye
to his family and past identity in Miami and started over from
scratch in New York. Jake's contact with his eldest son had been
limited to birthday phone calls and erratic visits ever since. Now
was a time of healing, and a time of forgiving, too.

"How do you say mushroom in Italian?" Jake asked his son on
their way to the studio of the popular live television talk show in
Milan, "Porta Bella."

"Uh, fungi, I think. Hey, Pop, you're not going to tell another
one of your jokes in Italian, are you? You'll blow the punch line like
you did the last time," Jake Jr. said, looking in fond amusement at
his father.

"Whatta ya mean? I didn't blow it. They just didn't get it, that's
all," Jake insisted.

"How do you expect them to get it when instead of piscada for
fishing you kept saying pishatta—taking a piss for Chrissakes!"

"Yeah, well you were laughing hard enough."

"Are you kidding? I thought I'd bust a gut lookin' at the expres-
sions on the faces of those old Italian matriarchs. But seriously,
Pop, this is like the Johnny Carson show of Italy. You'll be seen by
everyone from Milan to Sicily. And I've lined up a little surprise for
you this time, so don't blow it!"

"What surprise? I don't like surprises."

"If I told ya, it wouldn't be a surprise, would it? Relax—you're
gonna like it."

Jake sat next to the suave talk show host, cigar in hand,
displaying his best show biz manner before the multiple television
cameras and large studio audience as he quipped and joked in his
halting Sicilian Italian and characteristic Runyanesque style.

"So how many times have you been married?" the talk show host
asked in flawless high Italian.

"Five," Jake replied.

"What happened to your first wife?"

"She died from eating poison mushrooms."

"What happened to your second wife?"

"She died from eating poison mushrooms, too."

"And what about your third wife?"

"Broken skull."

"How did that happen?"

"She wouldn't eat the mushrooms," Jake dead-panned as the audience laughed appreciatively.

"With your permission, Champione, we couldn't have your beautiful wives here tonight, but I think we have planned something that you will like even better," the host said smoothly, changing the subject. "You have not seen your father, Guisseppe La Motta, for over 25 years. We have taken the liberty of bringing him here tonight from his home in Trieste for a very special father and son reunion."

Jake's eyes widened in astonishment as he watched his eldest son lead his aging father slowly across the stage. He was smaller and more bent, and his thinning hair was much whiter than Jake remembered. His long Sicilian nose had taken a sharper curve toward his thin, compressed lips; his once fiery eyes smoldered like burnt-out embers in their deep, hollow sockets. But his step was still firm and straight, and the color rose in his robust cheeks as Guisseppe embraced his first-born son, his tears staining Jake's scarred face as he kissed him freely on both cheeks.

"I love you, Pop—forgive me," Jake mumbled as the tears rose in his own eyes and he beheld his father through the dim years of the painful past.

He was just an ordinary, harmless little old man, after all.

Jake wandered all by himself down the thick red carpeted aisle of the majestic Dorothy Chandler Pavilion, ogling the endless rows of jealously guarded seats filled with Hollywood's glittering royalty, lost in the sea of famous strangers as he wondered vaguely where he ought to be. He had passed unscathed through the receiving gauntlet of whirring cameras, protruding microphones and hungry, screeching fans clamoring for a taste of stardom, and now stood in proper black tie, embossed invitation in hand, looking uncomfortably for his precious reserved seat.

Noticing Jake's bewildered expression, a pretty usherette came to his rescue, glanced at his glossy invitation, and led him down the aisle to a single seat near the front of the cavernous auditorium. Jake sat imperviously among the hopeful faces and stared contentedly ahead at the huge proscenium stage dominated by a giant center screen. No one and nothing could touch him now. Tonight was his night. Gradually, the privileged audience of Hollywood elite grew expectantly silent, the shimmering house chandeliers dimmed, the strategically placed live television cameras started to roll, the music swelled as Oscar's master of ceremonies, Johnny Carson, strolled on stage to enthusiastic applause, and the 53rd Annual Academy Awards, delayed twenty-four hours because of the attempted assassination of President Reagan the day before, officially began.

Long after the pre-recorded greeting from President Ronald Reagan, the familiar medley of best-loved classic film clips, the humble stammerings of grateful winners, the operatic serenade by Luciano Pavarotti, the honorary Oscar presentation to Henry Fonda by Robert Redford, past the several standing ovations and countless commercial breaks, came the moment Jake was waiting for. Nominated in eight categories, including best director in which Martin Scorsese had lost to Robert Redford in his directing debut for *Ordinary People*, *Raging Bull* had been generously represented in the winners' circle throughout the long evening. Now last year's best actress winner Sally Field descended the steep decorative staircase and walked determinedly across the stage to present the coveted Oscar for best actor.

Jake sat erect in his seat and tried not to notice the giant camera lenses he knew were focused on him as his name was pronounced for untold millions to hear.

"As Jake La Motta, a man whose violent career was only part of a violent life, and whose success in the ring was balanced by spectacular failures, the film "Raging Bull". . . . The winner is Robert De Niro. . . ."

Suppressing a strong impulse to rise from his seat and walk up onto the stage himself, Jake watched De Niro stride down the aisle and leap gracefully up the steps to claim his well-deserved prize. No longer the bloated bully he had become in the name of his art, De Niro, looking trim and fit in his well-tailored tux, his unpermed hair back to its casual length, and sporting a brand new mustache and Vandyke beard, grabbed his Oscar firmly in one hand and faced the audience and cameras self-consciously as he nervously accepted his award. "I forgot my lines, so the director wrote them down for me. Uh, I uh, I want to thank everyone—It's said so often, but it's true, and uh, what can I say . . ." He then proceeded to thank just about everyone who had anything to do with the film, including "Vickie La Motta and all the other wives, and Joey La Motta, even though he's suing us . . . I hope that's settled soon enough so I can go over to his house and eat once in a while . . . um, and Mardik Martin and Paul Schrader who wrote the script, and, of course, Jake La Motta, whose life it's all about . . ."

Jake applauded loudly along with the rest of the audience, a fixed smile frozen on his lips that his fading eyes denied. All at once, he felt a pang of loneliness, as if he were the only one in the tremendous auditorium clapping by himself. For the first time he noticed the unfamiliar faces around him. Not one of them was clapping for him. It was De Niro's night, not his. Having shed Jake's sinister persona along with the pounds, De Niro had quickly moved on to newer challenges, leaving Jake trapped forever on screen as the benighted, self-defeated loser. He had only been the vehicle for De Niro's success. Now the ride was over, and there was no one left to share his glory or his grief.

Jake sat alone for a long while as the theatre slowly emptied. Then he got up and sauntered down the deserted aisle toward the door clearly marked EXIT.

PART V

Catharsis

Nineteen

Augie drove his faded orange Nova slowly up the circular drive sliced neatly through the clipped, manicured lawn and halted behind the shiny blue Cadillac parked conspicuously before the Long Island suburban ranch house. Rick had been adamant about Augie's picking him up at his home on time, and it was exactly nine A.M. as Augie rang the pleasantly chiming doorbell and a pretty, well-groomed brunette promptly answered the door.

"You must be Augie. Just a moment, I'll call Rick," she smiled politely and disappeared into the meticulously clean foyer. Moments later an obviously pained Rick strode stiffly through the doorway, pulling the heavy white wooden door firmly shut behind him as he headed awkwardly toward the passenger side of his Cadillac, his head cocked rigidly to one side.

"I won't forget you for this, buddy. If I had to drive with this goddam pinched nerve, I'd probably kill myself. You're a real pal," Rick muttered between clinched teeth as he unlocked the car door.

"Yeah, sure, sure, Rick. But wait a minute—I thought we'd go in my car here. I can't drive that tank in the city. I can't even reach the pedals. I might kill somebody!" Augie protested from the driveway.

"I'm insured for millions. I don't care if you hit God. Just get me to the friggin' doctor," Rick asserted, sliding carefully onto the plush cushioned seat.

Augie shrugged resignedly and slipped obediently behind the wheel of the oversized three-year-old '78 Cadillac.

"Wow, it feels like I'm drivin' the Queen Mary!" Augie ex-

claimed as he nervously turned the key in the ignition. "But Rick—
did the engine start? I don't hear nothin'.."

"That's 'cause you're used to drivin' that six cylinder
lawnmower. She's on. Just slip her into drive and let's get the hell
out of here before I go crazy."

Augie lurched into gear and inched cautiously out the driveway,
glancing anxiously from side to side as he eased onto the quiet residential street.

"Eh Rick, was that your wife that answered the door? She's really a nice lady—very pretty, too. Whoever thought you had such
an attractive wife at home all this time."

"Yeah, she's a real sweetheart. We've been married twenty-nine
years now. I don't know how she put up with me all this time. I've
had millions of broads—millions. . . . But she's one in a million—a
real lady," Rick replied, squirming uncomfortably in his seat. "Hey
Augie, step on it, will ya? At this rate I'll be dead before we get
there."

"Sure, okay, Rick, but tell me, how did you get this pinched
nerve or whatever it is? It must be really bad, uh? You're acting
like a cripple or somethin'."

"I hope nothin' like this ever happens to you, buddy. It's like a
fuckin' hot poker shooting down your whole back. It's an old war
wound from my street fighting days—back when I was rough,
tough and stupid—like Jake. We'd steal anything—cars, money,
women, you name it."

Rick rambled on, his eyes half-closed against his pain, as Augie
drove timorously along the Long Island Expressway.

"I came over from Italy at the age of nine to nothin' but Bronx
scum. It was steal or starve. But I always wanted to make somethin'
of myself. I didn't enjoy gettin' my brains bashed in like Jake. I
wanted to be an actor—get into the movies where the action and
the money was. One day I hitched a ride to Hollywood with nothin'
but dirt in my pockets. I drove a cab, hopin' to meet some horny
star or big shot producer who thought I'd look good opposite some
new starlet he was banging. I met loads of hungry actresses, and I
fucked 'em all, but I almost starved waitin' for a producer to give
me the time of day. So I wound up back in the Bronx carryin' a rod
for the mob. I only got pinched once, but it was a long fuckin'
stretch. I came out eight years older and a hell of a lot wiser. Some

relatives got me into the dress business, and I've been makin' a decent living ever since. . . . I never gave up on the idea of making movies, though. I've produced a few lulus in my day. I've come pretty damn close, but I never got that one goddam break. I thought I had it made this last time with *Raging Bull*, but . . . . Make a left here."

Augie struggled in frantic silence behind the steering wheel as he desperately dodged the aggressive cabs and impatient traffic of Manhattan's congested East side.

"Pull over in front of that building. I'll be right back. Just stay double parked here. If some son of a bitch cop chases ya, just go around the block," Rick charged, and made his tortured way across the busy avenue, disappearing into the lobby of the chiropractic office building.

Augie had dutifully circled the block for the sixth time before he spied Rick's towering pain-racked form limping toward him.

"Geez, ya don't look much better. What did the doctor say? Are ya goin' to be okay, or what?" Augie asked anxiously as Rick sank wearily into the seat next to him.

"Aw, it's a waste of fuckin' time and money. There's nothin' much they can do. I just gotta put up with it, that's all. Life is full of pain," Rick muttered darkly, the tears rolling down his ashen face.

"Yeah, but can't they give ya somethin' to make you feel better—a pill or somethin'?" Augie asked sympathetically.

"Yeah, some lousy muscle relaxers, but all they do is dull the pain. They don't get to the root of it. They don't make a pill for what's botherin' me. Sooner or later all the crap catches up with you—all the fighting and clawing and scratching to get ahead—all the lying and cheating and scamming to win—all just to wind up naked on a metal slab in some lousy mortician's lab with a silly fuckin' grin arranged on your face. Ya learn to live with a certain amount of stress, and then one day ya start to crack from the pressure—like a rotten worn out bridge," Rick rattled on in his hurtful stupor.

"Life is short—how long can ya live? I've made a couple of bucks. I'm a lucky guy. I love my wife, I have a good family, I consider myself a success. But I always figured we'd make out better on *Raging Bull* than we did. The whole goddam movie industry is driving me crazy. We should've made millions with the Academy Awards and all. But where the hell is the money? Sure, they paid me off. They didn't want any co-stars, co-producers—nothin'. But we didn't see a dime of the net. What net? I should've known better than to make a deal on the producer's end. They fix it so the books are always in the red. Hell, I've done it myself for Chrissakes! It's gotta be gross all the way, or you're just jerking yourself off. Jake thinks I screwed him. He thinks the whole world screwed him. He went through all his advance money like Grant took Richmond, and now he's back on the balls of his ass, like always. I haven't seen the fat fuck in over eight months. You know the way Jake is. It's very difficult to be his friend forever. Things happen. Things are said and never confirmed and it causes a certain amount of animosity. But with me and Jake it's different. We've been like family all these years, and all of a sudden, somethin' like this happens. . . . Ya know, Augie, Jake likes you. I've known him for over forty years and he never liked anybody, but he likes you. You tell it like it is, you don't pan it or smear things over. You're good for Jake. He doesn't have too many friends. You oughtta stick by him. You're a good listener. He's gonna need somebody like you around when he comes down off that pink cloud he's been riding," Rick sighed, finally winding down from his delirious monologue.

"Hey Rick, ya know what? Jake is over at Patsy's right now giving some interview to these guys from Swedish television or something. He told me about it the other day. Why don't we go over there and surprise him? I know he'd like to see ya. He's always askin' me how you're doin' and all. It's a shame two good friends like you and the Champ should break up over a dumb movie, for cryin' out loud. How about it, whatta ya say, uh?"

Augie maneuvered the unwieldy Cadillac into the parking lot across the street from the family-owned Italian restaurant in the heart of Manhattan's theater district where Frank Sinatra and other show biz notables were known to discreetly hang out. Augie and Rick entered the unobtrusive glass doors marked "Patsy's" in faded gold lettering and stood uncomfortably by the intimate front bar cluttered with the autographed likenesses of famous customers. Included was a prominently displayed photograph of Vickie La Motta brazenly baring all in a transparent negligee that left little to the imagination. The quietly elegant room was nearly empty as the red-vested waiters prepared the tables for the nightly perform- ance. Recognizing Rick's familiar silver-haired profile, Sal Scognamillo, Patsy's ubiquitous owner and host nattily attired in his perennial sharkskin suit, walked quickly over to greet him.

"Hey Rick, long time no see. How ya doin'? Ya know, Jake's here. He's upstairs with a couple of reporters—foreign guys. How about a drink at the bar on me?" Sal offered.

"Thanks Sal, but I'll take a rain check. Okay if we go up?" Rick half-smiled, masking his extreme discomfort.

"Sure, of course. Go on, they're in the back," Sal replied, re- turning calmly to his business.

Augie followed Rick up the red carpeted angled staircase to the top dining room where Jake sat in a corner table with two very blond young men, his back to the wall as he expounded between puffs on his trademark cigar into the recording microphone placed importantly before him. Jake stopped in mid-sentence, his face registering his shocked surprise as he suddenly noticed Rick and Augie coming towards him from across the room.

"Hold it guys. These are a couple of friends of mine you should meet," Jake told his Swedish interviewers.

Rick forced a toothy smile and extended his large, well-shaped hand across the table in a firm handshake as Jake beamed up at his old partner, an expression of genuine pleasure lighting up his dusky face.

"It's good to see you, pal," Rick said simply.

"It's good to see you, too," Jake echoed. "Hey guys, meet Rick Rosselli, the guy who worked on the book with me. If it wasn't for Rick, there wouldn't've been a book or a movie, and that's the truth. And that's Augie, the president of my fan club. Anything you want to know, just ask him," Jake attested as Augie glowed appre- ciatively.

"Hey, the drinks are on me. Whatta ya got—amaretto?

"Amaretto all around," Rick boomed to the suddenly attentive waiter as he and Augie joined the table.

"To the good times, pal," Rick toasted, raising his glass high as the drinks arrived.

"Yeah, the good times," Jake repeated, clinking his glass with Rick's.

Jake downed his shot heartily, never dreaming it would be the last time he ever saw Rick alive.

Jake had spent the worst New Year's eve of his life, drinking himself into a dejected stupor before the blank television set in his desolate studio apartment. When he arrived that cold, drizzling New Year's day at the drab funeral parlor in the old Bronx neighborhood, pale, shaky and sweaty from his dismal night-long vigil, he still couldn't believe it. Larger than life Rick, so full of vitality, sass and bold bravura a few days ago, had asked his wife casually if she needed any more money for the slot machines. He strolled confidently over to the crowded roulette table, placed his last fifty dollar bet on lucky black seven, and dropped dead of a massive coronary on the floor of the Las Vegas gambling casino. True to form, Rick had gone out in typical style, always leaving them begging for more.

Jake stood nervously smoking a cigarette near the entrance of the gloomy room crowded with milling mourners whispering their respects to the family members. It was with a welcome sigh of relief that he recognized Augie's familiar, drawn face coming anxiously toward him.

"Champ, how are ya. This is terrible, this is terrible. Who would've thought—Rick—he was so, so alive, and now . . . Ya never know, uh? Ya just never know," Augie shook his head sadly.

"I hate these things. . . . Whatta ya do here? What's the first thing you're supposed to do? I don't know. . . . I hate these things," Jake muttered miserably, his whole body trembling in near panic.

Augie grabbed Jake by the lapels of his damp, wrinkled jacket and pulled him toward him.

"Jake, what are ya, sick? Calm down. Whatta ya do? You sign the book, leave a boost, you walk up, kneel down, say a prayer, pay your respects to the family, and that's it. What else can you do?" Augie said poignantly.

Jake approached the elaborately enshrined mahogany coffin as if he were facing his own firing squad. Kneeling stiffly over Rick's lifeless form, Jake gazed on the gently smiling face of his erstwhile best friend, entranced by the serenity of the still image before him.

"Maybe he's in heaven, and I'm still down here in hell," Jake thought wryly. "You screwed me many times, Rick, I know, but what the hell. How many honest guys do ya know? And besides, we were friends since we were kids. How can ya forget that? Greed makes ya do a lot of things. . . . Maybe I shoulda trusted ya more, but you know I never trusted nobody, not even you. Remember that night before the Kefauver business when you came over at two in the morning and said, 'If ya sing, stupid, these guys have guns— they'll blow ya away. . . .' I always figured you was just doin' your job—you wasn't lookin' out for my ass. But then again, maybe you was. . . . Maybe you was all along. . . . I guess it really doesn't matter any more—not to you, anyway. . . . "

His impromptu prayer finished, Jake stood up abruptly, mumbled his respects to the doleful family, pulled his jacket collar up against the cold gray rain, and left the wretched scene behind.

Twenty

Theresa Miller sat with her girlfriends at the bar of the glitzy Las Vegas Frontier Hotel tipsily sipping her fourth margarita, an insipid smile creeping across her pretty face. "Well, Theresa, another lost weekend in junkie paradise, and then it's back to the same old boring California suburban grind. I'll drink to that."

Theresa raised her glass to her lips, closing her eyes on the scene about her, as she savored her ennui. Half-opening her deep green eyes, Theresa focused blearily across the gambling tables through a pair of open doors leading into a side room where two burly, barechested men in satin trunks posed obligingly in a mock boxing ring before a troup of photographers. A bevy of scantily costumed show girls draped themselves around them. Her sleepy curiosity aroused, Theresa placed her empty glass on the bar, slid smoothly off her stool, and made her way across the thickly carpeted main concourse. Slipping quietly into a corner twofer, Theresa propped her chin coyly on her hand and gazed bemusedly at the clowning antics of the obviously well-acquainted boxers. Noticing their monogrammed shorts, she recognized RG as Rocky Graziano, whose friendly grinning image was vaguely familiar. But she was puzzled as to the identity of the heavier, more somber bearer of the initials JL. She stared unabashedly at the latter's ravaged face, impressed by the deep furrows etched into his sallow cheeks. "Now there's a man who's lived," she said to herself. Catching her eyes upon him, he boldly returned her gaze, his eyes lighting up for a moment's glow as he smiled a surprisingly innocent smile. Theresa felt herself smiling warmly back.

The open house press show over, the photographers packed up and fled, the show girls dispersed amidst winks and empty promises, and the posing gladiators of yore climbed down over the ropes of their ringed stage to don their streetclothes. JL pulled a pair of trousers casually over his trunks, slipped a polo shirt over his head, and walked directly over to Theresa.

"Come on, you and me are going for a drink," he stated emphatically, grabbing her firmly by the arm and leading her toward the bar.

Too high to protest, Theresa surrendered passively to his command.

"I guess you know who I am—Jake La Motta. So who are you, you gorgeous, sexy creature," he rasped, eyeing her petite figure up and down approvingly as he swung her onto the bar stool.

"Theresa Miller. So that's what JL stands for. I was wondering. Were you a champion, too?" Theresa asked with a disarming smile.

"You gotta be kidding. You mean you don't know who I am? Haven't ya ever heard of *Raging Bull*? Don't ya go to the movies?"

Theresa shook her head innocently.

"What are you, some kind of alien or somethin'? My face is plastered all over this joint!"

"I guess I didn't notice," she shrugged with a small voice.

"So how come you're sittin' here havin' a drink with me. I could be just some bum tryin' to pick you up."

"How do you know I'm not some flirt tryin' to pick you up?" she asked coyly.

Jake grinned back, enjoying the provocative exchange. She was no young chick, but she had a sweet, youthful, wide-eyed look and a trim little body. She had that wholesome, well-groomed attractiveness and white gleaming smile you see in home product commercials. And the sparkling green eyes that complemented her auburn hair were sensitive and warm. With her simple but classy white linen dress and the expensive looking jewelry she was wearing, he figured she was some well-to-do runaway housewife from suburban boredom slumming for a weekend fling in sin city. Then again, maybe she was just a smart operator with a class act. You just never know. . . .

"Look, I gotta go see Sinatra's show with Rocky tonight. It's business, or I'd ask ya along. How about meetin' me back here about two and we'll hit a few tables. Do you do much gamblin'?" Jake asked pointedly.

"I'm not much of a gambler, but I take my share of risks," Theresa smiled mysteriously.

"Yeah, I'll bet you do. Be in this spot at two, or I'll give ya a beatin'," Jake grinned and disappeared into the noisy melee of crap tables, roulette wheels, and flashing one-armed bandits.

By 2:45 a.m. Theresa swallowed the last of what she had resolved to be her final drink and slid resignedly off her stool, determined to chalk up Jake La Motta as just a phony bum she had regrettably met, when she felt a strong arm grab her elbow and steer her in the direction of the nearest blackjack table.

"Let's go, baby. I feel hot tonight. Maybe you'll bring me good luck," Jake rumbled as he slipped his arm familiarly around her waist and gave her a hard squeeze, peering lasciviously down the low cut front of her black beaded evening dress.

Theresa looked up at his gnarled, inebriated face in surprise.

"Bet you thought I wasn't gonna show, uh? Sorry about that, but I couldn't get away. I had to get paid. Here's twenty-five hundred bucks in cold cash. Let's run with it—win, loose, or draw." Jake rambled on, slapping a wad of bills onto the table and retrieving the neatly stacked 100-dollar chips the dealer shoved toward him.

Less than an hour later, Jake forlornly watched the croupier expertly hoe his last chips away. "Well, that's it. I'm tapped out. Lady Luck flew the fuckin' coop. Hey, Theresa, how much you got?" Jake slurred thickly as he grabbed his umpteenth brandy from the constantly passing tray of free booze.

"I don't have that kind of money, and if I did, I could think of a lot better use for it. Why don't you call it quits, Jake. We could go someplace and talk or something," Theresa urged invitingly.

Jake looked at Theresa through his booze-soaked eyes, half-considering her proposition as he wondered vaguely how she might be in bed, when the dealer discreetly shoved a 2000-dollar stack of chips toward him.

"Compliments of the gentleman at the next table, Mr. La Motta," the croupier murmured, nodding to a short, stout silk-suited Edward G. Robinson character sporting a diamond pinky ring that could choke a horse.

Jake turned and looked quizzically at the high-rolling stranger, who smiled and nodded imperceptibly back. With a careless shrug of his shoulders, Jake placed the stack of chips on the board and played his borrowed hand. He lost. The dealer promptly replaced the stack of chips. Jake played a second hand. He lost again. Again, the stack of chips was placed before him. He played and lost a third time . . . and a fourth. On the fifth try, with 10,000 dollars in the hole, Jake finally beat the house with a two down and a ten, six and incredibly lucky three showing. He had broken his losing streak.

Jake played on in extravagant style, tossing generous tips of 100-dollar chips in all directions, as he steadily downed an endless stream of alcohol and gleefully piled his mounting chips before him like a profligate, mad Midas. Theresa looked on in awe, appalled and fascinated by Jake's display of devil-may-care abandon. As Jake's booze-induced stupor began to insure the inevitable loss of all his winnings, she unobtrusively slipped the dwindling pile of chips into her black beaded bag before his careless indulgence could squander it all.

His frenzied fling with Lady Luck at last spent, Jake returned his 10,000 dollar stake to his anonymous benefactor, woozily pocketed the miscellaneous remaining chips, and, leaning heavily on Theresa's proffered shoulder, swayed his way up to his complimentary hotel room. The pale, January dawn barely penetrated the heavy orange velvet draperies of the room as Jake and Theresa, full of the thrill of first meeting, made tenderly passionate love.

Theresa awoke some time after noon with Jake snoring loudly next to her, somewhat embarrassed to find her naked body lying beside the equally naked body of a complete stranger. The madcap events of the night before tumbled past her hungover mind's eye like the jumbled colors of clothes spinning behind the windowed door of a giant washing machine. Slipping carefully out of the tangled, oversized bed, she quietly retrieved her hastily discarded clothes from their various locations on the floor, grabbed her bulging beaded bag from the mirrored walnut dresser, and retreated to the sanctuary of the bathroom, locking the door shut behind her.

Theresa emerged some moments later, her outward composure restored despite the deep creases in her evening dress. Her freshly scrubbed face had a healthy glow all the more youthful for the lack of the valuable jewelry she had purposely left lying temptingly on the bathroom counter.

"All right, so you're Jake La Motta, champion big shot. Let's find out just how big a man you really are," she thought slyly as she contemplated Jake's still snoring form entwined among the bed covers.

Theresa scribbled a hasty note telling him to meet her downstairs at the coffee shop, placed it prominently on the bedside table, and clutching her still bulging beaded bag, slipped noiselessly out of the room.

Jake entered the 24-hour casino coffee shop with a vague sense of uneasiness. He felt like hell and probably looked like it, and he was having a hell of a time trying to remember exactly what he had done the night before. The note stuffed in his pocket was signed Theresa, so that must be her name, but he wasn't at all sure just what she looked like. A cute little brunette number pushing forty with big bedroom eyes—that described half the broads in Vegas, he thought wryly as he blearily surveyed the bustling room packed with a motley crew of jaded, sloe-eyed show girls, weary, worn-out prostitutes, woefully hung-over tourists, and would-be high rollers crying into their coffee over the fortunes they carelessly lost the night before.

A pert, pretty brunette in a crisp Kitty Foyle blouse motioned Jake over to her corner booth. As he made his uncertain way toward her, the dawn of recognition spread across Jake's bewildered face.

"Good morning. I ordered you some coffee. You look like you could use it," Theresa said, smiling up at him.

"And you look like a juvenile delinquent. Why'd you run out on me?" Jake said gruffly as he squeezed into the tiny padded seat opposite her.

"Well I do have my own room, you know. I wanted to change into something fresh."

"Why? You were fresh enough for me. Tell me something. What the hell happened last night? I seem to remember being on a winning streak, and then, nothin'. What did I do—blow it all again?"

"Oh, you were on a streak all right. Some man in a silk suit kept backing you till you won, and then you kept playing until you lost. But don't worry, you paid him back—about ten thousand dollars, I believe."

"I paid him back? Whatta ya know. I must be gettin' honest in my old age. Ya know, it's funny bein' a celebrity most of my life. Complete strangers treat me like a brother, and my own brothers treat me like a complete stranger. . . . By the way, you left this in the bathroom. I figured you forgot it or somethin' when you was washin' up."

Jake pulled a handful of Theresa's jewelry from his pocket and laid it on the table before her.

"Ya know, if this was a few years back, you never would've seen it," he confessed.

"Then you never would have seen this."

Theresa opened her beaded bag and dumped a large mound of high numbered chips on the table before Jake's stunned face.

"I took the liberty of saving these for you last night," she smiled cagily.

It was the beginning of a beautiful relationship. . . .

Theresa and Jake spent the next few days stuck together like glue. Accompanying Jake on his rounds of the various Las Vegas casinos, promoting the next scheduled fighting events through personal appearances and interviews, Theresa found herself deeply impressed with Jake's professionalism and wry, ready wit. Unaccustomed to Theresa's attentiveness and shy, lady-like demeanor, Jake found himself pleasantly enamored of this unlikely new woman in his life. When it came time inevitably for them to depart from the Las Vegas airport for their separate destinations—she back to her Newport Beach, California, suburban home and he back to his mid-town Manhattan high-rise apartment—neither wanted their brief but momentous encounter to end. As Jake kissed her tenderly good-bye and walked jauntily out of view, Theresa gazed thoughtfully after him, wondering if she would ever see him again. She could swear he had tears in his eyes when he gruffly whispered in her ear, "See ya around, kid."

Twenty-One

Theresa stood anxiously by her over-stuffed suitcases near one of the sliding-door entrances to La Guardia airport trying not to panic and run to the nearest ticket counter to check in her return flight to California.

Okay, so she had taken Jake at his word when he had called her a few lonely months after their Las Vegas affair, demanding in his gruff way, "Come live with me in New York. I'll give you twenty-four hours to think about it." So she had thrown caution to the wind and in one impetuous moment decided to close her small interior design business, leave her half of their Newport Beach home for her remarried ex-husband to sell, divide her best jewelry and furniture between her two college-age daughters, pack what few winter clothes she owned, and hop on a plane bound for New York and whatever mad adventures awaited her there. And so, having rashly torched all the bridges of her safe, secure existence behind her, here she stood, a small, timid stranger in a strange, hostile land with no one in sight to greet her. So what?

"You're a big girl now. Theresa. You don't need anyone to hold your hand. Nobody forced you here under penalty of death. It was your decision. . . . Only why isn't Jake here to meet me?" Theresa lamented to herself as she struggled with her heavy bags out into the harsh, cold late February New York afternoon.

Finally managing to secure a taxi, Theresa scrambled into the rambling back seat of an old Checker cab, lurching suddenly to the widely spaced floor as the driver sped down the winding airport exit ramp.

"Where to, lady?" the hardened cabby cracked.

Theresa rearranged herself on the seat and rummaged through her large, cluttered shoulder bag for the scrap of paper on which she had jotted down Jake's address.

"Uh, 400 East 57th Street," she read aloud. "Is that very far, driver?"

"Naw, just down the Expressway, over the 59th Street Bridge and you're there. But this is rush hour, lady. I don't guarantee nothin'," the cabby replied by way of the rear view mirror.

Theresa sat back in the capacious seat and let a heavy sigh escape her lips. She hoped to God Jake would be there when she arrived. What if he had gotten the date mixed up and gone out of town or something? What if he had changed his mind about her coming since they had spoken and was afraid to face her? What if she was making the biggest mistake of her life? she thought dreadfully as she gazed out the dirty window at the grim industrial landscape whizzing by her. Theresa's heart gave a small leap in spite of her fears as the Manhattan skyline loomed suddenly into view along the horizon—cold, impersonal and implacable. "I'm at your mercy now. Do with me what you will," she whispered to the intimidating wall of concrete, brick, steel and glass.

The cabby waited impatiently as Theresa struggled with her unwieldy bags onto the sidewalk at the bustling corner of First Avenue and 57th Street, speeding off to his next fare almost before she could shut the heavy creaking cab door behind her. Lugging her worldly belongings into the glass-doored lobby of the imposing pre-war building, Theresa marched determinedly up to the small concierge desk and announced herself with as much authority as she could muster. "Please tell Mr. La Motta that Theresa Miller is here."

The skeptical man behind the desk pushed a button on his switchboard, muttered something unintelligible into the house phone, and said curtly, "You can go up—6-G."

He nodded knowingly to the curious doorman, who lumbered over to her parked bags and carried them in sullen silence into the cramped elevator as Theresa followed meekly behind. It seemed a small eternity before the doorman slid open the folding cage doors and unenthusiastically set her bags onto the nondescript dark carpeting. Theresa stepped gingerly into the long, low dim hallway.

Her heart pounding furiously, she wandered with her bags past the uniform rows of closed brown doors until she at last stood before what she fervently hoped was Jake's apartment. She knocked lightly, holding her breath in the face of her unknown fate.

Jake's bloated, red-eyed, unshaven mug appeared in the doorway. He was naked from the waist up, his substantial belly protruding over the waistband of his plaid boxer shorts, a half-empty can of beer gripped in one hand as he held the door grudgingly open with the other.

"Uh, Theresa, what are you doing here?" he said dully.

"Jake, it's Friday. Don't you remember? I told you I'd be arriving today. You told me to pack up everything and move to New York. You said you wanted me to come live with you. You said you needed me. . . . " Theresa's voice trailed off pathetically.

"I said all that?" Jake muttered. "Well, you're here now. Come on in. . . . Is all that your stuff?" he grumbled as Theresa sidled through the doorway, baggage in tow.

"I brought as little as possible. I didn't know what kind of closet space you had . . . " she began, her voice breaking off abruptly.

Theresa uttered a sharp little cry at the sight of Jake's Spartan studio, her face registering her shock as she stood in the middle of the woefully tiny room and beheld the uneven, cracked dirty cork floor, the smudged, dingy gray walls, the filthy, streaked windows in their crumbling casings, the two rusted folding metal chairs beside a rickety table, the single folding cot, and a miniature old love seat covered with a dirty and torn spread shoved negligently into one dusty corner.

"Oh my God, what have I done?" she thought frantically as she stared in utter dismay at Jake's grinning face. She was a hell of a long way from California.

"Hey, come over here you sexy creature," Jake rasped, grabbing Theresa and pulling her roughly toward him.

As Jake pressed his lips on hers, Theresa found herself responding against her will to his raw, uninhibited primal force, shutting her eyes tightly against the banal reality of her strange new surroundings.

It was well past midnight as Theresa left the shadowy, sheltered alcove of Sutton Place Park, so tranquil in its cool, dark solitude by the silently flowing East River. She headed reluctantly back across deserted 57th Street, huddled deep in her California parka against the chill, gusty Manhattan March night. It had been a lonely three weeks since her unwelcome arrival in New York. Jake had remained less than hospitable, urging her to get a job—any job—while hoarding in his private closet what money he hadn't gambled away since his last winning bout with Lady Luck. Drinking by day and gambling by night, he seemed largely to ignore her unwanted presence, leaving her to her own limited devices in the depressing, cell-like studio while he cavorted about town on his mysterious nightly sprees. Knowing no one in New York, Theresa had found her prospects of penetrating the cliquish establishment of Manhattan interior designers highly unlikely, her hopes of easily resuming her former West coast trade sadly mistaken. She had vastly underestimated the daily expense of living in Manhattan, and the personal savings she had thought would be sufficient were dwindling by the hour. Jake's callous neglect in the face of her dilemma was difficult to bear, but the thought of retreating to her discarded past in California, her head bowed in bloody defeat and her tail between her legs, was far worse. She had made her bed, however hard and narrow, and now she must lie in it, alone if necessary. If only she had a bed, she thought woefully as she shuffled shyly past the unfriendly night doorman. She cringed in the corner of the maddeningly slow elevator, murmured a timid "good night" to the unresponsive attendant, and unlocked the door to her dingy cell. She had returned from her lonely midnight sojourn to curl miserably on the tiny worn love seat that was her only resting place and cry herself to sleep.

Casually attired in white jeans and sneakers on a mercifully warm, sunny April afternoon, Theresa scurried to keep up with Jake's brisk pace as they headed the few blocks down Second Avenue to their appointed rendezvous with Vickie and some marketing consultant purportedly interested in using Jake's name to promote a new line of diet pills. Having flown in from her Miami home to investigate the possibility of relocating in New York, Vickie, Jake's favorite phone pal and tireless topic of conversation, had voiced a persistent interest in meeting Theresa, an interest that was not entirely mutual on Theresa's part. Aware of Jake's peculiar preoccupation with Vickie and her every move, Theresa had felt an ominous foreboding at the prospect of becoming involved in what she sensed would become a situation far beyond her control.

"Hurry it up. You're gonna make us late," Jake growled as Theresa lagged behind.

Jake swaggered ahead into the cool, dark interior of Elmer's, a favorite haunt of well-connected businessmen, ex-pugs, and wiseguys, making a beeline for a center round table where Vickie reposed in solitary splendor, her long, slender evenly-tanned legs crossed provocatively beneath a stylishly short dirndl skirt. Jake leaned possessively over Vickie, giving her a devoted peck on her smoothly powdered cheek, and sat down obediently next to her as Theresa bounced submissively behind.

"Theresa, this is Vickie," Jake said unceremoniously as Vickie smiled condescendingly and Theresa piped a chipper "Hi," sitting demurely in the empty seat to Vickie's right.

"So where's the guy? I thought he wanted to meet me," Jake launched in without further introduction.

"Well, he was here, but he said he had another meeting and he couldn't wait," Vickie replied casually.

"Whatta ya mean, he couldn't wait? I thought he wanted to talk to me about promotin' some diet pills, or somethin'."

"To tell you the truth, Jake, he seemed much more interested in my idea of a Vickie La Motta cosmetic line," she purred, examining her perfectly manicured nails.

"What cosmetic line?"

"Oh, didn't I tell you? I've had this idea for youth-preserving natural cosmetics for some time now. I think it's a perfectly marvelous idea, don't you?" she asked innocently.

"But what about my pills?"

"Honestly, Jake, don't you think you should lose a few pounds before you set yourself up as a prime example of physical fitness?" she said with a sidelong glance at Jake's prominent belly.

"Aw, that's nothin'," Jake muttered, automatically sucking in his middle. "I could lose that easy. I've lost over 5000 pounds in my life—you know that."

"Well, you've certainly let yourself go, dear. Aren't you watching his diet, Theresa?" Vickie asked archly, suddenly switching her focus on Theresa's silent presence.

"Who, me? Well, mostly he eats out, I guess," Theresa shrugged evasively, having no idea what or where Jake ate on his solitary excursions.

"Look, Vickie, if you're gonna do this make-up thing, then give Theresa a job. She's gotta go to work so she can pay her own way," Jake interjected gruffly.

I suppose I could use a bright, attractive assistant. . . . We'll see," Vickie replied, eyeing Theresa critically. "I have to go to the little girls' room. Coming, Theresa?" Vickie asked pointedly as she rose from the table and sauntered toward the rear of the near-empty restaurant. "Jake, order us a couple of drinks—something cool and refreshing," she called over her shoulder as she disappeared around a dark corner. Theresa scrambled from her seat and dutifully followed Vickie into the intimate ladies' room, feeling very much like a helpless pawn in a life-size game of chess.

"So, Theresa, how has Jake been treating you? I hope you're not letting him get away with too much. You're much more than he deserves," Vickie cooed into the mirror as she expertly examined her flawless make-up.

"Well, it has been pretty rough, not really knowing anybody here. You're the first person Jake has introduced me to since I arrived," Theresa confided, feeling a compelling need to talk to someone.

"You poor thing, I bet he's got you locked up in that pathetic dungeon of his like a caged sparrow. Is he still hoarding the rolls of toilet paper? I spent years with a basement stacked with cartons of toilet paper," Vickie said as she carefully reapplied her lavender lipstick.

"How did you know? He's always yelling at me about using more than two sheets at a time," Theresa confessed, collapsing into peals of laughter.

"I know more about Jake La Motta than I ever cared to know," Vickie said with finality, dropping her lipstick into her bag and snapping it shut. "Well, it looks like I'll be moving back up here now. I simply can't afford the payments on the Miami property any longer. My son, Jack, will have to take it over. I don't have many girlfriends in New York, and you're going to need all the help you can get with Jake. I think we're going to get along just fine," Vickie winked seductively, linking her arm compatibly in Theresa's as they emerged together from their private tête à tête.

New York came suddenly, magically alive for Theresa. Playing Vickie's faithful assistant and ubiquitous sidekick, she found herself attending exciting social events and frequenting exclusive Manhattan clubs she never dreamed existed. Vickie's lively night life led Theresa through a fascinating, decadent labyrinth of all night discos and private after hours hideaways patronized by the sort of worldly men that Vickie preferred and Theresa regarded with awe. It was a whole other world, and by contrast Jake's frugal, seedy, mean little realm seemed poor indeed. Deep under the influence of Vickie's spell, Theresa developed a casual aloofness to match Jake's disregard. It mattered little to her when the three of them were out together if, according to Vickie's whim, Vickie was introduced as Jake's wife while she remained obscurely nameless, or, if Vickie so desired, she was conspicuously placed as Jake's girlfriend while Vickie roamed footloose and fancy free. If Jake could take it, so could she.

Spending most of her time with Vickie, Theresa found her undisguised contempt for Jake rubbing off on her. She withdrew further and further from Jake and his lonely little world. High on the thrill of her first autumn in New York, Theresa confided to her best friend Vickie that she planned to leave Jake for good by Christmas, never noticing the gloating glint in Vickie's eyes as she smiled her triumphant smile of approval.

Christmas Eve found Theresa huddled dejectedly alone under a worn blanket on her tattered love seat in Jake's studio, vainly fighting back her unbidden tears and the hacking cough she had developed while wondering desperately what to do. Jake was out carousing in his favorite after hours gambling dens in his usual cavalier fashion, while Vickie was entertaining her latest clique of admirers in her posh Park Avenue apartment. Her hot and heavy friendship with Theresa had perceptibly and inexplicably cooled over the past few months. Theresa's brave, bold autumn plans for independence crumbled slowly before her swollen, reddened eyes as, friendless and jobless as the day she arrived, she contemplated her bleak future.

The apartment door slammed open with a violent bang, jarring Theresa from her thoughts as Jake stalked heavily into the room. Obviously drunk and in a nasty mood, he stood swaying before her with a mean scowl scarred across his face. Theresa knew he had taken another heavy beating at the tables.

"I need some fuckin' money. Give it to me," he slurred thickly.

"Jake, you told me never to give you that money. You'll only go out and lose it again," Theresa reasoned with him between her persistent coughing.

"I said give me the money," Jake growled menacingly, taking a few threatening steps toward her.

"No, Jake. You'll only regret it tomorrow. You know you're going to lose it. Please, listen to me," Theresa pleaded.

"Give me the money, Theresa, or I'll strangle you, you bitch," Jake snarled, his eyes mad with booze and desperation.

"Go ahead, then. Take it. Lose it all! What do I care. It's not my money!" Theresa cried, sick with fear and aggravation. Leaning over to her sewing basket on the floor, she pulled out a wad of bills and threw them despairingly in Jake's sneering face. As Jake scrambled greedily on the floor for the scattered money, Theresa ran desperately into the bathroom, a sudden rush of thick black liquid gushing from her mouth. Leaning wretchedly over the bathroom sink, she vomited convulsively as her stomach divulged itself of a belly full of blackened blood.

Stuffing the wayward bills into his pockets, Jake headed blindly for the door, stopping in his tracks as he saw through the half-open bathroom door Theresa hunched miserably over, hugging her stomach.

"What's the matter with you? I didn't come near ya," he muttered defensively.

"I'm sick, Jake. . . . I'm very, very sick," Theresa whispered weakly, her frightened face pale and trembling.

Jake stepped into the cramped bathroom and glanced into the blood-stained sink.

"Jesus Christ—that's blood! Stay here—I'll call Vickie for help," Jake exclaimed, suddenly sober.

Jake went quickly to the phone and dialed Vickie's apartment.

"Hey Vickie. It's me. Theresa's sick. She's throwin' up blood. I don't know what to do. You'd better get over here," Jake rasped into the phone.

"Don't come unglued, Jake. She's probably faking it. She told me months ago she was planning to leave you tonight," Vickie replied coolly.

"Whatta ya mean, leave me? She's got no place to go. I think she's really sick.

"Well, that's what she told me. If you don't believe me, ask her yourself. Look, I have an apartment full of people here. It's Christmas Eve—I have to go," Vickie said curtly and hung up.

Jake walked leadenly back to the bathroom where Theresa sat hunched over her knees on the floor, her face white as a sheet.

"Please Jake, help me. Take me to the hospital," Theresa implored, looking up at him pitifully.

His face grave with fear, Jake helped Theresa to her feet, tossed her coat around her shaking shoulders, and escorted her down to the deserted, snow-covered streets in grim silence. He hailed a passing cab to take them to the nearest hospital emergency room.

Theresa was admitted immediately to Lenox Hill Hospital with a bleeding peptic ulcer. Weak from her loss of blood, she was prescribed a week of complete bed rest, intravenous feeding, and no aggravation—a welcome respite from the hectic rat race of her stressful, nomad existence. Lying quietly alone in her very own comfortable hospital bed, Theresa calmly began to sort out the maze of the past year since Jake had charged recklessly into her life. There were no visitors to disturb her. Theresa knew Jake well enough by now not to expect him to overcome his deep aversion to hospitals and unexpressed shame and guilt long enough to comfort her. She knew Vickie simply didn't give a damn. Lonely but temporarily safe from the daily ravages of survival in cold, hard, grasping Manhattan, Theresa pondered the significant absence of her two dubious "benefactors."

Vickie's devious ploy to turn her against Jake from the very beginning was pathetically obvious to her now. How could she have been so stupid not to see through Vickie's phony smile and false compliments—all the lurid, wild stories of the past designed to paint Jake an unforgiveable monster and Vickie his innocent victim. Some victim! All Vickie wanted was for Jake to be alone and miserable so she could twist him around her little finger as easily as she always had without any outside interference. No wonder Vickie had seemed so pleased about her decision to leave him! Her little scheme had almost worked. Jake was no white knight, but maybe if she had tried a little harder to understand him instead of running like a scared rabbit from his crude, rough facade, she might have improved some of his self-destructive habits rather than made fun of them. Maybe all Jake needed, like any rundown, neglected empty house, was a little tender loving care. It wouldn't be the first time a woman had to reconstruct the man of her dreams from the rubble of his own abuse.

A friendly intern whose sympathetic ear she had bent during his rounds had given her a clue to Jake's erratic, violent disposition. Determining that Jake imbibed often in brandy and heavy cordials like amaretto, the young doctor had told her that Jake seemed to exhibit a lot of the symptoms of a hereditary genetic condition he called intermittent Mediterranean porphyria. Certain wines and cheeses and especially brandies and cordials acted like chemical poisons to Jake, short circuiting his thought processes and causing him to behave violently or irrationally, especially when under stress of any sort. The only cure was to avoid the triggering substances. Theresa was sure Jake had never been given such a clear explanation of his disastrous Jekyll and Hyde behavior before. Maybe it would make a difference, and maybe it wouldn't, but one thing she knew for sure. She would never again allow anyone to take control of her life so easily, nor be driven to such a state of miserable distraction that her own body began to feed on itself.

Armed with fortified self-esteem and heavy doses of antacids, Theresa left the hospital ready to make a new beginning alone with Jake, if it wasn't too late.

Theresa's dramatic illness had a sobering effect on Jake. His reckless, self-defeating drunken binge had apparently run its course for the time being. Greeting her at his door with an awkward, little boy politeness, he hovered over her with a solicitous concern, his eyes avoiding hers in a contrite, humble reticence that Theresa found touching. Discovering for the first time that he could cook, Theresa stretched out on the brand new queen size bed he had bought for her and watched bemusedly as Jake puttered contentedly in the miniscule kitchen, preparing her a special pasta dinner which he served with a hungry eye for her approval. He even washed the dishes, tossing them still wet into the bare cabinets with a comical efficiency. It was a domestic side of Jake she had never glimpsed before. Regarding him with eyes untainted by Vickie's venemous influence as he modestly performed his small duties in the privacy of his home, no longer the strutting, cocksure, boasting champ he felt he had to be in public, Theresa began to fall quietly, steadily in love.

Inspired by what she was certain lay beneath Jake's tarnished surface, Theresa set about the formidable task of polishing his long-neglected exterior. Beginning with his sadly deficient personal hygiene, she shampooed, conditioned and trimmed his thinning crop of hair, manicured his rough, bitten nails, gave his pock-marked skin a cleansing facial, and introduced him to the concept of body deodorant. Invading the sanctum of his jealously guarded personal closet, she disposed of years of accumulated crud, unwashed, sweat-stained outmoded clothing, and worn, smelly sneakers, thoroughly disinfecting and airing out the reeking alcove. Appalled by Jake's atrocious eating habits, Theresa sat him down and taught him the rudiments of table manners, patiently demonstrating the proper use of knife, fork, spoon and napkin as though she were instructing a feral child. Unaccustomed to such attention and concern, Jake docilely accepted Theresa's gentle but firm guidance. The lack of pride in himself that had shown all over was gradually replaced by a new, positive self-regard. His chronic paranoia and hostile suspicions of others began to ebb as his newfound sense of well-being extended beyond himself to include the world around him.

Accompanying Jake on his long constitutional walks about town, Theresa smiled happily at her well-behaved man, pleased with the change she had wrought in a few short months. No longer squandering his time and money gambling and drinking, he had curtailed his alcohol intake to admirable moderation, conspicuously avoiding the deadly cordials and brandy. His waistline considerably reduced, he looked fit and fashionably tan in one of the tastefully coordinated outfits she had purchased for him. Left alone to share the small everyday moments of their lives together, they had grown ever closer and more compatible, content to bask in the warm glow of their relationship. Interrupting their comfortably silent stroll homeward, Jake dug into his pocket to hand a couple of bucks to a lone, dejected bag lady languishing in squalor beneath the 59th Street Bridge as Theresa beamed in secret admiration. It was more than she ever hoped for.

And then Vickie, swooping down upon them like a relentless harpy, struck again.

Impressed with the dramatic change that Theresa's nurturing had wrought in Jake, Vickie was no less scornful of the happily budding romance that had taken strong root between them. Knowing Theresa had grown beyond her sphere of influence, Vickie concentrated her suddenly renewed attentions on the unwitting Jake, whose blind devotion she had long exploited. Reversing her tactics, Vickie began calling frequently for Jake, inviting him to escort her to various affairs while coolly ignoring Theresa. Jake went blindly along with Vickie's every whim, much to Theresa's chagrin. No longer willing or able to stand silently by as Vickie played her devious cat and mouse games, Theresa preferred to remain home alone rather than witness the willful destruction of all that she had so carefully cultivated. Returning late and drunk from his slumming sprees with Vickie, Jake regressed to his old ways, treating Theresa with as little respect as he felt for himself. Alone and unhappy, Theresa felt the familiar, ominous pains of her ulcer returning. She hadn't the guts to force Jake to choose between Vickie and herself. It was no contest. She knew she would only lose.

The sultry summer sun filtered hazily through the soot streaked windows into the mean little room, lending a surreal effect to the nightmarish scene. Jake stood phone in hand with his ear glued to the receiver while Theresa paced frantically to and fro, her hands pressed tightly over her ears to shut out the obscene words Jake was loudly repeating.

"Hey Theresa, Vickie says you screwed this guy at her place one night. Is it true? She says you screwed every guy you met. Is that true? How many fuckin' guys did ya screw, ya bitch!" Jake shouted in rage.

"Stop it! Stop it, Jake! I can't stand it. You know she's lying. Why are you saying these awful things? Please stop," Theresa pleaded, her voice on the verge of hysteria.

"Why should Vickie be lying? Maybe you're lying. Vickie tells

me you're just hangin' around waitin' for the right time to leave—
you never gave a shit about me. Is that true? Ya better tell me,
Theresa—the truth shall set you free. Remember that—"

Theresa ran wildly to the phone and grabbed it from Jake's hand,
breaking the connection to Vickie's hateful, goading voice.

"I hate what she's done to you. I can't bear it any more—just
can't bear it," Theresa sobbed, sinking miserably to her knees.
"We were so happy once. Why did you have to let her destroy it
all? Why, Jake?"

Theresa wept convulsively on the floor as Jake watched her with
cruel detachment.

"If Vickie's lying, then tell me the truth. What was she doin' all
that time? What did she say about me? Ya better tell me,
Theresa—I'll find out," Jake persisted maddeningly, thinking irrationally that he could determine the true imposter by playing one
against the other.

All at once Theresa stopped crying and sat up, her eyes glazed as
if in a trance. For some moments she sat staring blankly ahead, rigidly motionless and apparently oblivious to her surroundings, lost
in a world of her own. Alarmed by her strange withdrawal, Jake
knelt beside her, shaking her gently to arouse her from her stupor,
suddenly fearing he had pushed her too far in his bizarre search for
the truth.

"Don't touch me. I'm leaving you," Theresa responded in a cold,
hard voice.

"You're leavin', uh? So Vickie was right. Where the hell do ya
think you're goin'. Ya haven't got a dime," Jake retorted.

Without another word, Theresa rose and walked to her tiny
closet, took out the expensive fur coat Jake had gotten for her
wholesale in better days, picked up her purse, and headed directly
for the door.

"I'll send for the rest of my things tomorrow," she announced
calmly and walked out, closing the door firmly behind her. This
time Jake had gone too far. She would make it on her own if it
killed her, but she would never put herself at Jake's mercy again.

PART VI

Karma

Twenty-Two

"Hey Jake, come on—the cars are leaving. Everybody's ready to go. Are you coming or not?" Joey called from the long line of black limousines filled with a host of close and distant relatives and friends who had traveled from near and far to pay their last respects to the universally loved Elizabeth La Motta.

Jake stood alone in the steadily pouring rain by the open grave, staring dejectedly at the elaborate gold coffin in which his mother lay in peaceful repose, her lingering, painful bout with cancer finally over.

"Go ahead, I want to stay awhile. . . . I just want to stay awhile," Jake muttered half to himself as he remained standing motionless over the descended coffin with his hands behind his back and his head bowed, as heedless of the waiting cars of near strangers as he was of the heavy summer rain dripping from the hastily erected protective canopy down the back of his simple grey suit, or of the quiet tears flowing gently down the deep crevices of his ravaged face.

Joey shrugged and stepped into the leading limo crowded with the immediate family of siblings and spouses, and the procession of mourners slowly drove off, leaving a lone car and driver waiting behind as Jake stood alone and remembered.

"I'm sorry, Mom, I didn't come visit ya in the hospital more often, but you understood. I just couldn't take seeing you suffer and not bein' able to help you. That last time I came and you looked up at me so helpless, I knew. I knew you was going to die on my birthday. Maybe you was tryin' to tell me somethin'. I never remembered my birthday. . . . Now I'll never forget it. . . . Don't worry, Mom, about the rain. Like you always said, it's only God's tears. He's cryin' for you Mom, and maybe for me, too . . . "

Jake tossed a final red rose onto his mother's coffin and, shoving his hands deep into his pockets, trudged away in the rain toward the patiently waiting limo. He could hear the shoveled dirt plopping onto the coffin as the graveyard attendants began their final task, each methodical thud resounding in his ears like the punch of a giant boxing glove. As Jake ducked into the rear of the empty limousine, the driver firmly closed the door behind him, snapping shut another chapter in his life.

The phone was ringing as Jake turned the key in the lock of his apartment door, returning alone and somber from his mother's funeral. Not in the mood to talk to anyone, he let the phone ring on before he reluctantly picked up the receiver.

"Yeah, who is it?" he muttered darkly.

"Jake? It's me, Sahra—I mean Sally. I've been trying to reach you. I heard about your mother. I'm so sorry, Jake. She was a beautiful person. Everybody loved Mom. I know she was a good person and God will reward her."

"Yeah, we buried her today. Ya know, Sally, she died on my birthday, July tenth. Do ya think God was trying to tell me somethin'?"

"I don't know, Jake, but our Lord works in mysterious ways. Our whole congregation has been offering prayers for her soul, and we pray for you, too, Jake. The Lord has called me to a full time ministry now. I call it Cast the First Stone Ministry. We work out of the Good Shepherd Lutheran Church here in North Miami. I wish you could come down here, Jake. The children and I could take you to church and hold a laying of the hands and intercede for you in prayer, and I know you would accept the Lord, Jake. You were always seeking God in your own way. I pray every day that you will find the Lord and be saved."

"Maybe you're right, Sally. Maybe that's what I need. I know I need somethin'. It's like I can't talk to anybody anymore. They all disappoint me, or maybe I disappoint them, I don't know. Nobody talked to me at the funeral. All my brothers and sisters, they only talk to me when they have to. And not one of my ex-wives showed up or even called, except you of course. Not even Vickie. I know how she hates these things, but ya think she could've sent a Mass card, or somethin'. . . . "

"Jake, where's Theresa? Isn't she with you?"

"Aw, she walked out on me about a month ago. I haven't heard from her since. I don't even know where she is. Maybe she found some other guy. I don't know."

"Oh, Jake, I'm sorry to hear that. Nobody should be alone—especially you. You need a lot of nurturing, I know. . . . I'm sending you a Bible, Jake. I want you to read it every day. 'Jesus is the only name given under heaven whereby men must be saved.' Read the words of our Lord and pray, Jake, and God will come into your heart."

"I'll try, Sally Bird. . . . I'll try. . . . "

Jake hung up the phone and sat thinking for a while, then he suddenly got up, poured himself a glass of white wine, and began rummaging through his reformed closet for his old solitaire deck.

"Theresa moved everything. I can't find nothin' no more. She probably threw out my lucky cards," Jake grumbled to himself. In his restless search, Jake came across a stack of letters from Augie piled neatly on a back shelf.

"Hey—little Augie. Why wasn't he at the funeral? He's everywhere—he shoulda been there. Boy am I gonna tell him off!" Jake said to himself, draining his glass of wine and going angrily to the phone.

"Hello," Augie's wife, Marie, answered in a gentle, high-pitched voice.

"Eh Marie, this is the Champ. I want to talk to Augie."

"Well, I'm sorry Jake, but Augie isn't here. He's in Beth Israel Hospital. He's very sick."

"Hospital? What's wrong. What's wrong with him? What's happening to everybody?"

"It's his back, Jake. He hurt it on the job. They had to operate. I can give you the number to his room, if you like."

"Yeah, give me the number. Give me the number. I'll call him."

Jake poured himself another glass of wine, circled the room a few times to collect his thoughts, and, with a heavy sigh, dialed Augie's number.

"Hello," came the small, raspy voice over the receiver.

"Hello Augie, this is the Champ."

"Oh Jake, God, am I glad you called. I'm gonna die in this place. I'm gonna die in this goddam place."

"Whatta ya mean?"

"The two doctors—Dr. O and Dr. No—O No, I say when I see them. They just left the room. I'm paralyzed. I'll never walk again."

Augie broke into tears, unable to hold back his despair, as Jake listened in silent sympathy, his heavy breathing punctuating Augie's convulsive sobs.

"Look Augie, you gotta be a man about this. You gotta take it," Jake said, breaking the long silence.

"Jake, that's very nice, but this ain't the ring. We're not fightin' Robinson here. I can't move—don't you understand? I can't move!" Augie cried hysterically. "No matter how tough I am, and I was a pretty tough guy—how can ya be tough in here? I can't walk. A woman could walk up and kick me in the nuts and I wouldn't feel nothin'! Don't ya understand what it is? Don't ya understand?"

"Take it easy. We're gonna pray together every night. I'm gonna call ya every night, and you can call me."

"Jake, I know you don't like to be bothered. . . . "

"I know. But you can call me. You're gonna make it."

"Yeah, but Jake, the doctors, they see me every day. They say I'll be in a wheelchair for the rest of my life. . . ."

"Augie, listen to me . . . "

"They run this sharp little wheel down my body, and when they get to my waist—nothin'! Jake, you're a fighter. These are doctors!"

"You gotta be a man. You gotta take it. We'll pray together, and every night I'll call you. You're gonna make it, Augie," Jake repeated steadily. "You're gonna make it. . . . "

Jake stood with his back to the wall, a glass of wine in his hand and a wry smile on his face as he watched Vickie across the crowded hotel ballroom make her play for a tall, handsome young football player who had caught her ever roving eye. Having brought her with him as his date to the black tie affair in Jersey City honoring past and present sports greats, Jake had discreetly retreated to the sidelines after the elaborate sit down dinner and tiresome speeches to allow Vickie a clear field in her relentless quest for ever newer and younger lovers. Her new status as *Playboy*'s oldest centerfold rendered her a popular center of attraction for the younger studs in the room, who hovered about her like so many worker bees around their queen as she willingly displayed her well-exposed charms before one and all. Increasingly uncomfortable with the dubious honor of playing Vickie's dummy escort, Jake tried vainly to ignore the snide remarks and thinly veiled snickers he knew were aimed in his direction as he stared stoically ahead and wondered how he had ever allowed himself to sink so low.

After an indecent interval, Jake decided to stroll back across the room and quietly remind Vickie of his existence. Passively parting the huddle of admirers surrounding her, Jake stood awkwardly by as Vickie continued her intimate conversation with the young quarterback next to her, totally ignoring Jake's presence. Embarrassed by the ridiculous image he knew he projected, Jake walked silently away with what dignity he could muster, and took up his distant station with soldierly pride.

He drank two more wines before he gathered enough courage to venture back into Vickie's queenly domain.

The look of discomfort on the faces of the embarrassed young athletes as Vickie repeated her performance before Jake's wounded eyes was enough to prompt Jake's second retreat.

On his third advance, seething with cold contempt he had never known before as Vickie cavorted brazenly on the lap of an unwitting linebacker, Jake had finally had enough.

"Vickie, I think we ought to leave now," Jake said with ominous control.

"Oh Jake, it's early. You're being such a bore," Vickie pouted back.

"I said now, Vickie, or you'll walk home," Jake rumbled.

"Oh all right, if you're going to get mad about it," Vickie shrugged, slipping off the lap of the abashed linebacker.

Jake sat beside Vickie in the rear of the rented limo in stony silence the entire ride back to Manhattan. As the car halted before Vickie's apartment and she leaned perfunctorily over to kiss him goodnight, Jake turned his head away in disgust.

"Goodbye, Vickie. I've lost what little respect I had left for you. I never want to see you again," Jake said with chilling conviction, his eyes focused adamantly ahead.

As the limo sped off, leaving Vickie standing perplexed on the sidewalk, Jake didn't have the slightest urge to look back.

A few days later Jake received a strange call from his son, Joey, in Miami.

"Hey Pop, it's me. I had to call ya. . . . I had to call ya and tell you. I did it, Pop. I shot up her whole fuckin' room—the Vickie La Motta shrine. All her precious shit—all the stuff my mother stole from you all those years. I took a gun and I blasted it all away—the whole fuckin' room. . . . I had to, Pop. I couldn't take it any more. She took you away from all of us. . . . I did it for you, Pop. . . . I did it for you. . . . "

Jake was beginning to believe in the concept of meaningful coincidence. The spell was finally broken . . . The exorcism was complete.

It was a cold, rainy, late November night, and Jake was glad to be inside his warm, dry but cheerless studio as he contentedly munched his favorite sausage and pepper sandwich before the TV wrestling match—a man's man in a man's world. He groaned inwardly, giving the telephone an annoyed look as its shrill ring shattered the peace of his reclusive cocoon.

"Who the hell could that be?" he grumbled as he stalked across the room to the jangling instrument.

"Hello," he mumbled, chomping on his sandwich.

"Jake . . . Jake . . . I need help . . . I'm sick . . . so sick . . . Please come and get me," came the frail, pathetic voice on the other end of the line.

"Theresa, is that you? What's wrong? You sound like you're dying or somethin'."

"I can't talk long . . . I feel so weak . . . I haven't eaten for days . . . "

A long fit of coughing and wheezing interrupted her quietly desperate voice.

" . . . I'm afraid, Jake . . . please come right away . . . I have no one else to help me. . . . "

Jake walked quickly through the rain down First Avenue towards the strange East side address Theresa had given him.

"I thought she had a place on the West side. . . . How did she get so sick? . . . What the hell is going on?" Jake asked himself in confusion as he ploughed worriedly on.

Turning the corner at 51st Street, Jake slowed his frantic pace as he searched for the right number. He stopped before a nondescript three-story building with a single glass door entrance bearing the name of some real estate office. There were no lights on inside. Jake double-checked the address with the slip of paper in his hand. There was no buzzer or mailbox. Theresa's name was nowhere to be found. Trying the door, he was surprised to find it open. Entering the small darkened office, he saw a faint light coming from the bottom of a narrow little stairway immediately to his left. He descended the steep stairs to a low-ceilinged basement store room, and there, huddled shivering under a thin blanket on a narrow cot in the corner, lay Theresa, deathly pale and ill. The tiny windowless cubicle was cold and damp, and the single shadeless lamp on the floor cast eerie shadows on the peeling walls and exposed pipes overhead. Jake stared in horror at the ghastly scene, reminded of the miserable days spent in solitary in the prison hell hole of his forgotten past. Theresa looked feverishly up at him from her pitiful berth. The tears sprang to his eyes as he beheld the wretched condition his blind selfishness had driven her to. He was overcome with remorse and compassion for this gentle soul who had tried so hard to save him from himself and who now needed him so desperately.

Jake walked over to Theresa, tucked the rough blanket tightly around her, picked her gently up in his arms, and carried her out of her dungeon into the stormy night.

"Come on, baby, we're going home," he whispered hoarsely.

Twenty-Three

⊂Ε "Aw come on, Theresa. It'll be great. It's the biggest fight of the year. Everybody'll be there. I'll be working, and we can get married in style at the same time. And we met in Vegas—that makes it even better. You're gonna love it."

"I don't know, Jake. It sounds kind of like a three-ring circus. I don't want to be married at a carnival side show. I want my daughters to be there, and I want it to be very special. Maybe we ought to wait until we get back and have a small, private ceremony here."

"Aw, you really want it. You're just actin' like a broad playin' hard to get. When the time comes, you'll come around. You'll see. We got time. I figured we could get married on April 14th—the day before the fight, and taxes, too."

Theresa was standing in a pile of plaster, stripping down the walls. I got stuck with painting the closet. It was Theresa's idea to re-do the apartment from top to bottom—mirrors and fabric on the walls, marbled tile on the floor, new appliances in the kitchen, brand new furniture—everything. It was going to cost me a fortune, but if it made her happy—what the hell. Besides, it was going to help her get work as a decorator, too. And we could start inviting people over for a change instead of meeting in restaurants and saloons all the time. Since Theresa and me decided to get married, my whole life started to pick up again. Bob Arum of Top Rank had hired me to promote all of his fights, including the big Marvin Hagler-Thomas Hearns Middleweight Championship fight in Vegas. I'd be traveling all over the country making personal appearances in sixteen cities for two weeks prior to the fight. The

250

money was good, but the work was better. I liked being active and feeling useful again. I didn't like being a bum. If Theresa hadn't come into my life when she did, I probably would've destroyed myself. Now she was all I lived for.

But like I told Theresa about the wedding: Don't try to change my style. This was going to be my sixth trip to the altar—I said I was going to keep trying until I got it right—and I wanted it to be the biggest event ever. With the whole boxing world and all the press in Vegas for the Hearns-Hagler fight, what could be better?

I knew when it came down to it, Theresa would understand.

Everybody was there. All the high rollers and hustlers, the fancy ladies and overdone whores with their white-suited pimps, the second-rate hoodlums and entertainers, the blue-haired biddies at the slot machines, all the wheelers and dealers and the baffled tourists and fight fans runnin' around with their twelve dollar T-shirts and autographed programs, and hundreds of media guys packed into the bars. When Roosevelt announced war with Germany and Japan, he didn't have this kind of press coverage— and that was the biggest fight of all. They were all there to see the two toughest middleweights in the division trade knockout punches before thousands of spectators and millions of closed-circuit TV viewers, but all I saw was Theresa and the familiar scarred mugs of the tough old fighters I used to know. Guys who didn't know how to quit, like Willie Pepp, Carmen Basilio, Gene Fullmer, Joey Maxim, Paddy DeMarco, José Torres, Billy Conn, and Sugar Ray Robinson. I hadn't seen Ray in years, but he was still the big, beautiful, black giant who kicked the shit out of me to win the championship. We hugged each other tight—not the kind of hug you give in the ring when you're just glad it's over, but the hug of two old veterans who survived six wars together. I couldn't have had a better best man.

Theresa and me and Ray and his wife Millie walked into Ceasar's Palace ballroom to watch Hearns's workout with his sparring partners before an audience of rollers, fans and photographers. Hearns turned to watch us, eyeing the way we handled ourselves. Three of the sparring partners came over and asked Ray and me for our autographs. We sat down in a front row of folding chairs and watched Hearns smack punches into the thick mitts of his sparring partner's hands. I remembered the trouble I used to have keeping sparring partners. They had to wear a padded body protecter to keep from getting hurt. Hearns looked concentrated and sharp, but he kept breaking his rounds to pose for the cameras. Hagler, the older workhorse, was off somewhere working up steam alone. Hagler was a southpaw, which gave him the advantage, but Hearns had the reach, which gave him the edge. Hagler was a stand-up fighter, but he'd have been more effective if he crouched the way I did with Robinson and tried to get inside Hearns's reach. But that was his style, and it was too late to change it now. It was going to be a close fight. It was the first real betting fight they'd had in a long time, and a lot of money was showing on both fighters, but my betting days were over.

"Hey, Jake," Ray nudged me. "Did I ever fight him?" he asked me, pointing to Hearns.

I looked at him, not believing what I heard. He wasn't joking. I'd heard Ray was sick, but I never knew how sick. He was only a year older than me, but he'd fought on ten years after I'd retired.

"Naw Ray," I said, "You'd have killed him."

He was still the greatest champion I ever saw.

Just like I'd said, the wedding took place in the ballroom of the Maxim Hotel and Casino on Sunday night, the night before the fight, with about 400 noisy people crowding the room. Our friend, referee Joey Curtis, set up the whole bash so it didn't cost us a dime. Theresa was happy as a lark. Her sister, Dana, was her maid of honor, and her two daughters, Stephanie and La Trisha, stood close beside her. Sugar Ray stood proudly to my right. Somebody stuck two fingers in his mouth and whistled to get everybody's attention, then the judge began. He got as far as the love and obey part, Theresa and I said we would, and I then kissed her.

"Wait a minute," the judge said. "Not yet."

I looked up. Theresa smiled, and the judge coughed. Then the phone rang in some corner of the room.

"What round is it?" I joked.

Everybody cracked up.

"We've got to finish," the judge said.

The room settled down a bit, and the judge continued, a little faster this time. In short order, he pronounced us "Mr. and Mrs.

Jake La Motta." Everybody cheered and applauded. It was the best wedding I ever had.

They opened the doors to the adjoining casino, and you could hear the clanging of slot machines as more people started to wander into the room. A piano player in a black cowboy hat started playing "The Nearness of You." Me and Theresa stepped onto the dance floor with everybody watching. We started dancing cheek to cheek, and Theresa whispered in my ear, "Jake, this one is going to last until we die."

You know something? I believed her.

Bob Arum had invited us to join him by the pool at Caesar's Palace at nine o'clock. When we arrived, we were greeted by a standing ovation of hundreds of people. There was a 50-foot long banner proclaiming "Congratulations Mr. and Mrs. La Motta—This Bud's on You." A giant six-tier wedding cake stood in the middle of the tiled terrace. "Entertainment Tonight" cameras were rolling on the whole scene. I was amazed; Theresa was ecstatic; her sister and daughters couldn't believe it. Bob Arum had arranged the whole thing with Budweiser as a surprise wedding reception for Theresa and me.

"Theresa, darlin', is this what you meant by a quiet, private little ceremony?" I winked.

"Jake, remind me never, never to question your judgment again," she smiled, and kissed me like she'd never stop.

Call it karma, or destiny, or whatever is behind my subconscious, but God had given me enough time to try and right some of the wrongs of my life. I've blown two fortunes—the two million I made in the ring and the half million I made on the movie—and five marriages, but I still have my health and my hopes and my attitudes, and I believe the Man Upstairs gives us enough time to balance the scales. God gives everybody chances, but who would figure I could have a book and a movie in my own lifetime, and wind up with a beautiful, loving wife like Theresa at my age? I've always been a loner, and, for that matter, I still am, but I realize while I was trying to accomplish all the things and hear the standing ovations, I was forgetting about enjoying the happiness. I was always trying to grab what was next. Maybe I didn't want to savor it because I felt I didn't deserve it. Maybe it was some kind of guilt. You live your life, and there are things you have to go through. You always wonder why, why, why, but there's a reason. For years I made people cry. Now, with my comedy act, I try to make them laugh. It took me 63 years to figure out, if you want to be healthy and happy in life, you have no alternative but to do the right thing.

And now, thirty-six years after I won the title, I finally get inducted into Ring Magazine's Boxing Hall of Fame. There were those who said I forfeited my right for consideration by posterity when I agreed to throw the fight with Billy Fox. I guess it took a new, more forgiving generation to recognize my accomplishments in the ring in spite of what I had to do to get my rightful shot at the title. As *Ring Magazine* put it, " . . . the election of Jake La Motta will raise a few eyebrows, if not a major ruckus . . . but 'The Ring' feels that to continue to ignore his place among boxing's immortals would be the height of hypocrisy . . . " As Jesus put it, "Let he without sin cast the first stone."

I stood outside the small midtown restaurant having a smoke before I went in to accept my plaque. It wasn't exactly the Hall of Fame room at Madison Square Garden, but it was good enough for me.

"Hiya Champ. Champ, how are ya?"

I looked up and saw Augie coming toward me. He was moving slow and painful like, with a cane in each hand, but he was walking.

"Look, Champ—we did it. We did it. Look, I'm walking! The doctors call me the miracle man. The prayers—all your prayers did it. I made it, Champ! I made it!"

"I knew you would, Augie. I knew you would. Like I told ya, whatever the mind can conceive and believe, the mind can achieve."

I stubbed out my cigarette and followed Augie inside, rehearsing in my mind what I was going to say. . . .

"If it is true that when God examines a man, He looks not for medals, but for scars, then in sixty-odd years of survival in and out of the ring, I feel I have truly earned the title Middleweight Champion of the World. Thirty-five years ago, I lost that title to a very worthy opponent, Sugar Ray Robinson. Today, you have given it back to me again. This time I have fought not to be a champion gladiator, but to become a champion human being. . . ."

What round is it?

THE END